PENGUIN CANADA

TEN THOUSAND ROSES

JUDY REBICK is one of Canada's best-known feminists and political commentators. She is the publisher of Canada's irreverent web magazine *rabble.ca*, author of *Imagine Democracy* and *Politically Speaking*, with Kiké Roach, and the Sam Gindin chair in social justice and democracy at Ryerson University. Judy appears frequently on radio and television and is a columnist for *Herizons* magazine. She is also a former president of the National Action Committee on the Status of Women, Canada's largest women's group. She lives in Toronto.

ALSO BY JUDY REBICK

Politically Speaking (with Kiké Roach)

Imagine Democracy

TEN
THOUSAND
ROSES

THE MAKING
of a FEMINIST
REVOLUTION

JUDY REBICK

PENGUIN
CANADA

PENGUIN CANADA

Published by the Penguin Group

Penguin Group (Canada), 90 Eglinton Avenue East, Suite 700, Toronto, Ontario,
Canada M4P 2Y3 (a division of Pearson Penguin Canada Inc.)

Penguin Group (USA) Inc., 375 Hudson Street, New York, New York 10014, U.S.A.
Penguin Books Ltd, 80 Strand, London WC2R 0RL, England
Penguin Ireland, 25 St Stephen's Green, Dublin 2, Ireland (a division of Penguin Books Ltd)
Penguin Group (Australia), 250 Camberwell Road, Camberwell, Victoria 3124, Australia
(a division of Pearson Australia Group Pty Ltd)
Penguin Books India Pvt Ltd, 11 Community Centre, Panchsheel Park, New Delhi – 110 017, India
Penguin Group (NZ), Cnr Airborne and Rosedale Roads, Albany, Auckland, New Zealand
(a division of Pearson New Zealand Ltd)
Penguin Books (South Africa) (Pty) Ltd, 24 Sturdee Avenue, Rosebank, Johannesburg 2196, South Africa

Penguin Books Ltd, Registered Offices: 80 Strand, London WC2R 0RL, England

First published 2005

2 3 4 5 6 7 8 9 10 (WEB)

LIBRARY AND ARCHIVES CANADA CATALOGUING IN PUBLICATION

Rebick, Judy
Ten thousand roses : the making of a feminist revolution / Judy Rebick.
Includes index.
ISBN 0-14-301544-3

1. Feminism—Canada—History—20th century. 2. Women's rights—Canada—History—
20th century. 3. Feminists—Canada. 4. Oral history.
I. Title.

HQ1453.R423 2005   305.42'0971'09045   C2004-906316-2

Visit the Penguin Group (Canada) website at **www.penguin.ca**

To Norma Scarborough
and all the unsung heroes of the women's movement

Because woman's work is never done and is underpaid or unpaid or boring or repetitious and we're the first to get fired and what we look like is more important than what we do and if we get raped it's our fault and if we get beaten we must have provoked it and if we raise our voices we're nagging bitches and if we enjoy sex we're nymphos and if we don't we're frigid and if we love women it's because we can't get a "real" man and if we ask our doctor too many questions we're neurotic and/or pushy and if we expect childcare we're selfish and if we stand up for our rights we're aggressive and "unfeminine" and if we don't we're typical weak females and if we want to get married we're out to trap a man and if we don't we're unnatural and because we still can't get an adequate safe contraceptive but men can walk on the moon and if we can't cope or don't want a pregnancy we're made to feel guilty about abortion and... for lots and lots of other reasons we are part of the women's liberation movement.

Always cast your heart over the hurdle first;
your body will be obliged to follow.

—JUDITH THURMAN,
ISAK DINESEN: THE LIFE OF A STORYTELLER

CONTENTS

INTRODUCTION

I N 1995 ALMOST EIGHT HUNDRED WOMEN marched from Montreal to Quebec City to demand the elimination of poverty. As they passed through towns and villages along the way, whole populations came out to greet them, and churches sounded their bells. One man, a rose grower in Drummondville, was so inspired that he brought ten thousand roses to Quebec City for the huge rally that greeted the marchers, and so, instead of placards, every person carried a rose. It is from this story that my book takes its title. The theme of the march was bread and roses, the anthem of the women's movement.

The symbolic meaning of the title is in the thousands of women who made the feminist revolution. A few have become well known, but there are so many women just as intelligent, capable and courageous. In these pages you will meet dozens of them, from a variety of class, ethnic and racial backgrounds, from a number of different political currents, and from many regions of the country. Like that rose grower from Drummondville, I hope you will find extraordinary inspiration in their stories.

The book was conceived as an oral history, reflecting the mosaic of the women's movement in Canada. Most histories are written from a single perspective. Feminism has taught me that your view of the world depends in no small measure on your location in it. What you see very much depends on where you stand. My experience in the world is as a middle-class, white, Jewish woman whose generation believed anything was possible. My political perspective as a socialist feminist provides a framework for understanding what I see. But feminism taught me to listen to other women. Opening my ears and my heart to them—Aboriginal, black, poor, immigrant, young and old, lesbian and straight, Québécoise, disabled; from the West, the North and the East; from rural areas and from small towns—opened my mind to new possibilities and enriched my life beyond imagining.

Sharing those stories was one reason to write this book, but there were others. When veteran feminist Kay Macpherson died in 1999, I started to feel an urgency to capture the extraordinary story of Canadian feminism while I could still talk to her generation of feminists. Before I had a chance to interview her, the groundbreaking Rosemary Brown, the first woman to run for the leadership of a national political party and the first black woman to serve in a provincial legislature, was also gone. Fortunately, I was able to talk to a number of other pioneers who blazed the trail for my generation and those to come.

When I graduated from McGill University in 1967, I wanted to be a journalist. Along with my male colleagues at the *McGill Daily,* I applied to a local radio station. "We don't hire girls in the newsroom," the station manager told me. "Why not?" I asked. "Because the men swear and they wouldn't be comfortable with a woman around." "I don't give a shit if they swear," I responded. And then I was doubly damned because not only was I a woman but a foul-mouthed woman. Remembering how far we have come in a single generation is also a way of making sure we never go back.

Another inspiration was Susan Brownmiller's *In Our Time,* a history of the American women's liberation movement that focuses on grassroots activism. Reading Brownmiller, I was struck by how much more interesting and effective the Canadian women's movement has been. Unlike in the United States, women's liberation in Canada started with an alliance between older feminists and young radicals. In Canada, too, socialist feminists played an important role from the beginning, making sure that the interests of working-class women were part of the movement. The resulting alliance between autonomous women's groups and women in the labour movement has made our trade unions the most feminist in the world. Finally, through the efforts of women of colour and Aboriginal women, we succeeded here for a time in creating a multiracial women's movement, with strong leadership from women of colour, Aboriginal women and immigrant women. To my knowledge, this has not happened anywhere else in the world. We haven't overcome the divisions created by racism, but we have learned a lot about constructing alliances across the differences created by race, class, and national and ethnic divisions, alliances essential to creating a better, more egalitarian, world.

Finally, over the last few years, I have happily been engaged with a new generation of activists, female and male, in the anti-globalization movement and on such projects as the New Politics Initiative, *rabble.ca,* the Toronto Social Forum and the Activist School. I have been glad to see the impact of feminism on all of this work. But at the same time, I realize that much of the experience of the second wave of feminism, that of my generation, is getting lost. Most assessments focus on what was accomplished, which laws were changed, the number of positions women now occupy. What is not mentioned is how those changes happened. It is not only that the wheel is being reinvented, which is natural for each generation, it is also that the rich experience of the women's movement, particularly regarding many of the same issues and struggles that preoccupy young activists today, is not easily available. Feminists of the second wave spent decades finding new ways of making decisions and of sharing power. Indeed, many techniques of participatory democracy that activists now employ were honed in feminist collectives and organizations.

So much of what passes for popular knowledge about the women's movement focuses on what was achieved by liberal, middle-class women who already had a certain amount of privilege. These women did play an important role, but there were many, many others: radical feminists, Marxists, anarchists, black consciousness militants, Quebec nationalists, union activists, left-wing NDPers and plain old kick-ass shit disturbers. Radical uppity women make people in power nervous, so they are disappeared from history whenever possible. Radical uppity women are everywhere in this book, and I hope readers will enjoy and learn from them.

THE WOMEN'S MOVEMENT in Canada was so vast and multi-layered that any history is of necessity selective. Naturally, my own experience and knowledge of the movement coloured both my selection of events and my decisions about whom to interview, but at the same time I have tried to include a wide diversity of perspectives. Where there were important differences, I have interviewed women from both sides. *Ten Thousand Roses* covers most of the key political and social issues of the final three decades of the twentieth century and looks at feminism in almost every region of the country. The focus of each chapter is an event or milestone. But there is much that this book does not address. Many national organizations have contributed mightily to the equality of women, each of which has its own important history. Many stories could be told of women's access to and rise in the professions, most particularly academia, journalism, politics, law and medicine. Eco-feminism and women's health can almost be said to constitute movements of their own, and feminists have made significant changes to the field of science. An entire book could be written on the gains of women in culture: In literature, publishing, music, theatre and film, women moved from the margins to the mainstream in a single generation. But I think that the stories told here will give readers a rich, if not complete, picture of the many facets of women's liberation in Canada.

Ten Thousand Roses is assembled from interviews conducted over a two-year period. In some cases, as readers will see, the words of individual women stand alone; other sections of the book read more like conversations. Because of the nature of feminist activism, several women appear more than once in the book. At times I enter the story myself, through excerpts taken from an interview conducted by my friend Kim Elliott. The stories women told me are organized in these pages by decade, although of course the actual work continued and did not divide itself up that neatly. The book starts in the early 1960s and ends with the 1995 Du pain et des roses march in Quebec. Some would say that the 1990s was the decade in which the women's movement died on the vine. I prefer, continuing the metaphor of ten thousand roses, to think of it as a decade that produced abundant rosehips, ready to seed the next generation of feminist fighters.

Through second-wave feminism, thousands of women transformed themselves from passive observers of the world into active agents of change. We changed many of the laws that were holding us back, and opened up economic and social choices barely imagined by our mothers and grandmothers. Young women who find themselves accidentally pregnant no longer face a choice between the horror of a backstreet abortion and the "humiliation" of bearing a child "out of wedlock." One of the most powerful effects of feminism has been to open up our society to new kinds of relationships and new ideas about family and gender roles. It is hard to imagine the lesbian and gay liberation movement making the gains it has without feminism. But feminists have failed to uproot patriarchy. Male power continues to dominate in politics, in corporate boardrooms and in too many families. Women and men around the world are paying the price in the suffering, death and destruction caused by war and violence.

Over the past fifteen years, we have seen a significant shift to the right in our country, which has included cutbacks to the funding women's groups had grown dependent on. We have also seen a massive decentralization of power to the provinces, which feminists always knew would deal a blow to women's advocacy. Since the neo-liberal agenda has failed to deliver the more prosperous society it promised, there is a new opening now for activists to make social demands, such as a national child care program. However, there are few strong voices for feminism at the moment, and new strategies for achieving victory are urgently needed.

When I started working on this book, I thought its main subject would be the outstanding character of Canadian feminism, its diversity, its sophistication and its success, and indeed that story is found within these pages. But the personal is political, as we used to say, and so there are also the individual stories of brave women who saw injustices and decided to fight them. They were part of a river of change that swept our country and ultimately the world.

One of the hardest things for me to explain to others is the joy of fighting for social change. We are programmed in this society to believe that we can't change things and that it is foolish even to try. But as you will read in these pages, ordinary women decided to rise up against a world that limited their possibilities. They fought to realize their dreams and the dreams of other women, and in the process their lives were changed forever. The joy in that struggle, as well as the pain, jumps out of every interview in this book. In these days of cynicism and individualism, I hope it will inspire a new generation of women and men to realize that anyone can be part of making a revolution.

PART I
The 1960s

birth
control
handbook

ONE
THE SEEDBED

The sight of women talking together has always made men uneasy;
nowadays it means rank subversion.

—GERMAINE GREER

W HEN THE PARIS SUMMIT on disarmament broke up without solutions in 1960, *Toronto Star* journalist Lotta Dempsey wrote a column
calling on women to do something about the threat of imminent nuclear
war. Thousands of women responded. A few of them met with Dempsey, and
from that meeting came a new group called Voice of Women. Within
months, five thousand women across Canada had joined.

VOW's members had much in common politically with first-wave
feminists, who had fought for women's suffrage and believed that having
more women in public life would create a more just and more peaceful
society. But Voice of Women was also, as pioneer feminist and scientist
Ursula Franklin points out, "the seedbed for the second wave of feminism."
Organizing in the middle of the Cold War, the group courageously stood up
to the anti-Soviet hysteria of the time, insisting that women from the Soviet
Union and Canada could get together to talk about peace. According to
founding member Muriel Duckworth,

> Voice of Women founders had the idea of women as lifegivers. That was
> the basis on which a lot of women joined: accepting that women are
> lifegivers and therefore we cannot go out there killing people.
>
> Voice of Women had our first international conference of women for
> peace in 1962. Almost as soon as we were founded, we began connecting
> with women all over the world. One of the chief underlying principles

was that the women of the world were not our enemies, and we were not going to behave as if they were. We were going to make contact with them no matter where they lived.

As Ursula Franklin recalls, this personal contact between women permitted them to move past the stereotypes the Cold War had created:

Voice of Women invited Soviet women to come to Canada and talk about early childhood education in '62 or '63. We had to raise all the money, and it took great courage from both the Soviet women and the Canadian women. When the Soviet women arrived, they were naturally apprehensive. I noticed one had a cold, so I grabbed my handbag and gave her some vitamin C, and she smiled with relief. Now what man would do that to break down barriers? That commonality is also part of feminism.

One of Voice of Women's most effective early campaigns was to collect baby teeth from mothers across North America. The teeth, which showed high levels of strontium-90, a product of radiation, were used to pressure U.S. President John F. Kennedy to stop aboveground nuclear testing in Nevada. VOW also focused its efforts on the Canadian government, as Muriel Duckworth explains:

We took the strong political position that Canada should not have nuclear arms. We were very, very upset when Prime Minister Lester B. Pearson allowed them. Pearson was supposed to be the man for peace, you know. But he brought nuclear arms into Canada on New Year's Eve, 1964, sort of secretly. It was a shock to everybody that he would do that so soon after he became prime minister.[1] The Voice of Women also took a very strong position on Canada not getting involved in the Cuban Missile Crisis.

The risks Voice of Women took promoted in action the idea that the women's liberation movement would later develop, as Ursula Franklin points out:

---

1. In 1963 nuclear weapons were a major election issue in Canada. Pearson called for the addition of nuclear weapons to Canada's arsenal, a position opposed by then prime minister John Diefenbaker.

Protesting the Pearson government on nuclear arms lost Voice members, and we lost members by bringing in the Soviet women. We undertook these actions in the full knowledge that they were difficult and controversial and that we'd lose members. But it was an enormous contribution to the liberation of women to show women on the practical level that you could take these risks and survive. Many women feared that their public gestures would affect their kids at school. There were some divorces, but we didn't lose our jobs. Voice of Women was about politics and sharing food and resources, and there was a great deal of friendship on a daily basis. We made considerable gains of knowledge and social perspective. The empowering part of it came from doing something that was so uncommon and unpopular, and surviving and doing it cheerfully.

Women learned how to organize through Voice of Women, how to hold a press conference. Voice was always a bilingual organization. We worked out the language differences by having people speak the language they were most comfortable in, and by placing bilingual people with those who weren't. Later, women went into politics, consciousness-raising, equity and the law, the National Action Committee on the Status of Women, the environmental movement, and many went into the fight against nuclear power.

VOICE OF WOMEN was ahead of its time. In general, the second wave of feminism is agreed to have started in 1963, with the publication in the United States of Betty Friedan's *The Feminine Mystique*. Years before young radicals discovered feminism, the generation of women before them was starting to push against the constraints of what Friedan called "the problem with no name." "The problem," she writes, "lay buried, unspoken, many years in the minds of American women. It was a strange stirring, a sense of dissatisfaction, a yearning that women suffered in the middle of the twentieth century ... [A woman] was afraid to ask even of herself the silent question—'Is this all?'"

While Friedan summed it up, Canadian women had been reading about this "problem with no name" for several years by that time. Doris Anderson had taken the helm of the women's magazine *Chatelaine* in 1957—the first woman in that position—and begun to publish feminist articles long before the mainstream had a notion of the women's movement to come. In her autobiography, *Rebel Daughter*, Anderson describes why:

It became obvious to me that many of our readers shared a common problem—frustration.... With children in school and time on their hands, many were bored and longed to get a job.... But husbands often considered a working wife a reflection on their masculinity. "No wife of mine is going out to work!" was a common rallying cry.

With a sense of irony, Anderson recounts what happened when Betty Friedan asked if *Chatelaine* would serialize her book: "We discussed it and decided that we had already printed all that stuff."

No one could have realized that Friedan's book would spark such widespread recognition among women. Dorothy Inglis, a founder of Voice of Women and later of the St. John's Women's Centre, describes her reaction:

I read it thoroughly, and all my friends read it. At every party, it was the topic of discussion. It was a revelation to me that other women were feeling what I felt. I hadn't enunciated it to myself. I missed being a social worker, which I had given up once I got pregnant. I loved social work. Now I was a stay-at-home mother except over the summers, when I would fill in for social workers on vacation and my husband would pitch in. I had three small children I adored, and I loved being a mother and was very happy with my husband. But I also felt that I was a person, although I wasn't able to say that; I wasn't even conscious of what I was thinking. And then there was this book. It said I didn't have to feel guilty. I didn't know other women had this funny feeling.

Women everywhere began to act on their new awareness. In 1966 Thérèse Casgrain, a leader in the Quebec's women's struggle to get the vote and a VOW activist, founded the Fédération des femmes du Québec. That same year, led by feminist Laura Sabia, a group calling themselves the Committee for the Equality of Women in Canada formed in Toronto to campaign for the establishment of a Royal Commission on the status of women. In 1967, after the committee's polite briefs were ignored by the federal government, Sabia upped the ante. "We're tired of being nice about trying to get an official enquiry into women's rights in Canada," she told *The Globe and Mail.* "If we don't get a royal commission by the end of this month, we'll use every tactic we can. And if we have to use violence, damn it, we will." Pearson set up the Royal Commission later that year, and the commission's cross-country hearings provided a rallying point for the emerging women's movement.

IT WAS NOT JUST Friedan's generation that was waking up to the world around it. Young women, entering university in larger numbers than ever before, were drawn into the student activist movements of the time. The 1960s was a decade of revolutionary change. National liberation struggles against colonialism and imperialism were on the rise across Asia, Africa and Latin America. The United States and Soviet Union continued to battle for world hegemony, but the Cold War's hold began to be burned away first by the American civil rights movement and then by an unprecedented youth radicalization. The civil rights movement had been protesting what amounted to apartheid in the southern United States since the 1950s, and both the non-violent struggle led by Reverend Martin Luther King and the more militant Black Power movement, led by Malcolm X and the Black Panther Party, inspired young people and people of African origin around the world. The first mass resistance in the United States to the Cold War was against the war in Vietnam. In Europe, young people took inspiration from the anti-colonial liberation struggles against their own governments. The student revolt and subsequent mass strike in May and June of 1968 in France were widely seen as a revolutionary mobilization that inspired young activists on both sides of the Atlantic.

In Canada, the decade began with the Quiet Revolution, which swept Quebec into the twentieth century with dramatic flair. In a few short years, under the leadership of Premier Jean Lesage, the Quebec government loosened the grip of the Catholic Church on education, modernized labour laws, abolished the law that declared married women minors and nationalized hydroelectric power. By mid-decade, three of Quebec's brightest leaders, Pierre Trudeau, Jean Marchand and Gérard Pelletier, dubbed by the media "the three wise men," had accepted Prime Minister Lester B. Pearson's invitation to participate in his government in Ottawa. Despite that Pearson was prime minister for most of the decade, it was Trudeau's leadership and charm that defined the Canadian government in the 1960s.

The student, anti-war and civil rights movements in the United States, as well as the revolutionary youth movements in Europe, inspired young people in Canada to activism as well. In the spirit of the times, they organized, occupied, demonstrated and insisted on being heard by those in power. Organizations such as the Student Union for Peace Action, the Canadian Union of Students, Students for a Democratic University and the Union générale des étudiants du Québec represented what came to be called the New Left in Canada. In 1969 the Waffle, a mostly young left-wing national-ist current, challenged the New Democratic Party leadership and ran up against the party's anti-Communism; the Waffle itself was not Communist, but the League for Socialist Action, a Trotskyist organization, was active within its ranks. The Front de libération du Québec, formed in 1963, identified the struggle for Quebec independence with the black liberation struggle in the United States and the Algerian anti-colonial struggle. While the FLQ's numbers were small, the group's influence, particularly through their writing, was especially strong among youth.

The creative political thinking and actions of these young activists transformed North American culture and society. Their challenges to authority on everything from sexuality, the nuclear family and the length of one's hair to the nature of democracy itself had a fundamental and lasting impact. But the young women in these radical movements played just as subordinate a role to male activists as their mothers did to their fathers. When they got tired of walking three steps behind their men, they too revolted. They called their movement "women's liberation."

It started in Canada with the Toronto Women's Liberation Movement, founded in 1967, and mushroomed from there. The Feminine Action League was established at Simon Fraser University in Burnaby, soon followed by the Women's Caucus in Vancouver. By 1969 similar groups existed in Regina, Saskatoon, Winnipeg, Ottawa, Kingston, Guelph, Hamilton, Halifax, Sudbury, Thunder Bay, Edmonton and Montreal. A mimeographed article entitled "Sisters, Brothers, Lovers, Listen …" was passed eagerly from hand to hand among women in the New Left. It denounced the "male chauvinism" of their comrades and ended with the declaration, "We are going to be typers of letters and distributors of leaflets no longer."

Men on the left did not watch this development passively, as Vancouver activist Jean Rands recalls:

> The student movement was dominated by articulate young men who were arrogant and full of themselves. Women were intimidated, and there was a lot of nasty, misogynist stuff that happened. When the student left organization at Simon Fraser University invited some left-wing activists from Germany to speak, the women's caucus there decided to hold a meeting with the woman member. The male left was so outraged that we would have a woman-only meeting that they tried to drown us out.

Everywhere that women stood up, men freaked out. Denise Kouri remembers what it was like for Saskatoon Women's Liberation, one of the most active groups in the country:

> Our group of activists was small, and people were such jerks to us. When we were doing the women's educational table on campus, the engineers rigged up a cannon and bombed us with oranges. Men would actually say things like, "You're ugly and just need a good fucking."

But the hostile male reaction simply spurred young feminists on. In fact, it was often this reaction that caused things to click for them, as Waffle activist Martha Tracey recalls:

> One of the epiphanies for me was a Waffle meeting in Regina. A woman and three men were planning to move east, and I remember that one guy got up and talked about how three very important people to the organization were leaving. It was so abundantly clear who he was leaving out. At that point I had really thought that we were equal in the organization, and I was absolutely appalled. It was a very emotional moment for me.

Feminism reached deep into all the radical circles in Canada. Akua Benjamin arrived in Canada from Trinidad in the middle of the radical ferment in Toronto's black community:

> In those days there were lots of support groups for African liberation movements. There was anti-racist organizing. There was the White Paper on Immigration in 1966, and, of course, the student struggle at Sir George Williams University in Montreal in 1969.[2] We had all kinds of rallies and forums to talk about these various issues.
>
> The women were the workhorses in these organizations. We did the cooking and the cleaning. The men would get up and talk and talk. Men were the leaders, and we were told to do the grunge work. Anne Cools came to one of these meetings, and she blasted the men. She challenged us

---

2. In 1969 students at Sir George Williams, led by black activists Rosie Douglas and Anne Cools, protested against a professor who was accused of racism, and in the ensuing struggle computer data and university equipment were damaged.

women in the room as to why we were not talking. In those days, I just sat quietly in the back of the room. I would sit there and sweat. I was afraid to speak, afraid that I would get shut down. Anne cursed the men out, saying, "fucking" this and "fucking" that. We had never heard a woman talk like that. She really empowered me. After that I thought, "I'm going raise my voice."

In Quebec, radical youth identified closely with national liberation struggles, seeing Quebec as akin to a Third World country. The women's movement was closely linked with national liberation, as described by union activist Monique Simard:

In the late 1960s, feminism was emerging in Quebec, but it was very, very interlinked with all the other social movements at the time, the nationalist question, the trade union movement. The slogan of the women's liberation movement was, "There can be no liberation of Quebec without women's liberation, and no women's liberation without the liberation of Quebec." So it was a total environment.

I supported le Front de libération des femmes du Québec, FLF. I was not a member, but I was around. There were huge demonstrations at that time. There were taverns, pubs, forbidden to women, and there was this huge demonstration where women went into the pubs and were chained together so we could not be removed. We were all arrested.

Probably the most famous women's action of the 1960s was the protest against the Miss America Pageant in Atlantic City in 1968. But a year later, Canadian women carried out an even more effective protest against beauty pageants. At the time a young student who had just discovered feminism, Judy Darcy tells this story:

In a meeting in December 1969 of the Toronto Women's Liberation Movement (TWLM), there was discussion of the Miss Canadian University Pageant that was slated to happen in January of 1970. Miss Simon Fraser University was planning to disrupt the pageant, but when the organizers got wind of it, they decided to disqualify her. Feminists needed another protest candidate, and women asked me.

I went to a meeting of the student government and asked if I could be Miss York University. They were shocked and wondered what I was up to.

After a debate they said, okay, but don't tell us what you're going to do. I didn't have to go through any process; I just got declared Miss York University. I went undercover to pageant preparations for several days, sneaking out for strategy meetings. As part of the contest, we had blind dates and went out to events with these guys. They were placing bets on us. It was an excruciating experience for a young feminist.

On the night of the pageant, there was a demonstration outside as we walked in on the arms of our blind dates. The pageant started, and we had to walk in a T formation. I was one of the seven semi-finalists. I'm sure the judges knew what I was up to, and they thought it would be a choice thing to do. They awarded Miss Congeniality, and then it was the drum roll and the envelope please. Janille Jolley, a member of TWLM, came in from outside chanting and demanding the right to speak. This was being televised. She marched up to the podium and got in a spat with the MC. They stopped filming. She denounced the beauty pageant, and the MC tried to stop her by saying she wasn't a contestant. Then I was allowed to speak. I yelled, "It's true, it's a meat market, and they do exploit women." We marched out singing "Solidarity Forever." We came this close to having Miss Memorial University and Miss Queen's walk out too.

I was terrified, and the media report said I was crying. It was incredibly stressful and scary. It was like going back into an incredibly oppressive culture after I felt I had left it all behind. I did it for the movement. I felt it was important to put aside personal considerations for the cause. Once it was over, though, we felt proud of it. It got a lot of coverage, and it had a ripple effect. We made a powerful statement, and it did make a difference.

Protesting mainstream notions of female beauty was important, but the focus of women's liberation groups was much broader: Feminists organized to give women control over their own bodies. In the middle of what was called the sexual revolution, abortion was illegal, as was distributing birth control information. Women across the country did abortion referral and set up information tables on campuses. *The Birth Control Handbook* published by the McGill Student Society in 1968 became an underground bestseller across North America. In part because of women's organizing, the House of Commons passed an omnibus bill in 1969 that covered abortion, birth control and homosexuality. The new law decriminalized homosexual acts between consenting adults and made birth control legal, but it placed serious restrictions on abortion. Feminists continued to organize.

Women's health and sexuality were common topics of discussion in the consciousness-raising groups that women began to set up across the country. Talking together in small groups in someone's kitchen or living room, women began to realize that what they had thought were personal problems were really social and political. Friedan's "problem with no name" turned out, for many young women, to be the sexist nature of relationships. "The personal is political" became the movement's *cri de cœur*. Regina union activist Pat Gallagher recalls the power of those first experiences of female solidarity:

> *I was in a very oppressive marriage, and it was very revealing to me that I wasn't a crazy person for feeling really upset about being in an exploitive relationship. The women's liberation movement opened up a tremendous number of doors for me. All of a sudden I felt released.*

As a way of reclaiming their bodies and their sexuality, women in consciousness-raising and self-help groups often devoted some time to examining their vaginas. As these three Saskatoon feminists remember with considerable amusement, it was an important step in their liberation:

AUDREY HALL: Self-examination was very popular. CBC came to my house, and a group of us got together with our speculums and our mirrors, reclaiming our cervixes. I wrote an article for *Canadian Nurse* about it.

DENISE KOURI: People found it pretty shocking. I remember a more traditional left-wing woman saying to us one time, "While you're looking at your cervix, we're looking at the world."

GWEN GRAY: Ah, but we found the world in our cervixes.

Learning more about themselves led women to wanting to learn more about one another. There has since come to be an enormous body of work written about women through the discipline of women's studies, but in the 1960s, there was almost nothing. In 1968 Greta Hofmann Nemiroff, a professor at Sir George Williams University turned on to feminism by reading Betty Friedan and Simone de Beauvoir, decided with a friend to create and teach such a course. Their class was packed, as Greta remembers:

> *A lot of what we integrated into the course came from the students themselves. They did their big assignments on things close to their hearts. We*

would begin to develop a database of the research these students did. One woman's grandmother had been a labour organizer in the needle trade in Montreal. She did a project on this. She brought us the soup that her grandmother served. We were looking forward to homemade soup, but it turned out to be a can of Campbell's soup, as an example of what a working woman needed.

BY THE END OF THE 1960s, there were three streams of feminism in Canada: VOW peace activists; the middle-class mothers and career women who belonged to established groups such as the Canadian Federation of University Women and the YWCA; and the young radicals. Since many young feminists had come from the anti–Vietnam War movement, Voice of Women saw them as important new allies. And despite the slogan of the period, "Never trust anyone over thirty," young feminists quickly saw how much they had in common with these activist women. In 1971, VOW organized public meetings and conferences all across Canada where Vietnamese women spoke to hundreds of American women, who came to Canada to meet them and were supposedly their enemies. Young feminists welcomed and supported this important contribution to the anti-war movement. As a new decade dawned, the three streams of feminism flowed together to form the second wave of the Canadian women's movement.

PART II
The 1970s

ABORTION IS OUR RIGHT

WOMEN'S LIBERATION MOVEMENT

Feminism isn't an employment agency for women;
it's an alternative way of ordering the social space,
in which women are the prototype rather than men.
It is based on collaboration rather than competition.
As a youngster, I still remember my feeling of joy
that one could look at the earth differently.
That's feminism: everything is differently oriented.
Seeing the same world through different eyes.

—URSULA FRANKLIN

THE REVOLUTIONARY FERVOUR of the 1960s continued into the early years of the next decade. Political divisions inside the American New Left led to political splits in the largest student organization, Students for a Democratic Society, with a faction calling themselves the Weathermen (and later the Weather Underground) opting for a declaration of war against the U.S. government. As their tactics escalated from vandalism to bombing key government buildings, including the Capitol, the Weathermen went underground, and for a decade evaded a massive FBI manhunt. The 1970 Kent State massacre, in which the National Guard fired on a crowd of demonstrators in Ohio and killed four university students, combined with the rising death toll of American soldiers to turn the tide of public opinion against the Vietnam War. By 1973, in a tremendous victory for the anti-war movement, all American troops were out of Vietnam. On September 11, 1973, the democratically elected Marxist government of Salvador Allende in Chile was overthrown in a violent coup backed by the United States, raising serious questions among radicals throughout the Americas and Europe about the possibility of achieving revolutionary change through peaceful means. Between 1972 and 1974, the Watergate scandal exposed corruption in the highest office of the American government.

In Canada, the FLQ also moved toward the increasing use of violence. From the mailbox bombings it had conducted in the mid-1960s, the group graduated to kidnapping Quebec cabinet minister Pierre Laporte and British trade commissioner James Cross. The Canadian government's proclamation of the War Measures Act on October 16, 1970, in reaction to the kidnappings, suspended civil liberties. More than 450 people were arrested in Montreal, and troops occupied the city's streets. Laporte's body was found in the trunk of a car; James Cross was released early that December. The New Democratic Party was the only mainstream group in English Canada to oppose the declaration of the War Measures Act. But while most Canadians supported the federal government's actions, most Québécois saw them as an attack on the growing sovereignty movement. In 1976 the newly formed Parti Québécois was elected under the leadership of René Lévesque. The monumental struggle between sovereignty and federalism that defined the decade was epitomized in the battle between former allies Lévesque and Pierre Trudeau.

For those on the left, the invoking of the War Measures Act was a watershed. It provided clear evidence that the Canadian government, like its American counterpart, was prepared to go to extremes against opposition; many of those arrested in Quebec were socialist activists who had nothing to do with the FLQ. Leftists became much less idealistic about how quickly revolutionary change would happen. Those who remained politically active went in a variety of directions. The Waffle, which had significant female leadership, continued to gain influence inside the NDP. But although the group mounted a significant challenge at the NDP's 1971 leadership convention, developing strong platforms on women's liberation, the environment and Canadian nationalism, its failure to win led to the Waffle being driven out of the party. Marxist-Leninist groups in Quebec, following the teachings of Mao Tse-tung, experienced extraordinary growth, with a membership of almost seven thousand young militants. In English Canada, a portion of the Waffle leadership formed the Revolutionary Marxist Group (RMG), a small Trotskyist organization that later merged with the League for Socialist Action (LSA). These far-left groups declined significantly as the decade progressed, with much of their female leadership going into the women's movement and the union movement. One of the most significant differences between the women's movement in Canada and that in the United States was the importance here of socialist feminists.

The 1970s saw the flowering of the women's movement in Canada and around the world. In 1970 Shulamith Firestone's *The Dialectic of Sex*, Germaine Greer's *The Female Eunuch* and Kate Millett's *Sexual Politics* made radical feminist and socialist feminist ideology available to a wide audience. *Sisterhood Is Powerful*, an anthology edited by American feminist Robin

Morgan, defined the newly emerging women's movement in the United States. By 1975 feminism was so pervasive that the United Nations declared it International Women's Year. In Canada, the decade began with two monumental events for women: the report of the Royal Commission on the Status of Women and the abortion caravan.

In its three years of operation, the Royal Commission had gathered research, held public meetings throughout the country and received briefs from 480 individuals and organizations. When the commission was established, Elsie Gregory McGill was the only self-proclaimed feminist,[1] but by the time the hearings were over, the remaining four female commissioners— Quebec academic Jeanne Lapointe, Alberta farmer Lola Lange, New Brunswick judge Doris Ogilvie and the chair of the commission, Frances Bird—were feminists in their own right. The commission's 1970 report, with its 167 recommendations for changes to government policy, became the focus of the more established women's movement of the time.

Young radical women, however, were less interested in lobbying than in direct action. Women's groups and feminist services such as women's centres, rape crisis centres, shelters and transition houses emerged rapidly in every region of the country. Many grassroots organizations were funded through Opportunities for Youth (OFY) and the Local Initiatives Program (LIP), federal government programs designed to channel—some might say co-opt—the energies of radical youth. In 1973 the Women's Program of Secretary of State was established to fund women's groups doing advocacy. It was not only government funding that permitted women's groups to flourish, it was also the easy availability of both jobs and unemployment insurance. Feminists didn't hesitate to quit their jobs for movement work or to go on and off unemployment insurance to keep an organization running.

Women's writing and publishing were indispensable to the feminist revolution. They put "woman" into the popular slogan, "Freedom of the press belongs to the man who owns one." *Kinesis,* Canada's first feminist

---

1. The daughter of British Columbia's first woman judge, Elsie Gregory McGill was an electrical engineer and aircraft designer. In the 1960s she devoted considerable time and energy to women's organizations, serving as national president of the Canadian Federation of Business and Professional Women's Clubs from 1962 to 1964. As a founding member of the National Action Committee on the Status of Women, she was involved in its activities until her death. She was so ahead of her time that she kept her own name when she married in 1943, probably the first woman in Canada to do so.

newspaper, hit the newsstands in Vancouver in 1972. Numerous feminist newspapers and magazines followed, including *Broadside* in Toronto, *Upstream* in Ottawa and the *Northern Women's Journal* in Thunder Bay. *Les Têtes de pioche* and *La Vie en rose* were enormously influential in Quebec. Women formed their own publishing houses as well. Canadian Women's Educational Press, later known as the Women's Press, started off with several feminist kids' books and anthologies, such as *Women Unite!* and *Women at Work*. In Vancouver, the women of Press Gang trained as printers and then went on to produce classic early titles such as *I'm Not Mad, I'm Angry: Women Look at Psychiatry.* Feminist cultural activism carried into film with the National Film Board's launch of Studio D, which produced and promoted films by and about women.

While many feminists continued to organize around abortion and women's health, others turned their attention to economic and legal equality, daycare and violence against women. There was tremendous feminist activism in and around unions. Aboriginal women began organizing in the early 1970s to fight sexual discrimination on reserves and in the Indian Act.

Many of the Royal Commission's recommendations centred on increasing the number of women in public life. The decade opened with only one woman in the House of Commons, NDP MP Grace MacInnis. Women for Political Action, a multi-party coalition, held a national conference in 1973 to debate strategies for increasing the number of women in Parliament, and in 1974 two members of the group ran as independent candidates. But although women in each of three major parties set up women's committees, there was little improvement in the representation of women until the 1980s. Rosemary Brown became the first black woman elected to a legislature when she won a seat in British Columbia in 1972. In 1979, fed up with the slow progress women were making in mainstream politics, seven hundred women attended the founding meeting of the Feminist Party of Canada. But the Feminist Party never ran a candidate, and women continued to struggle for representation in the male-dominated political parties. Flora Macdonald, a staunch promoter of women's rights throughout her life, blazed a trail for women in politics working closely with feminist advocates. Even then the path was not always easy. When she was first elected in 1972, almost anything out of the ordinary made her the centre of public attention.

I worked twice as hard as anybody. You had to work hard. I had decided early in my career in the House that I would change the custom that only dresses were suitable, so one day I wore a pantsuit into the House of Commons. It was a beautiful pantsuit. I had bought it in France, and it was good quality. That became a front-page photograph right across Canada. Not long afterward, Margaret Thatcher became the leader of the British Conservative Party. She went to New York to do interviews, and on the way back she stopped off in Ottawa to meet Robert Stanfield, the leader of the Progressive Conservative Party. He had a small luncheon for her, and after the lunch Mrs. Stanfield and Mrs. Thatcher and I were standing together. Mrs. Stanfield, who was always direct in her questioning, said to Mrs. Thatcher, "Do people single you out as a woman because you may do something differently?" Mrs. Thatcher said, "I'm not quite sure what you mean." Mrs. Stanfield said, "Let me give you an example. Flora here wore a pantsuit into the House of Commons, and it became a front-page picture across the country. Would that sort of thing happen to you?" Mrs. Thatcher replied, "No, but then I would never wear a pantsuit into the House of Commons." You never can tell where the criticism will come from.

Canada's two currents of feminism emerged from the two generations of women: those trying to reform the system to improve the status of women and those who believed that a more radical transformation of society was necessary to achieve women's equality. These two currents worked together in uneasy alliance. But it wasn't only the generation gap that divided the women's movement. Soon after the first women's liberation groups were formed in major cities, significant political differences began to emerge. Socialist feminists believed women's liberation could be won only through an anti-capitalist transformation of society. Radical feminists saw patriarchy as the major problem. Much of the debate in the 1970s would centre on these differences in analysis, strategy and tactics.

TWO

SPEAKING TRUTH TO POWER
The Status of Women Committees

What I wanted more than anything was to be able to look after myself and make sure that every other woman in the world could do the same.

—DORIS ANDERSON, *REBEL DAUGHTER*

C ANADA'S FIRST PROVINCIAL COMMITTEE on the status of women was formed by a group of far-seeing feminists in Manitoba in 1967. Around the same time, women in Ontario had initiated a campaign calling for a Royal Commission on the status of women. The call came most vocally from Laura Sabia, president of the Canadian Federation of University Women (CFUW). Founded in 1919, the CFUW had emerged from the first wave of feminism, when women fought for the vote, and remained active since then. In the United States, established groups such as the League of Women Voters kept their distance from the radical young women agitating for equality in the 1960s. In Canada, such organizations did their best to work with young feminists. The best example of that uneasy unity was the Strategy for Change conference held in Toronto in 1972. Kay Macpherson described the gathering as the women in hats and gloves coming together with the women in T-shirts and jeans. The conference set the stage for many future developments in the women's movement, most importantly the founding of the National Action Committee on the Status of Women, which became Canada's largest women's organization, representing more than six hundred women's groups. From the first, NAC represented both conservative women's organizations, such as church groups and the YWCA, and radical groups, such as rape crisis centres, as well as women from all three major political parties. NAC's initial focus was to lobby the federal government for implementation of the recommendations of the Royal Commission, so many grassroots activists saw the organization as a liberal women's group at first. Nevertheless, over the years, many of the key debates of the women's movement took place on the floor of NAC's annual general meetings. NAC's first three presidents were Laura Sabia, Grace Hartman and Lorna Marsden: a Progressive Conservative, an NDPer and a Liberal respectively.

Women across the country formed their own action committees to follow up on the Royal Commission's recommendations. Two of the most active of these were in Vancouver and St. John's. In 1997, at the twenty-fifth anniversary of the Vancouver Status of Women, pioneer feminist politician Rosemary Brown, also a VSW founding member, recalled, "We were so naïve in those days. We thought if we could just explain the problems that women were facing to politicians, things would change." Through these status of women committees, women worked at the national, provincial and local levels to achieve political change. Their activities focused on lobbying, education and, on the local front, providing services to the women in their communities.

Manitoba Action Committee on the Status of Women

Susanna June Menzies

When I left the public service to have my first child in 1958, I realized that I had been earning an income and contributing to a pension and all the rest of it. All of those things stopped instantly, and I was regarded as a dependant of my husband. There weren't any laws about equality in marriage or anything like that. I was treated on the same basis as my child, in spite of this tremendous contribution I was making to the economy. A transfer of wealth, let's say, from me to the family, from me to the economy, without any recognition whatsoever. It was a gradual recognition, but that is when I became a feminist and decided to work to change the laws.

The other thing that was quite crucial for me was the United Nations conventions, the human rights conventions, the status of women conventions. I had joined a study group on the status of women in Ottawa, through the University Women's Club. I started researching the laws in Canada to see how well we complied with the United Nations human rights declarations, and I was astonished to find out that we were far below acceptable standards. I'd had the advantage of going to university and having independent employment, but what I assumed was there in the laws simply wasn't.

When my husband and I moved to Winnipeg in 1961, we had two children. At the time, a group of sole-support mothers were parading on the legislative grounds, wanting their maintenance orders enforced. Donald Bruce MacDonald, who was a United Church minister, invited them to meet in his church. Then he called me and said, "I have these women and I don't know what to do. Will you come down and talk to them?" So that was my first opportunity to put a public face on the private knowledge I had been accumulating. Here were specific examples of people being treated very, very poorly. All of the contributions these women were making were totally ignored. They were considered to be parasites on the economy because they needed support.

On the first night we met, the group told me they had an appointment to speak at the legislative assembly the next day. After we talked, they asked if I would put something together. So I wrote all night and put together what I knew about human rights—the rights of children, maintenance rights, this kind of thing—into a brief using their specific examples. Really, that was the beginning of my feminist work.

When the Royal Commission announced that it would be travelling across the country, we were already quite active in our various groups. Thelma Forbes, a member of Duff Roblin's cabinet, invited us to come to a meeting in the legislative buildings.[1] She thought it would be good for the Manitoba women's groups to come together and discuss what we were going to do. By then, some women had already submitted a brief to Duff Roblin, asking him to have a pilot commission in Manitoba, which he did not do.

We had set up our volunteer committee in 1967 to do the same thing we had asked Duff to do. It was organized along the same lines as the U.S. status of women commissions we'd been hearing about. We named all the categories that we were going to investigate, and we got a chairperson and volunteers for each of these committees. We travelled around the province. Not very many of us; we travelled in one or two cars. We had hearings, and people from the smaller cities and towns and rural districts came to tell us of their experiences. Then we went back home and wrote this all up. We

---

1. Duff Roblin was the Conservative premier of Manitoba from 1958 to 1967.

had our findings privately printed, and each committee presented its own brief to the Royal Commission.

After the Royal Commission reported, we came together again to form the Manitoba Action Committee on the Status of Women, because we were going to work for the changes that were recommended. It was 1971, and we were the first provincial action committee in the country. One of the major issues we worked on was the Murdoch case. Irene Murdoch was a farm woman in Alberta. Her husband was away a lot of the time, so she ran the ranch and the farm, and she was a very capable woman. Her husband was quite abusive; she had been battered. She left him, and then she claimed her rights to the farm. If she had been a brother or a partner or anybody else, she would have got it. But she was denied because she was a wife. She was denied her rights in dower because she had left the homestead, she had left the husband, even under those circumstances. So she was out on a limb without anything.

Immediately after the Murdoch case was decided in 1971, I was going up to Gimli to speak to a group of farm women. I knew people were wondering what the case was all about. So often people don't become aware of the issues until they find themselves perhaps bereaved, perhaps unemployed, perhaps a single parent, and then suddenly all of the problems hit them with a bang. Since I would be talking to farm women, I got a couple of my friends to come with me to put on a skit. It would be called "The Balloon Lady." We would have this lady floating along, upheld by inflated balloons. The balloons would represent marriage rights, pension rights, employment rights, and all the rest of it. We talked about Mrs. Murdoch and her experiences, and with each group of rights she thought she had, prick, the balloon would be burst. At the end, the balloon lady was flat on the ground without any supports.

It struck the farm women like a thunderbolt, because suddenly each of them realized, "I am Mrs. Murdoch." Requests for us to put this skit on just soared. We went all over the province talking to various groups, and the skit became very well known. Each time we performed it, there would be discussion afterward. Women would stand up in the audience and tell their own stories. The skit was different each time, because we weaved in stories and experiences we had learned about, what laws they related to and what injustices there were. It was a tremendous communications vehicle. We did more to promote the rights of women with that skit than with anything else.

The Royal Commission report contained 167 recommendations, and the various women's organizations in the province worked together to implement the resolutions. In 1972 Laura Sabia called a meeting in Toronto, for the same purpose nationally. Jean Carston and I went from Manitoba. When the group was deciding what to call the new committee, we suggested it be called the National Action Committee on the Status of Women, so that each province could form its own committee and we would have the same cohesiveness. That was argued back and forth. It is quite funny. Everybody else there seemed to be from Toronto. They were from all the national organizations, but they were from Toronto. So Jean got up to say something, and this woman said, "Oh, yes, but you're provincial, and we are national." This amused us highly. But they did decide to call it the National Action Committee. Then Laura said, "Look, we'll call it the National Ad Hoc Committee on the Status of Women. All of these recommendations are laid out, and they shouldn't take any time to implement. We'll call ourselves ad hoc, and then we can drop it." Of course, things didn't happen that way.

STRATEGY FOR CHANGE

Flora MacDonald

There wasn't anything in the way of a women's organization in the 1960s, other than in the political parties. In political parties, women's committees were always looked on as adjuncts, or something to help out when the time came, but not to make decisions. But Laura Sabia headed the Canadian Federation of University Women. Every year they met with cabinet and brought recommendations. They were a non-partisan organization that represented a great swath of women's groups all across the country. Among other things, they were always lobbying for better representation of women in Parliament, particularly in cabinet. This was while Lester Pearson was prime minister, and there was one woman, Judy LaMarsh, in the cabinet. Mr. Pearson said, "You know, I have a woman in the cabinet." Laura said, "Well, we want a Royal Commission on the status of women to find out where women stand." He wasn't at all willing to listen to what she said. But then she said, "Well, then, I'll have two million women march on Parliament." It was really because of that threat that reconsideration was given to setting up the commission.

Laura was amazing, a very colourful, well-spoken individual. She came from an Italian background, had grown up, got married to a doctor, lived in St. Catharines, became active on city council, then became mayor and then a radio host. Her broadcasts were listened to everywhere. She personified a kind of leadership that attracted many people.

Kay Sigurjonsson

In the late 1960s, I was a very young staff member at the Federation of Women Teachers of Ontario. My boss, Dorothy Martin, was in some ways very conventional, but she became involved in the little group around Laura Sabia that was demanding the government set up a Royal Commission on the status of women. Laura had announced that she would gather two million women and march on Ottawa, although she said afterward she knew about ten people who might go.

The reaction when the Royal Commission was first set up, from governments and from journalists, most of whom were men, was that it was a joke. "What's wrong with the status of women?" Women got really hostile to this, particularly as the commission went across the country. It held hearings in every province, and stories were coming out from ordinary women, terrible stories. I don't know how these women had the courage to show up. These were things nobody talked about—discrimination, unfair pay, the difficulties of bringing up children. So the media had to start taking the whole thing seriously. That was very enlightening for our membership.

The National Action Committee on the Status of Women was really founded in our office. Laura Sabia called a meeting after the Royal Commission reported, and we were the only people at the meeting who had an office. So we sent the notices out, and the group continued to meet in our office. It was agreed that we would have a founding convention of people from across the country. We called ourselves the National Ad Hoc Committee on the Status of Women. We laughed about it, because there were two women from St. Catharines and the rest of us were from Toronto. Anyway, we told the federal minister of labour that we represented the women of Canada, and he believed us. He gave us quite a lot of money for the conference. But the conference was organized by our staff. My secretary, Francis Orida, and I were NAC for a long time.

We had women come from across the country to attend, since we had money to pay for this travel. I think it was the first time in Canadian history that child care was offered at a conference. Our staff ran the child care. They were mostly young mothers themselves. The conference was held at the King Edward Hotel, a real dump in those days. Our staff had a few bedrooms full of the children who had come to the conference. I'm sure it would be illegal now, because we didn't have the facilities.

There were women attending who belonged to what was called the Women's Liberation Movement, very radical women. The strength of NAC from the beginning was that it represented everybody. Laura was very establishment herself. But she looked around the table at the first meeting we held after the Royal Commission report and said, "Where are the young women?" I was insulted, because I was quite young. But she meant, where are the radical women? She made a real effort to reach out to the radical groups, all of which despised her. I remember once that Laura said something about a young girl doing something or other. She meant a young woman. People hissed, shouted at her. She took a lot of very rude behaviour, but she was determined to have everybody there.

So, everybody was there. Some women had hitchhiked to come to the meeting. Women were billeted. All of that was organized by our staff, too. Women brought babies on their backs, and then at the same conference you had women from the Business and Professional Women's Club and the Canadian Federation of University Women. Laura didn't know any rules of order. She had chaired meetings for years, but she didn't have any idea how to run a meeting. So there was chaos as we were trying to bring everything together at the end. Believe it or not, Barbara Amiel took the minutes of that meeting.[2] Laura had hired her good friend, who wouldn't have had any sympathy for anything that was said or done, but who did a very good report on the meeting that went to government. On the last day of the conference we were trying to come up with some resolutions and Laura put her foot in her mouth, as she often did, by saying, "We've got to get these unions on side." One of the trade union women stood up and defended her union brothers. We thought the whole thing was going to fall apart. But it didn't fall apart. It was astounding.

Thérèse Casgrain, who was there, was the grande dame of Quebec feminism. She had fought for the right to vote, which women didn't get until the 1940s in Quebec. Florence Bird, or Anne Frances as she was known, was also at the conference. She had been the chair of the Royal

---

2. Barbara Amiel is a right-wing journalist who has opposed most of the demands of the women's movement.

Commission. Florence Bird had gone to one of the great women's colleges in the U.S. with Katherine Hepburn, and Thérèse Casgrain came from a distinguished French-Canadian family. I think they didn't know quite what had hit them when these loud young women would stand up and heckle. They were no respecters of persons, these tough younger women. But it wasn't so serious that anyone marched off in a huff.

In the early years, NAC was pretty establishment. I was on the executive for a while. It was pretty middle class and respectable for a long time. But that was a useful thing. Governments gave us a lot of money to open an office, have a newsletter and keep things going, because we didn't look as dangerous as we were.

Madeleine Parent

I had been doing trade union organizing among women since 1942. As the women's movement began to develop in Quebec, I didn't join, but I followed it and was quite pleased about it. I was also working in Ontario a lot with the Confederation of Canadian Unions.[3] I had followed the proceedings of the Royal Commission, and especially its final report, and when there was an open call to attend the conference in Toronto, I thought it important to go. I thought working-class women should be represented. The government had allowed money for two women from each province and territory to attend but, low and behold, five hundred women turned up.

I was one of the speakers at the banquet on the Friday night. Several ministers had been invited, but they all refused. Government officials had told the organizing committee that Florence Bird, the chair of the Royal Commission, had to be the keynote speaker. In her speech, she said that the most important thing was that the women's movement should ask the government to set up an advisory committee on the status of women.

On Saturday we had workshops, and women civil servants were everywhere, pushing for the advisory committee. All the workshops except one came back with this key recommendation. Laura Sabia asked me what I thought about it. A friend of mine, Yvette Rousseau, was at the conference heading a delegation from Quebec. Yvette had been to a meeting of delegation leaders, and she told me the leaders were really being pushed to accept this recommendation. That's when I realized we were going to have to fight. Laurell Ritchie and I went to Kay Macpherson and

---

3. The CCU was formed to break with American control of the labour movement.

said, we have an opportunity here to set up an independent women's movement. The three of us went to Laura Sabia, and we said, this is the time to set up a movement; the recommendation for an advisory committee should not be part of it. Laurell and I then went to Yvette, and her group split on it. Monique Bégin led the group supporting the government position.

Next we went to the young women's, or radical, caucus. There were about sixty women there. We said to them, the enemy here is not these bourgeois women; they organized this conference, and we have to join with whoever is willing to set up a real women's movement. In the end they agreed. I called for a disciplined group at the plenary. If we started splitting off among ourselves, then we would certainly lose.

I opened up the debate, and it roared. It was filled with pros and cons right through. It was beautiful. It was the biggest, longest debate of the women's conference. We won, and it was decided that we would have our founding convention the next year.

Laurell Ritchie

I was twenty-two when I went to the Strategy for Change conference. I was working with the Canadian Textile and Chemical Union as an organizer at the time, with people like Madeleine Parent. She was a panel member at the conference, and I was working on media there, but it was Madeleine who made sure I got invited. We weren't used to meeting at places like the King Edward Hotel, but some of us had been involved in the first poor people's conference, so meeting with people from all walks of life wasn't an unknown. There were two groups there that I hadn't had any dealings with, people of colour from Africville and the National Farmers' Union.[4] I was struck by how much the struggles they described sounded like the struggles of women in the union.

Some of the people at the conference were intimidating, but knowing someone like Madeleine made it easier to be with them. There were women I saw as very upper crust. But there was an interesting and productive range of people. It was a diverse group by race, age and class, although there was a preponderance of white women. This was a Liberal conference with a

---

4. Africville was a black community located in Halifax, Nova Scotia. The Africville Action Committee formed in the early 1970s to seek redress for the expropriation of their land.

Liberal agenda, so there were many bureaucrats, women who introduced themselves as being from such and such a ministry.

The conference was important for young women who were used to demonstrations and marches but hadn't dealt head on with an agenda. It was an incredible experience to turn around the agenda. There were a number of clashes from the beginning. The farming women wanted certain things like the Kraft Cheese boycott on the agenda.[5] The middle-class women didn't feel that was appropriate. And there was antagonism toward the government's agenda. The keynote speaker on the Saturday morning was Elsie McGill, who represented the Business and Professional Women. She was radical, far ahead of some of the union women. She had a lot of stature, and she quietly supported the insurrection. There were six workshops at the conference: on political action, mass media, daycare and education, direct action techniques, community organizing and economic status.

About fifty to seventy young women who considered themselves radical held a meeting during the conference, and a couple of the older women attended as well. There was a wide range of issues, and people wanted a more radical approach, more action than just changing laws. Madeleine, Grace Hartman and Kay Macpherson forced us to think about the government's agenda and to put forward an alternative.[6] We produced a statement saying that the system was wrong, not just the status of women. We called for future conferences. One point had to do with natural foods, in solidarity with the Kraft issue for farm women. The hotel was owned by a corporation that made weapons, and it served Kraft cheese. We suggested the inclusion of sexual orientation in the human rights code as part of our statement. We suggested that the women's movement had to be separate from the power structure. There was thunderous applause when the resolution that called for an advisory council on the status of women was defeated.[7] It didn't express what we needed or wanted.

There was a recommendation at the end of the conference to form a national action committee on the status of women. So the year after

---

5. The boycott against Kraft was to protest unfair practices in their dealings with dairy producers.

6. Grace Hartman was the first woman president of the Canadian Union of Public Employees, from 1975 to 1983. She was also an active feminist with both Voice of Women and NAC.

7. Nevertheless, the Canadian Advisory Council on the Status of Women was established in 1973 by the federal government and went on to play an important role from time to time in feminist organizing. It was disbanded in 1995.

Strategy for Change, NAC was formed. The biggest problem for the organization was travel funds, and it was Toronto-based because of this. There were some vicious arguments about regional representation. A committee was set up as a visible minority and immigrant women's committee, but it was hard to get people to run with those issues. In the earlier period, it was regional representation that was the big issue.

St. John's Status of Women

IN CONVERSATION: DOROTHY INGLIS, BONNIE JAMES, FRANCES ENNIS, LILLIAN BOUZANE, HELEN FOGWILL PORTER, FRAN INNES AND BARBARA DORAN

DOROTHY INGLIS: Our local status of women group was marvellous. "Women's libber" was a terrible thing to be called, but I loved the term. The papers and radio weren't kind to us, so it took a lot of courage. But information was getting out and more and more women started joining the women's centre we had set up.

BARBARA DORAN: We invited this radio talk show host down to the women's centre. That would be '73, '74. We thought if we could get to him, we could get to every woman in Newfoundland. We cleaned up the place. We brought him down, and he spent a couple of hours. We had the women's centre gathering place, the library, the rape crisis centre, the twenty-four-hour counselling line, the resource centre: the whole nine yards. He looked around. He said, "I'm really delighted you've done this. I've been talking about this on the radio, and I've been speaking in ignorance." We fed him the doughnuts and the coffee and everything. He said, "I'm really glad I came. I read you wrong."

So the next morning we're all sitting around and we turn on the radio and this radio host says, "Good morning, my lovelies. You've heard me talk about them before, the crowd on Military Road, but yesterday I went down and saw them first-hand. I went down and knocked on the door, and this creature opened the door. Not a stick of makeup and no brassiere." That was me.

OTHERS: Barb was really cute then.

BARBARA: "I went inside Military Road," this radio host says, "and the first thing I saw was a huge poster of a pregnant man." We are realizing by now that we made a tactical error. "The poster told it all, because that's really what they want," he said. "They want us to be pregnant and at home so that they can run around. And now I'm ready for your calls."

BONNIE JAMES: Military Road was our first member-owned centre, and it is still there. We bought it. Twelve of us raised the down payment with a loan of $100 each on a purchase of $23,000. We had two small apartments that we could rent. It was the first women's centre bought and owned by a women's group in Canada, and we're still in the same building.

DOROTHY: You didn't get many women who were not middle class. I remember we went to that Strategy for Change conference in Toronto. Eleven of us went. There was this woman there and she said, "I'm sick of all of you. There are women who are not here because they haven't got the goddamn money for bus fare." Because of this, we decided we would have a drop-in centre at Military Road, so that women dying to get out of the house could just drop by. We had all kinds of table games and cards. They could have a cup of tea and talk. There was no feminist indoctrination at all. But another chauvinist talk show host heard about it and said, "Be careful, because those women at the women's centre, they're all lesbians and they're looking to recruit more women." Some women never came back.

LILLIAN BOUZANE: It's 1973; the Trudeau era is at its height. There's tons of money around. There was money there, and we tapped it. We did hire people, but we also had a lot of volunteers. I was off work, and from 1973 to 1977 I practically lived at the women's centre, and so did Wendy Williams and a couple of other women. We were all volunteers. We knew how badly off women were. We knew if we divorced we were on the street with nothing. All the legislation left us out.

BARBARA: Remember when we had the press conference on the Matrimonial Property Act? We invited the press along when we were going to lobby the ministers. First we went to the minister of social services. He sat back and said, "Wait a minute, now. You're telling me that my wife—who sits home on her fat arse watching TV all day and drinking Pepsi—my wife and I, if we separated, she'd get half the house. Is that what you're telling me? Get out." He and his wife had eight children. That was in 1979.

The press asked us, "So, how did the meeting go?" Oh, very well, we answered.

So we go into the next one's office, the minister of health. We go in and do the same spiel. He says, "Is this women's lib? Well, if it's women's lib, I'm all for it, and I'll tell you why. I was in a bar in Toronto last week, and this woman came up and sat next to me and said, "Can I buy you a drink?" If that's women's lib, I'm all for it." So we looked at each other and said, yeah, okay. He was really on board.

HELEN FOGWILL PORTER: But Newfoundland did pass a Matrimonial Property Act in 1979. Later we had a feminist minister, Lynn Verge, and the reason she was so good was that she went to that Strategy for Change conference in Toronto. She had a strong feeling about matrimonial property. She tells the story that when she and her husband bought a house, her parents paid the down payment and she was paying the mortgage, but she couldn't get a mortgage in her name.

FRAN INNES: Every piece of legislation we wanted changed, we went into the minister's office and explained what we wanted. Newfoundland was the only province in Canada where women didn't sit on juries. The minister of justice said, "No, that's never going to happen in Newfoundland. You wouldn't want to sit on a jury. You might have to stay in a hotel sometimes, you know." Imagine. He said this to all of us.

THREE

THE WOMEN ARE COMING

The Abortion Caravan

If men could get pregnant, abortion would be a sacrament.

—FLORYNCE R. KENNEDY[1]

T HE FIRST NATIONAL ACTION of the women's movement in Canada was the 1970 abortion caravan. Seventeen members of the Vancouver Women's Caucus, one of the earliest women's liberation groups, decided to travel to Ottawa to protest the abortion law that had been passed by Parliament in 1969.

Up until 1969, abortion was illegal. Many women risked going to back-street abortionists, who were rarely doctors, or tried to terminate a pregnancy themselves. Many pharmacists stocked slippery elm, which a woman would insert into her cervix, hoping for a miscarriage. Some desperate women douched with Lysol, threw themselves down stairs or, in the mythology of the pro-choice movement, inserted a coat hanger into their vaginas. One of the strongest arguments for legal abortion was the number of women resorting to these drastic measures. According to one estimate, thirty-three thousand illegal abortions were performed in Canada in 1959 alone. A botched abortion was the number one reason for hospital emergency

---

1. Florynce Kennedy was the first African American woman to graduate from Columbia Law School. She was a flamboyant civil rights and feminist activist in the United States, well known for her quotable quotes. This one comes from a 1973 speech.

admissions of young women in those years. But instead of making abortion completely legal, the 1969 law limited abortions to accredited hospitals and allowed them to be performed only when approved by a therapeutic abortion committee of four doctors, for reasons associated with the woman's health. That meant a woman often needed a letter from a psychiatrist to get a legal abortion.

The abortion caravan women set off from Vancouver with the goal of arriving in Ottawa in time for Mother's Day. They stopped in cities and towns along the way for meetings and protest rallies, getting extraordinary press coverage everywhere they went. In 1970 women's liberation was news.

As the first unified action of the women's movement, the abortion caravan revealed some of the differences emerging among feminists. Most of the travelling Vancouver women were active in the New Left and the anti-war movement. They had some political disagreements among themselves, but they managed to work together well until they hit Toronto, where socialist feminists and radical feminists had just experienced a split.

The caravan arrived in Ottawa to much excitement on Friday, May 8. More women arrived from Toronto and Montreal the next morning. On Saturday afternoon, 300 women and men marched on Parliament Hill and then held a meeting inside the Parliament Buildings. Angry that no representative of the government would meet with them, about 150 of the demonstrators headed to Prime Minister Pierre Elliott Trudeau's residence on Sussex Drive. Trudeau was not in town that weekend, but demonstrators managed to leave a coffin representing all the women who had died from illegal abortions at his doorstep. On the Monday, about 30 women chained themselves to their chairs in the galleries in the House of Commons, in tribute to the British suffragists who had chained themselves at Parliament to get the vote a century before.

Feminists saw Trudeaumania as sexist enthusiasm over the bachelor prime minister. For his part, Trudeau had little patience for the challenges coming from radical young women. Some of the abortion caravan women managed to meet with him months later in a Vancouver hotel. They made an impression. Maude Barlow, then Trudeau's adviser on women's issues, remembers that when she asked the prime minister to meet with representatives of the National Action Committee on the Status of Women, he responded, "Are those the same wild, wild women that I met with last year? If so, it may be counterproductive."

IN CONVERSATION: BETSY MEADLEY WOOD, ELLEN WOODSWORTH, BONNIE BECKMAN, MARGO DUNN, MARCY COHEN AND JACKIE LARKIN

BETSY MARY WOOD: The Vancouver Women's Caucus didn't last long, but it was the best group ever. It came out of Simon Fraser University. Ellen Woodsworth came from the University of British Columbia, but we were mostly from SFU. Driving to and from work is how I got into the women's caucus. I heard someone talking about it on the radio, and I thought, Wow! I lived in West Vancouver at the time, and all the women there were getting their tranquilizers and sleeping pills and wake-me-up pills. The NDP didn't even have a women's committee at the time. And here was this fantastic group that had everything together and was moving.

On Thanksgiving weekend of '69, we held the first western conference on women's liberation. There were about a hundred women there. The Vancouver Women's Caucus put forward the idea of a women's cavalcade to Ottawa.

ELLEN WOODSWORTH: We'd been having incredible discussions about what issue we could take up to mobilize all kinds of women, and abortion seemed like the right one.

MARGO DUNN: We decided on a caravan because it was linked a bit to the On to Ottawa Trek of unemployed people in 1935.

MARCY COHEN: At that point the law was interpreted in such a way that you had to say you were not together emotionally to get an abortion. You had to go to a psychiatrist. A law doesn't mean much unless you change the climate.

JACKIE LARKIN: It didn't take long to arrive at the slogan "Free Abortion on Demand." If you are going to take on an issue, you are going to go all the way.

BETSY: Doctors wouldn't talk to you about abortion in those days. You would ask them, and they would look the other way.

MARCY: My first commitment was more abstract. I was a student radical and I wanted to make a difference and take the world on. It didn't really matter what issue. I remember coming to Vancouver from Calgary and not fitting in, and then the women's movement happened and it was an explosion. I could think and I could express myself and I was a person.

BONNIE BECKMAN: I was so new to it. I had been involved in some political stuff, but men controlled it. Women's liberation, what was that? I found this group and came away with a clear concept of what was being said. My impression was that the first thing we were going to do was repeal the abortion law. When we finished that, we were going to get twenty-four-hour daycare. And when we finished that, we were going to get equal wages for work of equal value.

I had dropped out of high school and travelled around the world, and when I got back to Vancouver, I found all of this brewing. It was really exciting.

ELLEN: We wanted liberation. We were just women strategizing with each other. Talking about patriarchy, talking about capitalism, talking about how we could mobilize women. I was secretly and in a positive way reading lesbian literature, which I couldn't share with anyone. But I knew this was going to open up. Abortion wasn't my issue personally, but there was momentum on it.

BONNIE: I had been trying to get a tubal ligation, and the doctors wouldn't let me have it. So my issue wasn't abortion, either. It was trying to come together in something that gave us a common language. The abortion issue lent itself very easily to a focused mobilization. As we radicalized, we were thinking what had big control over our lives—men, the media, advertising and the state. Abortion was a great example of something you could go after the state on. All we had to do was change the law.

MARGO: Abortion is the issue that has mobilized more women than any other. I feel as strongly now about it at the age of sixty as I did in my twenties.

BETSY: When the Women's Caucus started out, there were four things we stood for: equal pay, child care, abortion clinics and birth control. When I went to the Women's Caucus, I didn't go because of abortion. I went for equal pay. But no matter what our primary issue was, everyone worked on preparing for the abortion caravan. Seventeen women from Vancouver made the trip.

BONNIE: We travelled in two cars and a van. Before we left, someone painted "Smash capitalism" on the van. We got to Kamloops and met in a church basement. There was a big debate. Some people wanted the slogan off the truck and other people were defending it, and the discussion went on and on. I hadn't participated in all the ideological discussions of the women's movement. I put my sleeping bag off in a corner and went to sleep.

BETSY: The slogan had never been talked about in the group, but there it was. I just about died. "Smash capitalism" is fine, but that wasn't the time or place for it. I felt we could gain a lot of support, and "smash capitalism" could cause us to lose people. The debate continued as we travelled.

We got fantastic publicity. We had sent out our poster, which was fabulous, to every paper across the country along with our schedule. Everywhere we went there was publicity waiting for us. In Calgary, I opened up the paper and I couldn't believe it. It seemed to me that the paper was all about reproduction, and before the caravan you wouldn't have seen that. That's how fast it changed.

ELLEN: I don't think any social movement since the thirties had planned something on such a national scale. We were consciously using the media and trying to figure out how to get other women to join the campaign and build on it.

MARCY: We had guerrilla theatre portraying a backstreet abortion all the way across, too.

It was a better time economically. I was a student assistant, but I stopped working and did the caravan full time, without pay of course. It was much easier to survive in those days.

JACKIE: I was a national organizer for the Waffle in Ottawa at the time. They released me and let me work on the caravan. There was a strong cross-country connection of socialists, students, women and anti-war activists. They were the framework for what happened.

MARGO: We sent letters to women's groups across the country, telling them we were coming. Could they find us a place to stay and give us a little dinner, something simple like chili? So everywhere we went we'd stay in United Church basements and there'd be chili. It was chili all the way.

BONNIE: As we entered a town, we'd sit on the back of the van with our banners and really make an entrance.

MARGO: The van had a coffin on top, which we had our luggage stowed in. The plan was ultimately to deliver the coffin to Sussex Drive.

Every day we had this routine: drive three hundred miles, do guerrilla theatre, eat and have a public meeting. We collectively decided who would deal with the media. Some women were experienced with the media and some hadn't done it before, and we rotated. It was very feminist, the entire internal organization. The public meeting would inevitably wind up with wrenching horror stories and tears. I still remember some of the stories. The meetings would go later than we'd planned. And then we'd go back to where we were staying and argue about taking "Smash capitalism" off the van and about whether or not we should be smoking dope on the caravan. Before we left Vancouver, we'd had a meeting with a radical lawyer who told us all the things we could get arrested for. We were ready to be arrested once we got to Ottawa. We had bail ready.

ELLEN: It wasn't until we reached Ottawa that we really confirmed what we were going to do.

MARCY: I know we'd already had an idea of going into the House of Commons, because I brought a mini-skirt to wear. We had tensions among ourselves about what we were going to do in the Ottawa action, and we also discussed this with women along the way. In Toronto, feminists were definitely positioned on different sides. People weren't talking to each other, and it galvanized the differences we had internally. I remember feeling that there was a lot of difficulty in Toronto, and later when we got to Ottawa.

The Ottawa women's group almost all came out of the left of the NDP and the student movement, so they were less ideological. We used to think of the Toronto women as too heavy, too ideologically intense. They were the heavy women's liberationists.

ELLEN: We had one meeting organized at the University of Toronto, and people were not friendly to us. It was a whole different feeling than going through small towns and cities, where we had a real sense of exhilaration. In Toronto, women were icy cold, fighting each other, unclear if they were going to come to Ottawa and take this risk with us.

MARCY: We had to pander to the socialist feminists, exaggerating our internal differences so that the socialist feminists in Toronto would go with us.

MARGO: When we arrived in Ottawa, we went to a meeting at a school with two hundred women. That was Friday night.

JACKIE: The demonstration happened Saturday. Women from Montreal and Toronto arrived on Saturday morning. The decision to go to Trudeau's house happened spontaneously.

MARCY: We had had a lot of demonstrations in Vancouver where we had taken over the streets, so at first the Ottawa demonstration seemed fairly tame. We were on the sidewalks, and we pushed people to take over the streets.

BETSY: And then the speeches were over and wham, people were saying, "On to Trudeau's house!"

MARGO: Before the demonstration, there was a big meeting in the Railway Room in the Parliament Buildings. I remember I had the tools of an illegal abortion in my bag: a garden hose, a hanger and a can of Drano. A security guard opened my purse, looked in, and waved me through. Grace MacInnis spoke at the meeting.[2] Henry Morgentaler spoke and was hissed for not being radical enough. Doris Powers, a woman from Toronto who was involved in an anti-poverty group, spoke too. I think it was her speech that kicked things over the edge. We were furious when we got out onto the streets.

BETSY: We had agreed that if John Munro, the minister of health; Trudeau; and John Turner, the minister of justice, wouldn't meet with us, we would issue a declaration of war against the Canadian government for May 11, 1970, at 3 P.M., the day after Mother's Day. I think Trudeau was off at some meeting and Munro had gone to Europe.

JACKIE: None of the ministers showed up. When we got to Trudeau's house, there were only two RCMP guys there. They didn't know what to do with us, so we just sat down on the grass.

MARCY: We had linked arms because we expected to be stopped, but they didn't stop us, so we just kept going.

BETSY: The RCMP came and asked each of us if we were the spokesperson for the group, and we answered, "There are no leaders here."

---

2. Grace MacInnis was the only female member of Parliament at this time. She represented the NDP from Vancouver Kingsway.

MARGO: There were all the angry poor women from the Just Society Movement, a Toronto anti-poverty group. I remember women saying, "We are going to stay here till Trudeau comes back." Gwen Hauser read a poem, and I gave the implements of illegal abortion to Gordon Gibson, Trudeau's staff assistant at the time, who had shown up. I remember people didn't know who he was.

MARGO: We could have gotten into Trudeau's house if we had been prepared to break a window.

MARCY: But then we would have gotten arrested. So we went back to the school where we were meeting to plan Monday's action at the Parliament Buildings. There had started to be some scuffling on the lawn at Trudeau's, and we didn't want that. About two hundred women came back to the school with us.

JACKIE: The idea was to have a quick meeting and then have a party.

BETSY: We were going to have a debate about Monday's action, but the debate didn't happen. This is where Marcy and I parted company for a couple of years. Even teenagers who came with the women from Toronto could go into the Parliament Buildings, but only three of us from Vancouver could go in, and I wasn't going to be one of them. Finally Mary Trew stood up and said, "Is this a plan to keep Betsy out?" and a woman said, "Yes." The reason given was to protect me. If we were charged by the police, there would be trips back and forth to Ottawa, and since I had four kids, I couldn't afford it, or so they said.

MARCY: We were all part of the decision. It was torturous, and there was a lot of discussion as to who could hold the position of the group. There was a feeling that some people had a different philosophy from the rest of the group about how we should be arguing our position on abortion and how to deal with the police or a trial.

ELLEN: Our differences were not only over the "Smash capitalism" slogan and dope smoking. We were debating whether we were for the right to abortion only, or whether we were fighting to smash a system.

MARGO: I was one of the people who also wanted to go inside, and I didn't have any of the jeopardies that we had defined—women who were not citizens or had criminal records, anything that would make their case more difficult than others if they were nabbed. It narrowed down in my mind to who had been in the leadership. And to me that meant Marcy, Ellen and Betsy. But there were these differences. There were lifestyle issues, issues around clothes, etcetera, and it was so important that the three women who might go to court be united. So I remember voting for someone other than Betsy.

MARCY: I had a lot of guilt about it. I knew that my feelings came from the experience of being in Toronto and seeing the divisions between the socialist feminists and the radical feminists. Seeing Betsy gravitate to the radical feminists made me decide that if we were going to be at risk, we had to make sure we could carry the struggle. There was a continual struggle in terms of our differences, and if we were going to carry through what we had started, then we had to be solid and not risk breaking apart.

ELLEN: We assumed that we were going to be arrested and that we would be in a political battle with the courts and with the media, and we wanted people to not be fighting each other too. We wanted to be able to continue mobilizing for women's liberation in Canada.

BETSY: The only division I saw was that this was not the place for "Smash capitalism" if you wanted to smash capitalism. Abortion was such a great thing for bringing people together, and that was what we should stick to. I felt we were safe. I wasn't afraid of going into the building because there was no way they were ever going to arrest us. But as sisters, everyone else was making up my mind for me.

JACKIE: I think a lot of what went on was the political immaturity of the movement. If we go out on an abortion demonstration today, we don't worry about the politics of who is speaking; we get a broad cross-section of people. In those days the big issue was, did you have the right politics behind what you said? Here's an example. About a month after the abortion caravan, I was in Toronto, and Peggy Morton, a Toronto socialist feminist, sat on the steps of a co-op with me and said, "You know, we made a really big mistake when we went into the House of Commons," and I said "Oh, yeah?" and she said, "We should have been saying, 'Victory to the NLF.'"[3] It's exactly the same issue. If you are supporting abortion rights, then really you are in favour of smashing capitalism: that's what you guys argued then.

---

3. National Liberation Front in North Vietnam. The radical slogan in the anti–Vietnam War movement was "Victory to the NLF," whereas the unifying slogan was "Stop the War."

Or if you are really going to support abortion, you have to be a socialist feminist. It's bullshit, but that's what we were arguing.

MARCY: I don't agree that we were arguing that.

BONNIE: I think there was a generation gap happening, because Betsy was almost twenty years older than the rest of us. For me, this was very much about the way I wanted to change the world. Betsy, you came at it from a single-issue point of view, but you should have been participating. We wouldn't have been there if it hadn't been for you. But those were the times we lived in.

MARGO: In the big meeting, there was a three-hour discussion about whether we should chain ourselves to the chairs in the parliamentary gallery. I remember someone saying we should chain ourselves like the suffragists did.

MARCY: I remember all this talking and talking and talking, and then suddenly it was Monday morning. We had borrowed a lot of things to get us ready to set off.

JACKIE: I remember digging through people's cupboards in co-ops trying to find nylons. We had to go out and buy gloves and purses.

ELLEN: We strategized about who would go into which gallery and who would start the chant. If one person was taken out, what would we do? Go limp?

JACKIE: I remember going up the elevator in the Parliament Buildings, and no one looking at one another.

MARCY: Standing in the line with all these people you knew, but everyone looked different because we were dressed up … our other selves.

MARGO: There were three or four men from Ottawa who were beards for some of the women.[4] I think there were thirty-five or thirty-six who went inside. There was also a demonstration outside that was supposed to act as a camouflage.

JACKIE: My chain didn't work in the end. My memory is that for half of the women who went in, the chains didn't hold.

---

4. Men who escorted the women to cover their true purpose.

ELLEN: We also had to figure out how to get those goddamn chains out of our purses quietly. We tried not to be noisy or obvious, but we were listening to the MPs trashing some men in Vancouver who were marching across the border in Blaine to protest the war in Cambodia. Many of these men were our friends and lovers, so things started to move really fast back and forth across the gallery, and then it was pandemonium, people looking up and saying, "What's going on here?" They couldn't figure out where the shouting was coming from. Some people started to be dragged away. We went limp and they would try to drag us and we would go limp again. It took them quite a while.

MARGO: There was a text, written collectively, we were going to read. One person was supposed to start, and then the next person would continue in the next gallery. That was the plan, but it didn't work out that way.

JACKIE: The police took our chains. They didn't arrest us, but ten women were taken down to the police station and then released.

MARGO: Meanwhile outside, about two hundred women wearing black headscarves walked two by two around the eternal flame. Our heads were bowed in mourning for the women who continued to die because of lack of access to safe abortion. At 3 P.M., we threw off the black scarves to reveal red ones and charged up the steps to begin the first action of the "war." We set fire to a placard containing the text of the law. Soon the women who had been in the House ran out to join us. We were surprised, but thrilled, that no one was arrested. The caravan shut down the House of Commons for forty-five minutes, and we got tons of media coverage.

A few weeks later, back in Vancouver, the Vancouver Women's Caucus had a meeting with Trudeau. We met him at the Bayshore Inn. He had phoned from his plane to say he wanted to talk to us, and we only had three hours' notice to get women down there. We activated our phone trees. We got to the room in the Bayshore before Trudeau did. We discussed making him sit on the floor but thought we wouldn't get away with it. We didn't want him sitting in the middle of the room, though, so we moved his chair off-centre. When he got there, we were relentless—it was great. And there was a lot of press.

BONNIE: I remember saying, "Look, we want this abortion law repealed," and he said, "Well, go and get the people to vote for it. You have the right to have it, but go and do the job." He wasn't against it. He said, "Go and convince people."

MARCY: The thing I remember about him was his arrogance. I remember him saying that if you needed an abortion and you had money, you could go to the States.

ELLEN: And we were shouting, "Just society, just for the rich."

FOUR

A NOT-SO-QUIET REVOLUTION
The Quebec Women's Movement

In the period from 1970 to 1981, women went from the "I" to the "we."

—MICHÈLE STANTON-JEAN

THE WOMEN'S MOVEMENT in Quebec had its own distinct pattern of development. In 1966 the Fédération des femmes du Québec (FFQ) was founded by famed feminist Thérèse Casgrain. Unlike NAC, in which the older generation of women's rights activists worked alongside young radicals, the FFQ kept its distance from the feminists who emerged as part of the youth radicalization of the late 1960s. Nevertheless, the FFQ was active in promoting key issues of equality for women. Le Conseil du statut de la femme, established by the Quebec government in 1973, worked closely with women's groups to bring feminism to women around the province, as well as advising the government on women's issues.

Quebec women did not get the vote until 1940, a generation after the rest of the country, although they held it briefly from 1791 to 1849. Because Quebec moved so quickly in the 1960s from a reactionary, Catholic Church–dominated society into the modern age, new institutions such as unions were much more open to radical change than were their bureaucratic English Canadian counterparts. Young Québécoise agitators met as much sexism as their English Canadian union sisters, but much less resistance to their demands.

Young women in Quebec were attracted by action on the one hand and cultural expression on the other. The major feminist social movement of the time was the pro-choice movement, which organized in the streets under the slogan "pour l'avortement libre et gratuit," free abortion on demand. Dr. Henry Morgentaler performed his first illegal abortion in Montreal in 1968; after advocating for liberalization of the abortion laws, he felt hypocritical turning away women who asked for the procedure. On June 1, 1970, Morgentaler was arrested. His trial and subsequent jailing remained the focus of the pro-choice movement in Quebec until the newly elected Parti Québécois virtually legalized abortion in 1976 by announcing it would not prosecute any doctor performing safe abortions. Abortion would remain restricted in the rest of Canada until the 1988 Supreme Court decision striking down the abortion law.

As much in touch with the French women's movement as the American, Quebec feminists began organizing events to mark International Women's Day, which had been celebrated in Europe since 1918. French feminism also influenced Quebec's emphasis on culture. Several publications representing the different stages of the women's movement were quite central. *Québécoise deboutte!* reflected the nationalist radicalism of the Front de libération des femmes in the late 1960s; *Les Têtes de pioche,* the radical feminism of Quebec intellectuals in the 1970s; and *La Vie en rose,* the entry of feminism into the mainstream in the 1980s.

While there were important links between Quebec and Canada, the women's movement in Quebec took on its own rhythms, as explained by former FFQ president Françoise David:

> *The FFQ in 1966 was practically the only feminist organization in Quebec. Afterward, in the 1970s, there were lots of radical women's groups, above all in abortion and violence against women. In the 1980s there was an explosion in Quebec of the women's movement; many, many groups not necessarily radical but feminist. Like the women's centres, the shelters. By the end of the 1980s, there were ninety-three women's centres, seventy shelters and twenty-five rape crisis centres. And not only that— almost every union formed women's committees. There was an organization of women farmers. There were even feminist groups in the Catholic Church and feminist nuns.*

Fédération des femmes du Québec

Ghislaine Patry-Buisson

In 1972 I was married but working, so I became aware of the discrimination against women. I went to the Fédération des femmes du Québec congress. The theme was the involvement of women in politics. Monique Bégin, Jeanne Sauvé, Albanie Morin:[1] a lot of women were there to discuss these things. What really struck me was that the conference was held in a convent. I wondered why. My husband used to go the CSN, the Confédération des syndicats nationaux, and it was held at a hotel or in an institute of popular education. I became an active member of the FFQ and agreed to be part of the program committee. I organized the congress in 1973, and we held it at Institut coopératif Desjardins. We had it on a long weekend. The executive asked, "How can we do that on a Monday, when the children are on holiday?" I responded, "The fathers will take care of the children, and the women will come." Our theme was single-parent families. My husband had done a study on female heads of families. They were recipients of social assistance, women with children. We decided that we had to have these women at the conference. We raised about $2000 to subsidize them.

Women didn't have money in those days to come to conferences. Even middle-class women didn't have control over their money. Women had to pay from their pockets. The conference charged twenty dollars for everything, including food. We filled the institute and had to put some women in motels. We had 150 to 200 women there.

In December 1973, when I became FFQ president, I was among the federation's youngest members. There weren't a lot of us. There were women who had been there from the beginning, women around forty-five or fifty. I was a little younger, thirty-six.

People say the FFQ at that time was all bourgeois women, but that's not true. There were university women there, but there were also women who were working and women who had stopped working. And there were trade union women. Yvette Rousseau was there when I was president. She was a

---

1. All three women were elected to the House of Commons in 1972 as Liberal members of Parliament. Monique Bégin was minister of health and welfare from 1977 to 1984. Jeanne Sauvé was a cabinet minister during the 1970s, then the first woman Speaker of the House in 1980 and the first female Governor General from 1984 to 1990. Albanie Morin was elected again in 1974 and died in 1976.

textile worker. Her husband had had a stroke. She kept him at home, had eight children and worked in a textile mill. She was certainly not a bourgeoise. The bourgeois women did have the idea of founding a movement to demand that women have equal status, so that they could sign legal documents, get promotions and so on. But such a movement needed women who saw these things as possible and who also had the time to work on them.

Thérèse Casgrain, they said she was a bourgeoise, but she ran nine times for the NDP and lived very modestly. She was for equality of women. Mme. Casgrain was not on the board when I was president, but she called me almost every morning. She would tell me, "I read this in the papers and you have to send a letter." She was still active, and she came to our conferences. In 1965 she had had the idea to regroup women's organizations to give a voice to women, because women were not in politics. The FFQ was the result.

The young radicals were involved in the women's centres. They weren't attracted by the FFQ. They supported women who needed abortions, and they organized buses to take them to the United States. Women's committees in the unions had begun as well.

It was not easy in the FFQ. From time to time I went to the International Women's Day events on March 8 and worked with union movements, but some women in the FFQ said, "Don't go, Ghislaine, you have to be careful of your image." It was not just a class difference. The women in the centres were educated, but they were more radical.

The FFQ took the position of free choice in 1976. When I became president in 1973, my objectives were to work for equal pay for women and for abortion. But it took time. The women's movement was not that progressive at the time. We had to wake up and learn. It was a movement of education. We said that the participation of women in politics was important. We had some progressive groups in the federation, but there were also the Christian women's movement and the individual members organized by region. We created a board with delegates from the associations and from the regions, but when we had a congress, all individuals had a vote. At the board, we took a vote on abortion and it was a majority vote. The regional councils were for it, and the YWCA and the University Women. The Christian women said they couldn't take a position, since the Church was against abortion. The Christian women were for it, but they couldn't vote that way. Same with the Jewish women.

January 26, 1976, the day we had our press conference on the vote, Morgentaler got out of prison. The next day the papers all reported that the FFQ had taken a position for abortion. We demanded the application of the Criminal Code, the establishment of therapeutic abortion committees, because we didn't have them in Quebec. We were worried about young women who were getting abortions under bad conditions in Montreal. We wanted women to have access to counselling so they could be better informed, and support for women who wanted to continue with their pregnancies.

The FFQ was an organization of feminists because it worked for women's rights. But the members didn't want to call themselves feminists. I remember big discussions where I would drag over the dictionary and show them what "feminist" meant. They didn't want to be associated with the radical women in New York who were said to have burned their bras, or to be seen as lesbians. Young women organized separately from the FFQ, because they saw us as bourgeois. That causes me pain, because the federation did a lot for women at the time. We shouldn't forget our history.

The Unions

Monique Simard

In 1972 after I graduated from university I went to work for the CSN, the Confédération des syndicats nationaux. My first job with them was working with unions in the hospital health sector. I started there a few months after a huge labour battle, the Common Front of 1972, in which all the public sector employees went on strike and the heads of the unions were sent to prison. It was a huge social uproar. There was this new collective agreement that was considered a huge success and a great victory for unions after the strikes and illegal strikes and imprisonment. When I opened the collective agreement, I noticed that the classifications and salaries were different for men than for women. Women did exactly the same jobs, but their salaries were less. I was completely flabbergasted.

I think this was my very first true rebellion. I was scandalized by this, by the salaries. This was signed, this was printed, and I could not believe it. So I was young, and I went to see my boss. The CSN was a huge organization. Essentially, the technical advisers, the organizers, the negotiators were men, and the secretaries were women. We were very, very few women to be hired as negotiators; out of maybe two or three hundred, we were less than five. One woman who worked there was Lucie Dagenais. She was kind of like my mentor. She had hired me, and she said, "You know, there is no women's committee here at the union. What do you say we form a women's committee based on feminist organization?" I said sure, of course. So we created this committee in 1973. In 1974 it was sanctioned and made official by the executive committee of the CSN. After that, all the other unions set them up, too.

The mandate of the CSN women's committee was to look into specific conditions for women and to make sure that they had equality not only in the workplace but also outside of it. This was way before we had charters forbidding discrimination. There was no maternity leave. Women had to quit to have children. They would lose their jobs. Salaries were always lower for women. Our four priorities in 1974 were free abortion on demand, free daycare, the right to maternity leave at full salary, and equal pay. So we had this group of women, now officially recognized as a committee within the CSN, with these four priorities. Then we had to go to the national convention to debate these issues and make them a priority for the whole movement. That was something else, because we had to go through all these levels of union officials, all men, all older than us. At that time, to talk openly about the right to choose was still difficult. The CSN used to be the Confédération des travailleurs catholiques. It had been secularized in the early 1960s, but still, it was still Quebec, le Québec catholique. It was very, very exciting, and very rewarding, because we were opening a new path, and we won.

Negotiations started again in the public sector. I was still at the hospitals, and I was placed on the negotiation team. I guess they thought I was good. I worked very hard on certain issues—with other women, not me alone— to say that full paid maternity leave should be a union demand priority, and also that differences in salaries for men and women should be eliminated. These were the two things that we really argued. That was in 1974, '75, '76. Now, we didn't achieve a full paid maternity leave, but we did win better conditions for maternity leave. And we also won the elimination of differences in salaries for men and women in the same jobs.

At the same time, things were advancing in society. It's interesting, because all of a sudden everything moved forward at the same time. We were advancing; the laws were advancing. It was a very positive time, very proactive, and we got results. We were always winning, always going forward. There was constant social progress, particularly in Quebec. Quebec in the 1970s was extraordinary. In 1979 I was chief negotiator for the Common Front, and I negotiated full maternity leave, twenty weeks at full salary, for the first time in Canada. We also negotiated full pay for abortion leave. That was very important.

There was a dynamic women's movement in Quebec. There were women's groups everywhere: newspapers, magazines, and, of course, autonomous women's groups. The autonomous women's groups, which mostly held a radical feminist analysis, accused us of collaborating with the enemy because we were in the unions and collaborating with men. But still we worked together well. We built a very strong women's movement in Quebec because we respected each other. We were complementary, and we recognized the complementarity of our work.

We organized the first celebration of International Women's Day in Quebec, on March 8, 1973. I was on the organizing committee. We met in a church basement. We were a group of women from autonomous women's groups and from the CSN. We decided to organize it jointly. We had lots of fun. The year after was bigger, the year after was bigger, the year after was bigger … by the end of the 1970s, early 1980s, we organized huge parties for March 8 with over twenty thousand women walking the streets of Montreal, always very joyful.

Sometimes there was friction, but the work that the radical feminist groups did helped us in a way. It permitted us to say, you see, this is where society is going. We are not as radical, we work within the unions, but you see that is where things are going in society. So they helped us to push, to put on that pressure.

I've always thought that the women's movement in Quebec was very, very democratic. I think this has a lot to do with the good job we did in the unions. We penetrated all social classes, all milieus and all regions. So there were the radical groups and us, and then there was Le Conseil du statut de la femme. That council was le féminisme de l'état, you know, state feminism, but it was very smart from the start, quite radical, and established offices in all regions in Quebec. So that permitted women from la Côte-Nord, l'Abitibi, everywhere, to interact on women's issues, share awareness, information. Everything was happening in a dynamic process that was widespread and in all sectors of society, which I think is still very important.

Les têtes de pioche

Michèle Stanton-Jean

In 1972 I was asked to teach what I think was the first course on women's history at the University of Montreal. Then an editor asked me to write a book on the subject. *Québécoises du 20e siècle,* a feminist reader, was published in 1974. Nicole Brossard, the poet, came to the book launch. She said, "I read this. I liked it. It was interesting." At the end of 1975, she called me and said, "Listen, Mme. Jean, our collective wants to do a journal. The international year for women is ending, and we need to do something. We'd like to have a historian in our collective. We'd like you to join." So I landed in *Les Têtes de pioche*.

For several months we discussed what we were going to do, how we were going to do it. We took what was called at the time a radical feminist approach. We used radical not in the sense of militant action, *faire des éclats*, but in the sense of roots, going to the root of questions about men and women. In other words, why was there discrimination? Why were there what we called at the time relations of power? We didn't like the language of dominated/dominator, because we didn't have the impression that women were dominated, but rather that they did not have the opportunity to take on their roles within the society. This is why the first article we published was called "Le Matriarcat québécois analysé par les reines du foyer" (The Myth of Quebec's Matriarchal Housewife). In Quebec there was this idea that women controlled everything, because there was matriarchy. Our point of view was that perhaps women had authority within the family, in terms of the children and so on, but for all kinds of other reasons women did not occupy the place they could at the scale of the social, the political. There was the theory of two spheres—the public and the private.

So this was our starting point. We were six or seven in the collective. Those who could afford it, each put in seventy-five dollars, and then we needed to find someone who could print something like three hundred copies per month. There was the idea at the time of consciousness-raising. So at the beginning of each meeting we took the time to talk about ourselves, and then we talked about what to put in the next edition. These were big discussions. I had this idea, with my background in education, that we should not be too rigid in the beginning. I wrote an article called "Quand tu seras prête" (When You Are Ready), which said that each woman will have her own revolution, her own growing awareness. We said, okay, we'll print this, but then each of the others would also print their opinion. It was very democratic. We wrote articles that were often at the heart of women's concerns without ever being discussed, like "We Are Tired of Being Tired" or "Mother's Summer Holidays," which said a woman always comes last because she has to buy shoes for her children, she has to buy this and that, then she looks at herself, and she always puts on her old bathing suit. The article ended by having her throw her old bathing suit in the trash can, saying, "Next year I will take a couple of days alone for my holiday." Some people—men and women—found this too radical. Even some of my family had reservations. After some years, my mother said that we were right! But there were women who wrote to us and said, "I cried when I read your magazine," because it went very deep for women. Women's voices were beginning to be heard at the Librairie des femmes (the women's bookstore). Women were beginning to speak of violence. Women would read this and say, "Wow. That is me. But I can't say that. If I said something like that!"

Some articles, like "Faites des mères," appeared in *Le Devoir,* where journalist Renée Rowan was a faithful reader of our journal.[2] Some people were saying that feminists didn't like children and stupid things like that. So I wrote an article titled "Les Féministes n'ont jamais rejetté les enfants" ("Feminists Have Never Excluded Children"). It said that feminists were asking for things like daycare, things to make it possible to have children, but also to make it possible to have a life. It was a fight, because they always tried to position feminists as bra burners.[3]

The title *Les Têtes de pioche* means hard-headed, to hammer in the nail. We must hammer in the nail, we said, we mustn't give up, we must continue. In the first issue we must have explained the name. *La Vie en rose* came later. It was sexier in format, more like *Chatelaine* or something like that. *Québécoise deboutte!* was perhaps before. *Les Têtes de pioche* was seen as much more radical.

We did this for two or three years. At the end there were movements that were more Marxist that wanted to work with us. But they didn't have the same basis for understanding the problem. It didn't work very well. Finally we didn't have any money left, and some women wanted to do other things. I was starting to work. It was a good period.

We tried to mobilize women during the referendum, which was held in 1980.[4] I was invited to speak at a big meeting organized by Lise Payette before the first referendum in 1979.[5] I asked them, "Are you sure you want

---

2. A Montreal daily newspaper popular with intellectuals in Quebec.
3. The myth is that feminists protesting the Miss America pageant in the United States burned their bras in protest, as draft dodgers protested the Vietnam War by burning their draft cards. In reality, the plan was to burn various symbols of women's oppression, including steno pads and high heels, but organizers couldn't get a fire permit, so they decided not to do it. Nevertheless, "bra burner" was a major epithet against feminism for many years.
4. The Parti Québécois government held a referendum on sovereignty in 1980. Another one was held in 1995.
5. Lise Payette was the first minister responsible for the status of women in Quebec from 1979 to 1981.

me to come? I'm not sure that you'll like what I have to say." I went and said, in the end, "Women have for a long time been saying yes—yes to marriage, yes to devotion, yes to goodness, yes to love. The practice of yes is a practice of women. Be careful not to be used." Although she was not very happy, I think Lise Payette thought that I was right.

We were interested in the national question, that is certain. But for us the priority was the advancement of women. We needed not to let the question of women be subsumed by the national question. In the nationalist action, for those who were separatist or other, we needed to clearly know what was going to happen for women, what their political participation was going to be. We were not going to wait, not going to put this on the back burner. No, no, no. Women were the priority.

The feminist movement, that is to say the more avant-garde radical feminists, had helped women pass from *je*—when you think it is only you who has problems, only you who are frustrated—to *nous*. The movement had collectivized the life of women, given a "we" to women, given a "herstory"—a term we liked very much but couldn't translate into French. In the period from 1970 to 1981, women went from the "I" to the "we."

The other important thing was that the struggle of women was very complex. In general, when you have a radical or revolutionary movement, like for instance with the Marxists, there are the enemies, the bourgeoisie, and the people in the revolution. There is always an enemy in the revolution. But for women, as we said, the enemy is in your bed. You live your private life with a husband, with a family who you love. It is very complicated to have an attitude where you say, "We are discriminated against" and your husband says, "But I'm not doing anything to hurt you." And you say, "I'm talking about the general way that women are perceived in scholarly books, in this and in that." So it was difficult, because most women continued to have relations with men. A woman could be a lesbian, but even then she had brothers, men in her family, sometimes children. It was very complicated to try to define the theory. If you think of the natives in Chiapas, they know who their enemy is. For women, it is more complicated.

La Vie en rose

Francine Pelletier

Sometime in 1975, I heard that the women's bookstore in Montreal was having an open house and I decided to go. It was this little, little place not even as wide as my house. I went in there and it was packed full of women, standing room only. Women were standing up and talking about their experiences as women: about being afraid to talk, about being humiliated. Everything from the pretty severe to the banal, and it all rang so many bells for me. It was like a religious experience almost. I recognized the pattern. My identification with men had been because I didn't want to be a victim, I didn't want to be a loser; I wanted to be on the winning end. I identified with just about everything those women said, so there was no going back. I had never known what solidarity meant, that great thing about the women's movement. It's not complicated. It's not academic. It's a gut feeling that you relate to and that you can share. You feel really connected to these women. I had never felt that. I come from a family that has no sense of family. I had no people and there, suddenly, I had people.

I immediately became involved. I got involved in a group to find a women's centre, and then I got involved in the big movement for l'avortement libre et gratuit, and from there in *La Vie en rose*. That moment was important, because the women's movement had the wind in its sails. *Québécoise deboutte!* was a feminist magazine and a rallying cry and very much like the feminism that was sweeping North America, but the women's bookstore was one of the few women's *places*. It was the most visible women's place. I had participated [in patriarchy], and it was liberating to decide that I would not participate anymore. Enough already! That was the euphoria of that decade particularly, feeling that women could come together and, without much ado, there was a great feeling that we could change things.

In 1979 five women got together. Most of us had been activists in the abortion movement. The idea was we all wanted to write. We thought that there should be some kind of vehicle, magazine, something more sophisticated. We really thought we could go mainstream with this. We were a little naïve. We started with zero cents, no focus group. We got together in someone's kitchen and brainstormed. *Ms.* magazine was a model, of course. We heard that *Ms.* had started as an insert in a mainstream paper. There was a left magazine in Montreal called *Le Temps fou,* so we went to them and said, "We want to be inserted in your magazine for a year." And they said yes. They gave us a place, so we started that way. I was the first staff person. It was a little insert, with maybe twelve pages. In 1981 we became a full-fledged magazine. And it was the best experience of my life.

It was as if you had embarked on a sea and the wind was carrying you. We were our own bosses. We ran the magazine by selling ads and getting subscriptions and grants. We always had trouble selling ads; for some reason, people think feminists don't buy cars or smoke cigarettes. It was up to us to invent it. We were really creative. We had fun. We had so much fun. We laughed and we had the "comité des lectures" (readers committee) and we had fiction issues in the summer. We were a fairly big success. We never had a lot of money, but I'm not sure we could have. We had embarked on a decade that was entirely different from the 1970s, but, of course, at the beginning of the 1980s, we couldn't have known that. At the beginning, anyone who was vaguely feminist bought *La Vie en rose*. By the end, women didn't want anyone to tell them what to think. It wasn't the same game at all. But it was a wonderful experience. Also, for me, my dream had been to write. This was the perfect way to put it all together. So I became a journalist and that was my training, *La Vie en rose*. Running the shop, writing articles. It was great.

It was the best, the most fun and the most inventive. We could stay clear of politics, so it was easier than trying to run NAC or another kind of women's group. I think, to a certain extent, what we tried to do was what Quebec women related to. Not a dour kind of feminism where you are always beating your breast. There was a more radical faction, but we were mostly moderates. Radicals were always suspicious of men and putting heterosexuality into question, as if it was a dirty word. We didn't have anyone who closely resembled Andrea Dworkin in Quebec.[6] I've always been allergic to that. Even in *La Vie en rose*, I remember undergoing questioning about why I was going out with one of the guys from *Le Temps fou*. I found that outrageous. That's the radicalism that I hate. The radicalism that I like is the persistence of someone like Françoise David.

I left *La Vie en rose* a year before it folded. I figured, now I have discovered my calling and I must venture forth. I was afraid that being labelled a feminist, I wouldn't get a job. But au contraire. It had a very good reputation, *La Vie en rose*. We had created something, a success story of the alternative press. Our circulation was twenty-five thousand. We had a bigger circulation than *Le Devoir*. We were the envy of all the other magazines in Canada.

---

6. Andrea Dworkin is a radical American feminist famous for her outspoken views on pornography and violence against women.

FIVE

BREAKING NEW GROUND
Organizing for Child Care

We have begun to raise our daughters more like sons ... but few have the courage to raise our sons more like our daughters.

—GLORIA STEINEM, 1995 SPEECH

C HILD CARE WAS A CENTRAL DEMAND of the women's movement from the beginning. As women entered the workforce in large numbers, they needed high-quality care for their children, and one of the major recommendations of the Royal Commission on the Status of Women was a national daycare program. In the 1960s women and some men also saw daycare as a way of collectively raising children and challenging the restrictions of the patriarchal nuclear family.

Co-operative daycares, run by the people who used them, were great for young activists and students, but the requirements of a fully functioning collective were onerous for working-class parents. To reach broad numbers of women, organizers in the child care movement needed to participate in the system, getting state subsidies for the daycare centres they ran and maintaining government-approved standards. Initially, governments saw daycare as a welfare service enabling single mothers to work. Only parents on social assistance could get their children into these municipal centres, which were run along authoritarian and traditionally gendered lines. Some other daycare was available, but it was commercial and run for profit. It was activists in the women's movement who introduced the idea that daycare was for the average family, and that parents should be involved in running the centres. Two of the most interesting early daycares were Campus Co-op and Devonshire, both set up on the University of Toronto campus.

During the 1970s, daycare organizing remained at the local and provincial levels. Finally, more than a decade after the first co-op daycares were established, the Trudeau government followed up on the Royal Commission recommendation by organizing the first national conference on daycare. The government planned to assemble various stakeholders in the field for some professional development. But Action Daycare, a Toronto-based group, seized the opportunity to connect with daycare activists from across the country and put forward their own platform.

CAMPUS CO-OP AND DEVONSHIRE CO-OP

IN CONVERSATION: SARAH SPINKS, JULIE MATHIEN, MYRA NOVOGRODSKY AND SUE COLLEY

SARAH SPINKS: We had a feminist group that met once a week or so. We talked about feminist theory, and some of us got tired of just talking. Many of us wanted to have children eventually, so decided we'd start a daycare centre. This was 1969. We wanted to do something concrete, something to get our hands dirty. We wanted to do something for the downtown community that included the University of Toronto. We negotiated for a house and paid a rental at 12 Sussex Street. We wanted it to be a co-op, but didn't know how many staff we should have, how many volunteer hours, and we had lots of discussion about how it would run and gender roles. We dressed boys in dresses and girls in pants. We had a very high parent-child ratio at first—one adult for every child at one point because of the volunteers. They knew the children and loved working with them. Then we went to one adult for every two or three children.

We put out a leaflet to the entire university, but we wound up appealing to intellectuals and hippies. We reached out to ordinary people working at the university, but we set the co-op up in a way that we later figured out wasn't that attractive to them. We hired two staff, but we expected parents to work and then do a volunteer shift at the daycare centre. We discouraged them from coming in and visiting their children. We wanted to make everything communal, and we felt you should be as interested in other children as in your own.

JULIE MATHIEN: Everything belonged to everybody. The whole doctrine of looking after each other's kids was, in principle, an important thing. Having parent volunteers was quite a new notion, the idea that one would be responsible in a broader sense for a community of children. That was a personally important thing for me to understand and act on. It is something that has stayed with me all my life. We were trying to break down the nuclear family, and though we live in them now, we have much more porous boundaries.

The campus daycares were crucial to the development of the child care movement in North America. In the late 1960s and early 1970s, women started going to graduate school in numbers that were unprecedented. If they wanted to have children, they had to use daycare. For the first time, middle-class families were starting to use daycare. The co-ops were different from the commercial daycare in the city or suburbs. They had free curriculum, they were cheap, and they were smaller too.

MYRA NOVOGRODSKY: I had come to Toronto in '68 from the U.S., where I'd been involved in the anti-war movement and the civil rights movement. I was desperate to find some action in Toronto, which I considered Sleepy Hollow at the time. I read "Sugar and Spice" on a train trip,[1] and I decided to find those people and see what was going on. I started as a volunteer at the centre, and within six weeks I was pregnant. I thought, this is a place I can have a child. These people are struggling, thinking of how to raise children in a non-conventional way. I was only twenty-three, and I was so grateful for that community. Even if we made some mistakes, there was such a positive feeling about children and the love we had for them. The community of volunteers was the new intelligentsia. Plus the friendships that were formed were outstanding.

Another part of the ideology was that everybody had to come to all the meetings. The gender issue was huge. You could be asked to leave the community if you weren't participating. You had to do shifts and a certain amount of work whether you wanted to or not. We had huge expectations. Parents, both men and women, had to come.

JULIE: We rotated the chair at meetings. We arrived at decisions by consensus rather than voting.

---

1. An article that Sarah Spinks wrote about the daycare in *This Magazine is About Schools*.

SARAH: The community attracted a huge number of male pioneers, men willing to work to change regular male attitudes. Men who wanted to be around children. We wanted the kids exposed to men and women who were challenging sexism. The daycare was one of the few places in the women's movement that was welcoming men.

JULIE: The kind of daycare my boys were in made them very socially adept, and it made them tolerant and good negotiators. They were led by adults to consider the other person's perspective. Kindness and creativity were important. It's hard to disentangle the way we were living and the daycare. It was all part of figuring out a new way of being. I had a great deal of difficulty in explaining it to our parents' generation. Many never got it. Snowflake, another feminist daycare centre in Toronto, opened after we did, and those people were even freakier than we were.

The provincial government wouldn't give us a licence. The fight was about fire regulations, the size of toilets and chair size. It was partly about mixing infants and toddlers, partly about people with bare feet working in the kitchen. It was also about the training of staff. Many of the things we did—maybe not the bare feet—are standard now.

SARAH: We didn't have the money for fire doors and other safety renovations. It cost $12,000 a door. We asked the university for money, but they wouldn't give it to us. So we had a demonstration, and then we occupied Simcoe Hall, where the president's office is, in February or March of 1970.

MYRA: We stayed there overnight. Initially, it was just the daycare cohort. Perlmutters, a bakery in Kensington Market, delivered bagels. It was a confrontation and we were making demands, and the whole thing was new. It was resolved really quickly.

SARAH: I don't think we started out assuming we would occupy. It was in the back of our minds, but I don't remember it being well thought out. We didn't do any kind of reconnoitre inside Simcoe Hall, something we would have done if we had planned it. We were pretty serious radicals.

JULIE: We were pushing the envelope in any number of ways. It was an occupation, it was on a feminist issue, and it was about daycare for babies and toddlers.

MYRA: People thought we were nuts starting kids at six weeks.

JULIE: The occupation was so successful that we got everything from the doors to a triple sink. But the day nursery people still didn't want to give us a licence. Our backyard wasn't the best, so we decided we needed to have a nicer one. One of the dads was a landscaper, and he drew up plans. There was no money from the province for this, so we called the university and said we needed four or five thousand dollars, and they said no. I called Claude Bissell, the university president, and he called me back himself. I remember telling him, "Well, President Bissell, Simcoe Hall is looking awfully empty these days." He gave us the money.

For the longest time, we held out on trained staff. The government took us to a hearing and tried to close us down. They stalled and stalled and stalled, and finally we agreed to trained staff, because the community colleges were graduating daycare students who had had placements with us and who we thought were acceptable. The government licensed us when we got trained staff. They were really afraid to shut us down.

In 1972 Sarah and I and a couple of other people went to the university and said we needed another building for older kids, the graduates of our first daycare. A lot of university people used the St. Andrew's Church daycare, but that wasn't a university daycare centre. They trotted us around to various buildings but kept saying we couldn't have them. We liked the meteorological building. We sat down with the university and said, "We'd like that building. It's perfect; it's got a big yard." We came to the conclusion that they were not going to give it to us, so we decided we would have to take it. The university wasn't using the building, but they wanted to develop it.

We held our planning meetings in people's houses. We were clandestine about it and had a phone system with passwords. The plan was that the minute everyone was in the building, I'd go to a pay phone and call the media. We scoped the place out, and the night before the occupation, three of us met and went to a window that we knew was open and broke into the building. We put a strip of masking tape down the window as a sign that we had got in. We broke in at 3 A.M. and spent the rest of the night in a room in the basement, because we didn't know if there were security guards there. Bob Davis, who was the editor of *This Magazine is About Schools,* had ice in his veins. He went to sleep, but I was terrified and stayed up all night. At 7 A.M., everyone came in with the kids.

MYRA: For the first two weeks, we all stayed there all the time. But no one was getting any sleep, so we cut down. By the end it was once a week you had to stay. We always had children sleeping there, too. They weren't going to come and yank us out with kids.

JULIE: We entered into a series of long negotiations with the university. They had security guards handing out notices when people entered the building because our being there was illegal, but they never kicked us out. We occupied the building for ten months, twenty-four hours a day.

In 1974 Ontario started its first wave of capital grants for child care. First the university tried to get St. Andrew's and Campus Co-op to amalgamate. That wouldn't have worked, because they were so different. Then they tried to make another place, Margaret Fletcher, the official university daycare. We said we wouldn't go in with Margaret Fletcher. What ended up happening was that both sites got capital grants, and the campus had two daycares.

MYRA: We were in Devonshire, the daycare we occupied, for thirty years in the end. When I look back, I'm amazed we had the fortitude to do that occupation for so long. We were so sure we were right that we held on. It became part of people's lives, and even if they weren't comfortable with the occupation, they did their part. And it didn't do the kids any harm. Many of the kids went on to achieve greatness academically as well as artistically.

SUE COLLEY: At the beginning the left was involved because the occupation was seen as so alternative. I was in the occupation at Devonshire, and people would debate things from the point of view of various left tendencies.

MYRA: There was a debate as to whether we should encourage schools to do junior kindergarten or not. Could we shape our kids better on our own, or should we demand that the state provide more education?

JULIE: By 1973, the infrastructure for a larger daycare movement had grown out of the Sussex daycare. We were putting out a tabloid called *Day Care for Everyone*. We were trying to set up co-ops in working-class areas, although we still hadn't learned; people were working in factories and then having to clean up at the daycare. We also started to engage with government and demand grants for community-based child care centres.

We had a meeting in the spring of that year with a guy from the day nurseries branch. He told us there were some changes coming and that we would be happy. That was when the province announced that child care centres wouldn't have to have as many staff. All the quality stuff was being stripped away because of pressure from the commercial daycares. The government had totally misinterpreted what alternative daycares were all about. Everyone got galvanized, and it was the beginning of a time when the non-profit sector, the municipal sector and the alternative sector worked together. We planned a big demonstration against the government's Birch proposals, which reduced requirements for daycare. There were still people among the Campus Co-op group who wanted nothing to do with government, so we left for the demo thinking that people would come but not being sure. Five minutes before it was about to start, Campus Co-op showed up with banners, and I was so happy I almost cried.

SUE: There was an evolution from the student movement to a more serious left movement. We tried to do a lot in alternative ways. It wasn't only daycare. There were communes, alternative bookstores, all kinds of things. A lot of them didn't work for very long. In daycare, we realized we really needed that subsidy. It became a practicality for the daycare movement to get involved with the state. You had to be, to get the services you needed.

That was the beginning of the notion that child care is a right. It was the beginning of thinking that child care should be a social service. That's how it related to the women's movement, too. If you didn't have child care, then how could women have equality?

JULIE: We were wrong about one thing, though. The lack of good daycare didn't keep women out of the workforce. There are still many women who go to work worrying about the care their kids are getting.

The National Daycare Conference

IN CONVERSATION: SUE COLLEY, MARTHA FRIENDLY, LAUREL ROTHMAN AND JULIE MATHIEN

SUE COLLEY: The National Daycare Conference was a federally funded conference organized as a follow-up to the Royal Commission on the Status of Women report, which had recommended universal child care. September 1982 was the date set for the conference in Winnipeg. In 1979 we had written a radical political platform for Ontario called the Action Daycare Platform. We demanded free universal child care. Julie Mathien took this into the provincial NDP and got it adopted and Pat Schultz and I got it adopted by the Ontario Federation of Labour. We were seeing a broadening of interest in child care issues in the social democratic movements. So we decided to bring our platform to the Winnipeg conference.

MARTHA FRIENDLY: We spent the summer before the conference calling and writing everybody across the country with this platform.

LAUREL ROTHMAN: By the time we got to Winnipeg, we had this little yellow book that called for universally accessible child care.

MARTHA: We had a debate about the wording for the booklet. Should we say "accessible" or "free"? We didn't use "free" for the conference, because free might mean there was no value attached to it.

SUE: The night before the conference opened, we had a meeting. We didn't know what was going to happen, but it was galvanizing. Two hundred people showed up to decide how to intervene in the conference, something none of us had ever done before. So we were really high.

MARTHA: Twenty of us came together on the plane from Toronto, and Aggie Lucas had these buttons about universally accessible daycare. At first everybody was friendly, and they all put on buttons. Then they realized what was going on, and by the time we got to Winnipeg, they took off their buttons. We formed into two distinct groups on the trip to Winnipeg. There was a social agency, early childhood group, and we were parents and feminists. At the conference there were more groups. There was a small for-profit child care group, and staff people who had never imagined anything like this.

JULIE MATHIEN: An alliance formed at the conference between the fence-sitting agencies and the for-profit group. That was somewhat of a problem then, and it kept being a problem later.

MARTHA: We went full speed ahead, although we didn't really know what we were doing. Something really important was that we had brought Ellen Roseman with us. She was a reporter for *The Globe and Mail* who was interested in child care. I had asked her to cover the conference, and we were the only ones she knew. She wrote about it every day, and her stories were on the front page. That made an enormous difference. There were people in the government who thought child care was to help poor kids. They weren't against child care per se; they just had a very social-work notion of it.

Renee Edwards, who became one of the members of the Katie Cooke Task Force, told me later, "We knew what you were talking about at the conference, but we thought it sounded really radical and really scary."[2] The conference was the first time I remember NAC being visible on child care.

SUE: By lunchtime of the first day, government bureaucrats were coming up to me and whispering, "What's going to happen next?" That's when I knew we had taken over the conference. We then had the confidence to move on and adopt the platform for universal child care, which became the basis of the Canadian Daycare Advocacy Association.

LAUREL: At the end of the conference, there was some acrimony. That was the first major cross-Canada perception of the difference between for-profit and non-profit child care.

MARTHA: If you supported for-profit child care, you weren't for public funding, universality, quality or paying workers decent wages. That still holds today. That's what the conference was really about.

LAUREL: The conference was an incredibly politicizing event, a real turning point. It might not have been so new for the activists, but for the front-line workers, it was an incredible experience.

MARTHA: On the plane coming home I sat next to someone who cried the whole time. She just wanted to be a teacher of young kids; she didn't want to do all this. She didn't like conflict. But most people found it incredibly exciting. When I speak now and ask people if they were at the Winnipeg conference, there are always a number of people who were, and they all say they found it exciting. There is money set aside for a third conference now, and several people have taken me aside and said, "You're not thinking of making it like the last conference, are you?"

SUE: The most concrete thing that came out of the 1982 conference was the appointing of the Katie Cooke Task Force. It reported in 1986, on International Women's Day, and said that Canada should have a universal daycare system.

LAUREL: Trudeau, who was prime minister at the time, would never have started that task force without the conference. It was obvious that child care had become a national issue, and it had to go somewhere. It was supposed

2. The Katie Cooke Task Force on Child Care was set up by then Minister Responsible for the Status of Women Judy Erola in 1986. Katie Cooke was a senior bureaucrat with responsibility for women's issues.

to be part of the Liberals' '84 campaign platform, but by then Trudeau was out the door.

MARTHA: There were three major occasions on which we almost got child care. The Katie Cooke Task Force was supposed to turn into a child care program, but Trudeau quit and the Liberals lost. Brian Mulroney tried to give us child care, but we didn't want what he was offering. The third time was when the Liberals got elected in 1993. Child care was in the Red Book, but the referendum and the deficit killed it. The Liberals were terrified about how much it was going to cost.

SIX

NO MEANS NO
Resistance to Male Violence

Men who want to support women in our struggle for freedom and justice should understand that it is not terrifically important to us that they learn to cry; it is important to us that they stop the crimes of violence against us.

—ANDREA DWORKIN

I N 1970 VIOLENCE AGAINST WOMEN was still hidden, a secret shame. It was the one issue on which the Royal Commission on the Status of Women was almost silent. Yet every time a women's centre or women's health centre opened its doors, women phoned or turned up with stories of male violence. The mainstream services available to women, whether police, doctors or hospitals, were patronizing at best, and at worst, inclined to blaming the victim.

American writer Susan Brownmiller's *Against Our Will: Men, Women and Rape*, published in 1975, was influential in developing a radical feminist theory of violence against women. "Rape is nothing more or less," Brownmiller wrote, "than a conscious process by which all men keep all women in a state of fear." Violence against women, she and others argued, was then a kind of terrorism aimed at keeping women "in their place." The solution was to empower women, first to overcome their fear, and ultimately to overthrow the patriarchal system. But there were major debates on the issue. Liberal feminists thought that violence against women could be curbed, if not eliminated, by persuading legal institutions to take the violence seriously. Socialist feminists were slow to respond since the issue did not fit easily into their political analysis. Everyone agreed, however, that the first steps were to create safe places for women fleeing abusive relationships and to increase women's economic independence.

From the beginning, most women's transition houses and rape crisis centres worked from a radical feminist analysis, countering the widely accepted notions that a woman's own behaviour brought on the beatings and that a man's violence against his female partner was a private affair. Anti-violence activists were not just battling backward attitudes; they were also fighting seriously regressive laws. In Canada, the law covering rape before 1981 refused to recognize rape within marriage, let men off if they "honestly believed" that a woman had consented to intercourse and allowed defence attorneys to question a victim on her sexual history, in the widespread belief that women who were sexually active were probably "asking for it."

Front-line agencies, rape crisis centres and transition houses were also in the forefront of the struggle by marginalized women to make a place for themselves in the women's movement. It was here that working-class women, lesbians, immigrant women and women with disabilities often had their first contact with feminists. As clients and as collective members, these women fiercely demanded that their voices and their experience be integrated into the work. Divisions were intense and in Vancouver led to a serious split.

VANCOUVER RAPE RELIEF

Lee Lakeman

I had come from Ontario to a conference in B.C. in 1975 or '76 that was billed as the first International Family Violence Conference. Gene Errington delivered one of the great speeches of the early movement about men's rage in women's lives. The male researchers at that conference were arguing that there was no such thing as violence against women, that it was family violence. But I also met women there who were talking about the direct confrontation by women of violent men.

The next year I moved to Vancouver. Vancouver Transition House was already up and running, with its position that transition houses should be mandatory services paid for by the government, a position I had not thought about before. Vancouver Rape Relief was four or five years old at this point. It was a collective, basically a rape crisis centre. I got hired onto the staff of five there and was involved in hiring three more staff within six months. So pretty quickly there was a new phenomenon.

Collectives offered a way of being in control of your work that didn't involve bossing anyone around or being isolated in a hierarchy, away from the wisdom and the intimacy of other people. I think the women who set up Rape Relief had learned a little bit from the Vancouver Women's Health Collective and a little bit from a women's collective in Berkeley. It was the practice of democracy. It was our version of what Paulo Freire talks about.[1] We thought you could see only one step ahead of what you were doing, and the collective was a way of practising democracy that gave you a greater and greater expectation of democracy. It wasn't that you practised perfection; it was that you were constantly moving in an open-ended way toward something better. There were a lot of experiments and debates and theoretical discussions: What did leadership and authority look like in that circumstance? What about our economic circumstances? We tried sharing incomes. We debated whether there should be paid staff at the centre or not.

When I came in, thirty women were in the collective. Five of us were full-time workers, and the twenty-five others were mainly women on welfare and women with low-paying jobs. I can count on one hand the professional women who worked in the collective. Overwhelmingly, it was an organization of poor women and women of modest means. There was a policy of dissuading lawyers to join, but mostly professional women just didn't get involved.

Because it was a collective, we never farmed out the cleaning, the maintenance, the schlep work. We didn't set up a hierarchy. Doing the dishes was an important part of the work.

In a collective, hopefully there's more leadership. The whole idea was to share the work, rotate the authority, protect and follow emerging leadership. We would rotate the position of chairperson from meeting to meeting, but if someone had a good idea, you might bend the rules of order to make room for it. One of our ongoing discussions was how to deal with the habit of undermining leadership. Every once in a while we would get into nay-saying: "Oh, you can't do that, no way," instead of being open: "Okay,

---

1. Paulo Freire is the author of *Pedagogy of the Oppressed* and the father of popular education; he believes education and action must go together.

say you are right: How would you do that?" To this day, we are constantly
in a debate about keeping authority and leadership separate.

In the mid-1970s, Rape Relief did three or four public education events
a week—talking to schools, community groups. Mostly we were invited to
come. We were participating in the B.C. Federation of Women.[2] We were
operating a twenty-four-hour phone line for women in crisis. We were also
organizing campaigns against specific attackers and attacks.

Not long after I arrived, a woman called about an optician. In the course
of examining the woman, the optician had dropped a contact lens down
her blouse, and he assaulted her in reaching down to get it. He did it again
when she came back for a fitting, and she realized that he was doing it to
other women too. We convinced a newspaper reporter to do a story, and in
the end we had fifty women come forward, one of whom had been raped
by this guy.

We wanted this optician to lose the privilege he had as a professional
to carry out these attacks on women. That didn't happen; the opticians'
college let him off. But this campaign set the tone for the campaigns that
happened after that. First we would get the crisis call. Rape Relief had to
be identified as a safe place to tell your story, a place that was interested in
acting on your story but also a place that would work with you and was not
going to take over your story. There was a date rape situation—we did a
few of them. They tended to be situations where the women involved didn't
think they could get the criminal justice system to act or thought the justice
system would act in the wrong way. I remember one situation in which a
woman had been seduced by a man in her apartment building. She didn't
want him jailed or criminalized, but she did want him to accept what he
had done. She thought he had committed rape, but neither she nor we felt
we could prove it. We talked to other women who lived in the apartment
building, and of course he had made passes at some of them, too. So in that
case, twenty of us went to this guy's door, well rehearsed in what we were
going to say. The hardest thing about doing a confrontation like this is to
take yourself seriously enough to meet ahead of time and prepare a simple
script. The woman prepares a line and the women accompanying her
prepare a line, and everybody has to be brave enough to say them. That guy
shut the door on us instantly. We always left the men the name of a men's

2. The BCFW was a coalition of women's groups across British Columbia formed in
1974.

group to contact, though, and sometimes we heard back. Almost inevitably, the man would describe it as a hundred women showing up at his door and yelling at him. The men were frightened and shocked and troubled by it all, and of course that's what we wanted. Then we would leave them to decide what to do with it.

Initially, what Rape Relief offered was support groups, phone counselling and some in-person counselling. In the early days, there was a lot of debate about the relationship between counselling and advocacy, and that remains a debate in the collective. What is a conversation and what is counselling? What is peer counselling and what is political organizing? We need to keep re-evaluating and rethinking that. One of my lines is that the brilliance of feminist services is to never resolve that debate. Everything needs to be tailored to the individual woman. The woman has to have food on the table and a place for her kids, so we do a bit of triage. But we are not going to be able to fix her life, and she has to know that from the beginning. And you better not be patronizing her, because she will pick up on that right away. Do you give a woman bus tickets to come to a group, or don't you? Do you go with her to welfare or not? Do you set up the agenda based on what she wants to do, or do you try to set the agenda? Do you want women who are fresh out of crisis to work in the collective? Do you want women to work in the collective who don't think they've ever been attacked?

We've always leaned to the idea that any woman who wants to work at Rape Relief should be able to do that and be as much in charge as any other collective member is. We may need to get some barriers out of her way for that to happen. If she needs a new pair of shoes to go to a speaking engagement, let's get her a new pair of shoes. We have women on salary, but we don't see anything wrong with volunteerism. We don't think of it as volunteerism, actually; we think of it as solidarity and self-aid. But that is hard, because the women on salary get more. We decided a long time ago that if we were going to have salaries, they had to be decent salaries, above labour standards.

Women against Violence against Women (WAVAW) was created in Vancouver in 1982 to provide an alternative to Rape Relief. There were some issues relating to individual women who had been part of the RR collective and then split with us. One woman thought that having subcommittees was a breach of collectivity. Another woman thought it was unacceptable to talk politics in the office. We used to take Friday afternoons for what we called loose talk, and we'd gather and talk about things. "Are you really including the Queen when you talk about all women?" "What is more important—socialism or anarchism?" We dared to think about reform versus revolution.

Some women in the community were appalled that Rape Relief was forming a group of men to raise money for the transition house we wanted, and there was also a group of women who were confronting me. The fights about men were the most bitter. There were women who were convinced there was no way to work with or speak with men where men would not win. For example, one of the debates was about the collective deciding to join a picket line. We felt that we had to respond to the situation of farm workers; both women and men were working in unbearable conditions, and we were eating that food. But there were women who felt we should stick to women's issues.

The Rape Relief collective was also in constant debate about whether or not we should assist the state in jailing men, and under what circumstances. A number of women split with us over that. We were raising the bar on women's responsibility. Now, I would articulate it this way: It is perfectly acceptable for me to support a woman in taking a man to court and giving the court material to convict him, and at the same time I can fight for better and more just sentences. But in those days it was an either/or. Either you used the courts and fought for longer and harsher sentences, or you were against the courts. Eventually the women's movement got very good at living with the contradiction. You had to deal with both. There were men that we didn't know what to do with but lock them up, and fast. And there were men who needed to be condemned by the community but didn't need to rot in jail. We wanted women to think through the consequences and not just think like victims. The more we experience ourselves as powerful, the more we can do that.

Some of our work involved challenging existing organizations. We did a confrontation of a postal worker who sexually harassed a woman on the job. The union was furious with us. But our position was: If you don't take this on as a union, we'll take it on as a women's movement. We expected unions to hold men accountable for their behaviour and to protect women workers.

We were also involved in pressuring people in various professions to change their behaviour. Sometimes we trained people, sometimes we met with them, sometimes we leaned on them, and sometimes we embarrassed them. We never trained them with the illusion that they were ignorant. But this work could be never-ending. At a certain point, for instance, we stopped training cops and stopped training emergency room nurses, because these were black holes where you could be taken up forever. In fact, there was no absence of knowledge—what there was was a refusal to change policy, a refusal to reward positive behaviour, on the part of the institutions.

I think we got credibility with women by being portrayed in the press as doing radical things and by the word spreading. Negative rumours travelled by word of mouth, too. We were constantly accused of things we never did. People would repeat these rumours and not seem to understand that they were doing the enemy's work for them. Rape Relief was audited again and again and again.

What was true was that we kicked back our salaries to get the down payment for the transition house. Once we got it, there were women who lived on unemployment insurance and worked at the house and there were women who lived on welfare and did the same. I was living in a co-op house with a man with whom I was lovers, and I got turned in. I quit welfare before it had a chance to cut me off. Rape Relief's funding had been cut 100 percent by the Social Credit government, so we decided to share our incomes.[3] Some women worked in a factory as well. We made up our minds that the government could remove our salaries, but they couldn't stop our work. We survived for ten years without government funding. By the end of those ten years, we had enough money to pay stipends to Rape Relief workers.

It was hard hanging on without government money. It was hard being very poor, very small, being worried that we were insular. The public attacks were very hard, too. Among other things, we were regularly accused of being homophobic, which was false.

When the B.C. NDP was elected in 1991, the collective badly needed to integrate more racially, and a woman in the collective argued that we had to change our position on seeking government funding. We realized we had to pay women of colour if we were going to bring them in, because it wasn't possible for women to live on welfare anymore. We made a point of going after South Asian, Aboriginal, Chinese and black women and building leadership from each of those communities. We had very few tensions throughout the process. We decided to hire women of colour for the core

---

3. The Social Credit Party held government in British Columbia from 1975 to 1991.

group, rather than for temporary contract positions. Where we could, we hired women of colour from the training group.

At one point we used to get $150,000 a year for five rape crisis centres throughout B.C. We shared that money among us. The province wanted to control each centre separately, but we were a collective of collectives. That's still going on in Quebec, but it's not going on here. Here the government has interfered so much, we barely have other rape crisis centres, and we don't have any coalitions that are not hierarchical and manipulated from the top. It's devastating, and it happened under B.C.'s NDP government. And now we have the budget cuts under the Liberals.[4] The social democrats set up the hierarchy and the right came in and lopped off the top and left the bottom scrambling. It has happened to health collectives, transition houses, rape crisis centres and women's centres.

You had to be totally unaware to miss out on feminism when I was growing up, and that's not true now. Today women have to fight for it and hang on to each other to keep the hope between them. There's the beginning of a reconnection to the anti-imperialist struggle, which I find helpful. There's a ground-to-ground connection with women in various countries. These women's services have saved a lot of women's lives in North America. They are a specific tactic that emerged at a particular time, a great moment of privilege. They are completely underestimated by the left and by Canadian political theorists, and they are being utterly devastated at the moment. Many women will die, and they won't even be counted. There will be a hell of a lot more who are beaten or captured. Transition houses and rape crisis centres play the role of revealing how much violence women face, but it is increasingly difficult to make the case. We are effectively decriminalizing violence against women. I know women historically have risen up every second generation. It's a stupid notion. Why can't this be the generation that doesn't let it go?

WAVAW/RAPE CRISIS CENTRE

Frances Wasserlein

My first job in the women's movement was as a summer student on a grant with Vancouver Rape Relief in 1978. That was a pivotal year in my life. Vancouver Rape Relief was a door into the women's movement not only for me but for other volunteers and women seeking help there.

---

4. The B.C. Liberals were elected in May 2001.

I got a job there because of Ellen Frank, whom I had met two years earlier at a huge demo organized by the B.C. Federation of Women to protest the firing of Gene Errington, who was responsible for Status of Women under the NDP government. One of the first things the Social Credit government did when it was re-elected in late 1975 was to fire her. It was the first demonstration I had ever gone to. Ellen Frank was the MC, and she talked about being a lesbian and about her work in the women's movement. She was a collective member at Rape Relief, and she was key in developing what turned out to be a fairly important relationship with the Vancouver police department in terms of having the police listen to women about rape. Vancouver was very early in providing rape crisis services. A couple of women put a phone in their house as early as 1972 and advertised their willingness to take calls from women who had been sexually assaulted— talk to them and try to find sympathetic services for them. The women taking the calls were hooked up with Vancouver Status of Women, which was in operation by late 1972. So Vancouver Rape Relief had deep roots.

I finished my bachelor's degree in 1980 and got a job as co-manager of Munroe House, which was YWCA second-stage housing for women who wanted to live with a bit of support after leaving violent and abusive relationships. In 1978 I had started an organization called Battered Women Support Services and volunteered there leading support groups. I was also involved in a battle that year against a government program that was giving $300,000 to anger management programs for men but not enough money to women's shelters.

At Munroe House, we started to get phone calls from social workers and people in provincial social service networks, and from other women's organizations, asking if we had had any recent contact with Vancouver Rape Relief. The callers would say that they knew women who had called Rape Relief and could not get service or were told that reporting to the police was not a good idea, because the justice system was controlled by race and class and the only men the police would arrest were poor and from racial minorities. So it seemed that if you were a woman standing in a phone booth calling Rape Relief, you had to answer a number of questions before anyone there would talk to you. These calls from social workers and feminists in other organizations increased in frequency and intensity. Women started discussing it, and it became clear that Rape Relief was not participating in general women's movement stuff. They had kind of vanished.

Then a number of things occurred at the same time, which worried us even more. What happened at the first of a series of meetings with Rape Relief was that we didn't understand them when they spoke. They spoke in this weird code that we later found out was a form of criticism/self-criticism.[5] There was a kind of formula: "This is what I see you doing, this is how it makes me feel, and this is what I want you to do."

That made us very, very worried, because one of the important women-operated services in our community appeared to have lost its collective mind. Then women who worked at Rape Relief started to be ejected in very poor emotional states. Some of them would talk to other women about it; others left town. In the unfolding of this, there seemed to be a connection with the relationship between Men against Sexism and Rape Relief. In the manner of the time, and perhaps unfairly, Vancouver Rape Relief was said to have married Men against Sexism. What had been a woman-only space was now occupied by men as well. I and others didn't think this was a good idea.

There seemed to have been a significant and fundamental change in Rape Relief's analysis that I would now describe as being based on identity politics. In the name of a class analysis, some terrible things were done to women who worked there and to some women who sought services. The exact same thing happened elsewhere in the women's movement ten years later, but that time it was about race. Those things led to the further co-optation of women's organizations into the 2000s, when it became possible for the government of B.C. to massively reduce government funding for women with almost no opposition. The roots of that depoliticization go back to that time.

Anyway, what happened was that a number of us held a meeting. The women at that invitation-only meeting had all worked at Rape Relief prior to 1980. We decided to gather information about what women's experiences with Rape Relief were, both to convince ourselves that it was necessary to stop this organization and to provide evidence to others so that they would agree with us. So we set out in secret to collect stories about what had happened to women who had worked or sought services there. This document came to be called "the dossier." After about two months, we decided to use these stories as a way to withdraw support from Rape Relief and to seek money to set up another rape crisis centre. A lot of concerns

5. Criticism/self-criticism was a method of dialogue developed by Mao Tse-tung in China and adopted by many radical groups in North America.

were put out into the open. Rape Relief was asked to provide info about what they were doing, and the upshot was a public meeting where a straw vote was taken to see if there was enough support to set up a new centre. Rape Relief denied the truth of what we said. In July of 1982, WAVAW/Rape Crisis Centre was established.

So there was a split with Rape Relief. A large number of labour groups and groups on the left which had never worked on these issues took it that Rape Relief was under attack by middle-class white women and decided that the correct thing to do was to support them. I think that was mistaken and short-sighted. I was intensely personally involved in this, because some of the key players were people I had known for some time. It was very painful. And at that time in the 1980s, when there was already a battle between the women's movement and the Socred government, the damage was great.

The split widened to such a degree that people became despondent about the women's movement, and then to have the Solidarity[6] thing, and to be completely sold out by the labour movement made it even worse. The radical feminist stream, who see themselves as combatting the effects of patriarchal social order, and women on the left have been more or less successful in making coalition on a variety of things that have come up in the last twenty years, but it has never been as cohesive again.

I have to say that I would now do things differently than I did then. I would not be willing to do the kind of secretive organizing we did. One of the consequences of that is that there is still this document very few women have ever seen. If we had not agreed to organize in secret, we would have in the end been more effective. I still think we did the right thing, but we could have done it more effectively.

Prince Albert Interval House

Priscilla Settee

Interval houses and safety homes for battered women started in the early 1970s, for Aboriginal women in particular. Aboriginal women organized the first safe house in Prince Albert, Saskatchewan. There was an incredible need for women and children to be safe. Women were telling each other

---

6. The Solidarity Coalition was a coalition of labour, feminists and community groups formed to fight the Social Credit government. When labour leaders arrived at a settlement with the Socreds on the eve of a general strike, many feminists and community groups felt betrayed.

about violence against them. We had our friends in other agencies, who worked within the system and helped us organize. They also had Aboriginal women on their boards. One service was the mobile crisis unit, which families could call at any hour of the day or night to report a personal or physical crisis. It was a natural co-operation. Prince Albert is such a small community that we've also always worked together with colleagues who aren't Aboriginal.

There wasn't any resistance to forming the interval house in Prince Albert. We used provincial funding. The Aboriginal community supported it as well. Our community tends to be male-dominated, but we didn't pose a threat to anyone. We were working with battered women who didn't have a voice. We were connected to the Saskatchewan Native Women's Movement, which was formed in the early 1970s and later became the Aboriginal Women's Network. It was hooked into the non-Aboriginal women's movement in Prince Albert but not in the rest of the province. So I went willingly to meet with the Saskatchewan Action Committee on the Status of Women, even though there was resistance from some of our members. They didn't always see the need to meet with other groups. We native women have always had to carve out our place. The Aboriginal women didn't necessarily see themselves as leaders, and they didn't think the non-Aboriginal women would value them. The all-white nature of the boards in other organizations felt like benign racism. There were different issues like this.

Interval House received government grants to keep our office going. We had a forum where you could introduce things and talk about issues affecting women. We talked a lot about violence but rarely got beyond the personal to the political. I was one of the more radical women, and I didn't feel I could bare my soul. This particular group of women was more grassroots. There was a lack of theoretical framework and political analysis. At times I worked with the left, but my main work was in the Aboriginal community. I felt I was a leader in both arenas, and the lack of political analysis was uncomfortable to be in at times. At that time there was little global perspective, and I feel we got stuck. I'd come back to my community and feel there was a real gap. It may have been my inability as a leader to bridge that gap. We talked about things as if they were our fault. It is different now.

I may have been one of the few Aboriginal woman working with the left in Saskatchewan at the time. We did some international work that was indigenous, and we felt it was relevant. I would have to say that I never felt at home in most of the mainstream Aboriginal organizations. They used to call me "the red beret." Some called me a communist. I was branded within my own community. It didn't isolate me, though. To me, organizing is exciting and part of life, and if I'm not doing that, I'm at loose ends. I'm a better listener now than I used to be. I'm not so sure I know everything. I have a better sense of what's important. In the early seventies, I took a woman's literature course at university, which impacted on me. Reading Angela Davis was a breakthrough for me.[7] I was more influenced by black literature than by feminist literature. It put me more in touch with myself as an Aboriginal.

In the late 1970s, we started organizing around International Women's Day in Prince Albert. Some of the women from Saskatchewan Working Women were close friends with us.[8] Working together was natural, and there was a lot of respect. Race wasn't an issue with that group. They supported us in our quests, and we went through a lot together. We were colleagues and friends. I think that where you lived in Saskatchewan made a difference in regard to racism and the women's movement. Saskatchewan is so small that you can't afford to offend people. There was always a level of respect. Aboriginal women had a home, and events brought us together. International tours, daycare, and violence against women—these were common issues.

Toronto Rape Crisis Centre

Deb Parent

In 1974 a small group of women got $8000 from the city of Toronto. Increasing numbers of women were wanting to speak of their own experiences with violence. This was happening on a grand scale, and no way existed for women to tell one another what was happening. With the Toronto Rape Crisis Centre, our goal was to end violence against women and create a service we thought would be temporary. We took 120 calls the first year, and the centre has been in operation twenty-four hours a day

---

7. Angela Davis is a well-known African-American feminist, left-wing activist and author.
8. Saskatchewan Working Women, formed in 1979, was a group of union and non-union women working to improve the conditions of women in the workforce and promote women in the labour movement.

since then. Thousands of women have put their time into it, heart and soul. Last year the centre took over fifteen thousand calls. It has become a feminist institution. But we had no way of knowing that at the time. It made so much sense to end the violence against women that we couldn't believe the problem would persist for long.

Feminist counselling was very much a response to traditional mainstream approaches to violence. Traditional counsellors and institutions were caught up in basic stereotypes. The principle of peer counselling with a feminist approach was revolutionary.[9] We had heard many stories of how women felt blamed or judged, and every feminist service was a reaction to patriarchy.

I got involved with the Toronto Rape Crisis Centre in 1980. I had moved to Toronto from Ottawa and gone on strike at Bell Canada. It was the first time the operators had been on strike, and there was a groundswell of community support. I went to a local feminist bar, an amazing hodgepodge of sex, drugs, rock 'n' roll and politics, trying to get support for the union. The idea of making good trouble was already there, but I was surprised that women in the bar didn't get the truth of this situation. They didn't understand that Bell had a huge share of the pie and that the operators had a very little one. But a small group of women from the rape crisis centre donated money and offered to come out and picket. The centre not only talked the talk but also walked the walk. They came out to the strike, and I started volunteering at the centre. Before long, I joined the centre staff. Even though I hadn't completed high school, they were willing to look at the work I'd done. I took over the public education role and spent the next twenty-two years in a variety of positions, getting paid to make good trouble.

What the women of the rape crisis centre did was give me a way to understand myself as a woman. They gave me a way to see myself in the world. My work there helped me understand why I didn't fit in. It gave me a sense of possibilities. The things that were part of me were a source of truth and strength. I had to work through my internalized sexism; to gain that understanding of the pain of my differences allowed me to love myself and other women in a new way. I was being paid, though not much, because every other year I was laid off. But now I had a vocation and a passion. This was a life, not just a job. Being the working-class kid who had

---

9. Peer counselling assumes that the person doing the counselling has a similar experience to the person being counselled.

never fit in and then finding a place where I was embraced and encouraged, where I had the resources to shape my work, was a gift.

When I came in, the collective consisted of thirty-five very active volunteers. You did a shift, a collective meeting every week, and other work like advocacy or education. I was the fourth staff member hired. Although the rape crisis centre's board was radical and revolutionary for its time, ideas were shifting, and the volunteers were constantly bringing in new ideas. We weren't all white, and we were Jews, lesbians, working class, disabled and so on. The board was resistant to the idea of looking at how we could hear each other and enact the necessary changes.

In the summer of 1981, I went to my first Canadian Association of Sexual Assault Centres (CASAC) meeting. There were fifteen members from Toronto and several hundred women from other rape crisis centres across the country. That was the first time we began to articulate a definition of violence against women that included racism, classism, sexism, homophobia and able-ism. It was a powerful experience but painful for many women. Many of us had just found a home in this movement as women, feminists and activists. This was a refuge. So to see that in this home there was a privilege corresponding to every oppression was difficult. There was a lot of pain and anger.

We were young. Now, part of our experience in mid-life is incorporating compassion with truth and justice; bell hooks's work on love synthesizes all the aspects of feminist analysis with a tender kick-ass approach.[10] But we didn't know at the time what tools would help us handle this. White, middle-class, heterosexual women were having a hard time realizing they had privilege. Resistance was high, because it felt like there was a division happening that was going to be insurmountable. And things got confusing. For instance, class is an amorphous thing to define. Many of us working-class women thought we were middle class, but when we went to the middle-class caucus, we realized that there was another part of our lives that was going to be on that see-saw between pride and pain. Some of us were lesbians, too, which felt like another division between us. We felt that women who were sexually involved with men had a harder time dealing with the issues. Lesbians could name male violence because we weren't in the position of having to reconcile our analysis with our relationships with men. Lesbians took risks to name male violence as part of patriarchy and male privilege.

---

10. Bell hooks is an African-American feminist writer who has written several books on love, activism and feminism.

We were familiar with attempts to see us as male haters, and we had to ride that backlash.

We were trying to develop an analysis and to deal with all the things that women needed. We knew we had to figure out a way to understand this. No other political movement was dealing with internalized differences. We didn't have anyone we felt we could turn to. It was incredibly challenging, because we were struggling with building a community and also dealing with who we were and weren't. We had to unlearn misinformation about each other. And we knew that the process was as important as the product.

This work continued when we got back home, of course. There was at one point almost 50 percent of the collective at a meeting who said, "What does all this have to do with rape?" We endeavoured to show that it had everything to do with violence. We had to understand the experience of whomever was calling us without presumption. More and more we were seeing marginalized women using the service because they had nothing else. So we also had to expand our vision of who was doing the work. We couldn't reconcile our differences at that meeting, and fifteen women turned in their keys to the centre. There was a fair amount of lesbian-baiting at that time. I was sad for everyone. But those of us who stayed knew our vision had to keep expanding.

The founders of the centre had left in '78, '79, when volunteers rebelled over a hierarchy. That struggle had happened, and the collective was reshaped, and now these other issues had reared their heads. The main thing was, how do we reshape our vision with compassion and not lose out?

When the NDP came into power in Ontario in 1990, we increased to eleven full-time staff at the rape crisis centre. That was our opportunity to hire more women of colour. Once women of colour were on board, there were struggles because the organization was mostly white. The majority of women of colour were also straight. We had some commonality, but it was challenging to hold both pieces at once. One of the reasons we got through our differences was that the white lesbians had been through the struggle before. We knew we had to ride it out. We had to let go of stuff to do it. Some women left because things weren't happening fast enough, but most women hung in. Women of colour had been articulating racism for many years, but it was harder when you had to articulate it across a table. Things that had worked for us as lesbians had to be deconstructed, and we had to see ourselves as privileged.

In retrospect, I think that identity politics was both necessary and limited. Without it, I don't think we would have as complex and broad and sophisticated an analysis as we do. Now we see a connection between all the different oppressions. Nobody else was bringing that experience as sharply to the table. In my individual growth, some kind of spirituality has had to grow. I think that's true in the feminist movement in general. We've given voice to our differences and understand privilege; now we have to talk from our hearts and not only from the sharpness of our experience. We can't feel guilty for our experience, either, because it makes us ineffective as allies. We need each other. People with privilege need to change. Nobody said the struggle was going to be easy. But if we can forgive ourselves and each other, and admit that we were self-righteous in our adolescence, we can see that we were finding our place in the world. If you hang in, something glorious can come out of that. The fact that the centres and shelters continue to exist and be active and that we haven't given it up is amazing.

SEVEN

SOLIDARITY AND SISTERHOOD
Union Feminists

I've seen the glass ceiling, and it's made out of golf balls.

—NANCY RICHE, FORMER CANADIAN LABOUR
CONGRESS SECRETARY-TREASURER

WHILE SOME FEMINISTS in the 1970s worked on developing women-only structures, others looked for strategies to transform the highly male-dominated labour movement. Women workers had been organized for many years, but women's issues were far from the top of labour's agenda, and women in the union movement were treated with the same patronizing sexism they faced in other institutions. However, with the rapid expansion of the public sector between 1965 and 1975 and the success of a series of militant strikes, female union membership was growing rapidly. Established leaders such as Grace Hartman and Madeleine Parent were joined by younger feminist activists who believed the working class would play a leading role in social change.

As the decade progressed, women's committees and caucuses formed inside unions and union federations. Thanks to their organizing, various trade unions fought successfully to gain paid maternity leave, equal pay for work of equal value, protection against sexual harassment, and rights for part-time workers. A series of first-contract struggles attracted the attention of the broader women's liberation movement, and picket-line solidarity formed the basis for an extraordinary alliance between feminists inside and outside the labour movement.

In 1975, despite massive opposition from the labour movement, the Trudeau government imposed wage and price controls. Although this led to a general downturn in labour militancy, women's union activism grew and grew. In British Columbia, a group of brash feminists decided to organize their own unions. In Saskatchewan and Ontario, women trade unionists and women outside the labour movement worked together to develop strategies for women's economic equality. Issues such as abortion and sexual harassment provoked tremendous debate within the union movement but, ultimately, feminists won excellent policy and action on both issues.

SORWUC and AUCE

Jean Rands

We formed a working women's workshop in the Vancouver Women's Caucus in 1970. The post office was paying women less than men, and we were demonstrating about equal pay and women being excluded from certain jobs. We demonstrated against the newspapers because they were listing help-wanted ads by gender: "Help Wanted Male" and "Help Wanted Female." But we soon concluded that we weren't getting anywhere by encouraging women to join unions. When I went to the Office and Professional Employees International Union (OPEIU) to investigate the possibility of organizing a union where I worked, they patted me on the head and the behind, told me I was cute and sent me away. I read through the BC Hydro collective agreement. All the categories in which women were allowed to work had separate wage rates for men and women, although the union had a fair number of women members. Other women were having similar experiences, so in 1971 we formed the Working Women's Association. We intended it to be a union but didn't know what that entailed. We wrote a constitution and bylaws. We had a founding convention, but then it turned out we weren't legally allowed to do it.

In 1972 we formed the Service, Office, and Retail Workers Union of Canada (SORWUC), with the objective of organizing those industries where women predominated. One of our founding members, Jackie Ainsworth, was working at a Denny's restaurant. The people there were in a rage about their working conditions. Jackie went to work one day and found a picket line. She had been talking about forming a union, but she didn't know the other shift was already organizing. They went on strike without a union. The biggest issue was sexual harassment. Women who talked about harassment or rape in those days were considered by men to be women who needed a good fuck.

Because SORWUC played a role in the Denny's strike, the union got a bigger profile, and SORWUC got involved in organizing a bunch of restaurants and bars after that. It wasn't ever certified in Denny's, but it was representing the workers there. The organization of the workers on campuses, the Association of University and College Employees (AUCE), started around the same time as SORWUC, out at the University of British Columbia campus. The OPEIU had refused to give these women any support. The women were pissed off by this and decided to form their own union. There was a movement for independent Canadian unions going on at the time.

AUCE had a founding convention in 1972–73, but they didn't manage to get enough people signed up. The following year I decided to get a job at UBC, working for the information office, where I could do union stuff. Jackie got a job at the library. We had to start all over again to get certified. Any membership form that was more than three months old didn't count, so we had to go back to people again. We were feeling intimidated, but we went ahead and did it. Ten people was the minimum we could get away with. We busted our asses and got some students to help us, people like Marion Pollock and Ginger Richards. We had no idea how many people worked on campus, and the people in the computer centre were anti-union snobs. But we signed up a whole bunch of people anyway and applied for certification around the time that B.C.'s NDP government was passing a new labour code. In the end, the B.C. Labour Relations Board decided to order a vote, and then we found out there were many more employees on campus than we had thought.

We put on a big campaign. The union-organizing drive brought people together, and we won the vote by a huge margin. We paid for things out of our own pockets; we had no money and weren't sure if we should accept donations from other unions, because we wanted to deal with them as equals. We got certified at the beginning of May 1974 and started bargaining. The university was so obnoxious. They gave us a wage proposal that we thought was a huge insult. We met in caucus, and we tried to remember what we'd seen on TV about breaking off negotiations. We called a special membership meeting to consider the university's offer and what we should do about it. We announced that members would also vote on whether to stay off the job that afternoon. The university sent out a memo warning that it would be an illegal strike and they would take action. Over nine hundred workers came to that membership meeting, and we stayed out for the afternoon. The meeting was spectacular. We had a fair amount of support among our supervisors, because we were seriously underpaid and under-respected. And there were all these women speaking for the first time in front of nine hundred people. We were really proud of each other. The university even had to pay us for that afternoon because they couldn't figure out who had been at the meeting.

There were twelve people on the AUCE negotiating committee, and we reported back at the regular meetings. We had a chair, but we all became experts on the various issues, and everyone spoke. We didn't have any outside help; we did it all ourselves. In the end, we got wage increases that, for the lowest-paid workers, were about 60 percent. My wages just about doubled. We got the right to have union meetings during work time, which helped membership participation. There was a lot of feminist stuff: We got a personal rights clause about not having to run errands and make coffee, and we got paid maternity leave.

AUCE got some support from the labour movement, but the people in CAIMAW, the Canadian Association of Industrial, Mechanical and Allied Workers,[1] argued against us going independent and encouraged us to join the Canadian Union of Public Employees (CUPE). We didn't want to do that. At first we made some trade unionists nervous because of our feminism, and others were nervous about our being a company union that would be in bed with the employer. But people joined at other universities and colleges, and Simon Fraser University got certified soon afterward. It was very exciting. It was an idea whose time had come—the whole thing about organizing in the public sector. The B.C. Government and Service Employees' Union (BCGEU) became a union at the same time. We had a couple of certifications under SORWUC by this time, but it was harder to organize in the private sector. People were more likely to be fired. Having an NDP government in power gave us more leverage at UBC, because management wasn't sure which side the government would be on.[2]

---

1. CAIMAW was an independent Canadian union affiliated to the CCU (Confederation of Canadian Unions), which was established in the late 1960s to fight the U.S.–based unions and work toward building democratic and independent Canadian unions. CAIMAW merged with the Canadian Auto Workers in 1992.
2. AUCE ended up joining CUPE in the early 1980s.

SORWUC started thinking in terms of organizing downtown, in insurance companies and banks. We decided to set up an office downtown ourselves. We had no money, which was frustrating. I used to hitchhike to other parts of the province in order to organize. But we wanted to mobilize the power that women had as workers to take on the oppression of women in general. Banks were a great example of women being ghettoized and exploited, and it was perfect that we should organize those. Jackie got a job in a bank, and it didn't take long for her to convince enough people in her branch to apply for certification. Was it legal to organize bank branches? We had a public debate going on in the press. We were leafleting and signing people up, and the response was pretty amazing. Hundreds of bank workers from all over the province got in touch with us, and we could barely keep up with the request for meetings.

I was working full time for the union, not getting paid, and also working part time as a temp. Jackie and another SORWUC organizer, Charlotte Johnson, worked downtown, so they could meet with people on their lunch hours. By the time the Labour Relations Board agreed to hold hearings, it was more than a year after the first branch had applied for certification. It was a long wait, and people were fired in the meantime. We didn't have a structure to defend workers, and the trade union movement wasn't as supportive as we needed. They wouldn't let SORWUC join the Canadian Labour Congress, and then they wouldn't support us because we weren't in the CLC. The final decision of the Labour Relations Board was that a bank branch was an acceptable bargaining unit. By the time we got to the hearing, we had concluded that we didn't want branch certification, though; we were hoping the board would consider a geographic unit, like, for example, all the branches in a small city.

Bank workers had stopped talking to us by this time because they were afraid their employers would punish them. So in some branches, we had no idea how the vote would go. We had twenty-five certifications, which didn't add up to that many members, and it was nightmarish negotiating with all these people. We didn't have money to pay people to sit at the table or to fly people in from across the province. We tried to get the banks to agree to negotiate with us as one entity, but most of them wanted separate negotiations for each branch. The Bank of Montreal did agree to bargain as a whole; we had great arguments with them.

It might have been possible to win that if we'd had the resources to keep up the campaign. But the local unions had given us as much money as they were going to. We took strike votes, thinking the only way we could get a collective agreement would be to have a strike in one bank and then organize a nationwide boycott. We held a conference to figure out how to run this huge campaign, but we decided to throw in the towel, stop organizing in the banks and give up our certification. It was the only thing we could do.

We got our confidence partly from the women's movement. We were intimidated, but we supported each other and kept reminding ourselves that organizing was our right. We did have lawyers for the Labour Relations Board hearings, but we believed that workers should be the ones negotiating, rather than trade union leaders. Collective agreements should be readable by workers, too—short and well indexed and written in plain language.

Why did feminists organize their own unions in British Columbia and not elsewhere? The main difference was the strength of the independent Canadian union movement here. The CCU in B.C. was ultra-democratic, though some were awful male chauvinists. Their constitution was awesome, with everyone working for the union being elected. This fit in with the feminist history in B.C., too.

Saskatchewan Working Women

IN CONVERSATION: PAT GALLAGHER,
SHEILA ROBERTS AND BARB BYERS

PAT GALLAGHER: Saskatchewan Working Women (SWW) came out of an interesting dichotomy in the labour movement. We wanted the ability to have a women's committee in the SFL, the Saskatchewan Federation of Labour, to raise significant issues. The SFL had no policy at that time on daycare or equal pay. It was really gross that there was such a lack of policy on women's issues. This would have been in 1978.

SHEILA ROBERTS: It really does go back to the Waffle discussion. The Waffle was formed in Saskatchewan in 1970. The "women's question" came up, and the women in the Waffle demanded a strategy. Men on the left were always dominating the debate, and the only way we were going to get past that was through parity. That was the big issue. There was a strong sense that trade union women did not have a voice in their unions. They weren't really organized as women. The larger women's movement was perceived as being white and middle class, and we saw that it was necessary for women to build something inside the labour movement. Through the SFL women's committee, we launched conferences in which all kinds of trade union women were involved, and they proposed that there be an organization of working women in the province. Then it just bloomed.

PAT: The majority of SWW members were trade union women, but we worked very hard in our original constitution for women who were not trade union members to be involved in it. That was one of the reasons we were constantly embattled with the federation, because they said only women who were in unions affiliated with the Canadian Labour Congress, the CLC, could belong. We got into a big pissing match about that.

SHEILA: Whether the women in SWW had to be union members was not a debate among women; it was a debate with the SFL's male hierarchy. The vast majority of the women involved wanted to include women who were unorganized. We put on campaigns around child care and around organizing unorganized women. We worked with SORWUC on some campaigns around bank workers, and the SFL didn't like that. We also did training projects with women so they could work inside their unions, get resolutions passed and get their voices heard. Women got confidence from each other. As a result, the future president of the SFL came up through SWW. The head of the Saskatchewan Government Employees Union came from SWW. The chairperson of the Labour Relations Board too. Nearly all of the women staff reps in unions came from SWW.

PAT: SWW gave women the basis to function as effective caucuses in their unions on key issues. There was the question of affirmative action. The daycare stuff was extremely key. There was a whole series of issues, and we gave women the background on them: tech change, part-time work, sexual harassment. A lot of the policy development on those issues was done in SWW meetings. Some of our meetings were fairly heated. Affirmative action went through various levels of debate. Then women would take the policies from SWW back to their unions and put them through their conventions as policy resolutions.

SHEILA: It was hard for women to be heard in the labour movement. It would be the standard hassle. You know, "Take a look at her short skirt" or "What are you doing, sit down, you don't have anything to say." It was difficult for women to cope with that. You're talking about an ordinary person, a working woman in an office job or a technical job. She goes to a convention, her first convention. She says, "Well, I want to talk about this," and someone in the union hierarchy says, "Oh, this is the way the convention runs and these are the rules of order and you can't do that." SWW helped women learn how to cope with that kind of harassment. And a lot of women started to run for election and take on union positions. There was no heavy-duty opposition, because the women were so well organized. Their background on the issues was so well done, and they generally won the debates.

BARB BYERS: SWW had a big impact on my life. First off, it was a place where people could debate and then walk out of the debate without feeling like they weren't going to continue to be supportive of each other. That taught me that you could do things differently than what I saw in the union movement. What I saw there was a lot of very divisive debate, with few solutions other than somebody getting to take a vote and somebody winning and somebody losing. In SWW we got into some pretty interesting debates about direction and strategy, but your position wasn't held against you, and we didn't tend to take votes in the same way. People tended to look for a solution to move things forward, and the solution couldn't always be the lowest common denominator.

ORGANIZED WORKING WOMEN

Barbara Cameron

The labour council in Toronto decided to hold a conference called "It's about Time" in 1975, during International Women's Year. I was a graduate student at the University of Toronto at that point, and a member of the graduate assistants' association. A lot of the debates in the women's liberation movement were about the role of the labour movement, and the people I most agreed with were the people in the Communist Party. I became a party member, and it was through that connection that I got to know the people from the labour council.

The motion that came out of the 1975 conference was to found an organization of labour women. An organizing committee got set up, and in '76 we had the founding convention for Organized Working Women. Strike support was a big part of OWW. And there was a coming together of the growing public sector movement and some left-wing people like Evelyn

Armstrong, who was with the United Electrical Workers. I've heard a tape of Evelyn getting up to speak at an Ontario Federation of Labour convention in the 1970s. The catcalls that faced a woman speaking at a labour convention then seem unbelievable today. All kinds of sexist comments were being yelled out, but Evelyn could really hold her own. She played a strong leadership role in helping train other women. She was pretty terrific. One of the things OWW did was bring the women's movement into support for the struggles of labour women.

OWW was an autonomous women's organization that prepared resolutions to go to Ontario Federation of Labour conventions. OWW members would also organize on the floors of conventions to push labour to take up women's demands. The leadership of the OFL started to realize that the people getting up in support of the resolutions on women were the male left, and they started to realize they'd better try to respond to the women, because they didn't want that kind of alliance going on. So it ended up being quite a creative dynamic.

For example, the OFL held a conference that helped found the Ontario Coalition for Better Child Care. This came out of a tension between some women close to the leadership of the OFL and Organized Working Women. It was quite a difficult political period, but in order to head off OWW, the OFL started to do things around women, so that was positive. OWW got a women's committee established in the OFL, and then organized to get women's positions on the executive. The labour movement was in a transition period, with the traditional leadership starting to recognize that now there was this whole public sector, and women were the next group that had to be organized. So it was a learning process on their part.

ONTARIO FEDERATION OF LABOUR WOMEN'S COMMITTEE

Deirdre Gallagher

When we talk about what women went through in their union work, we realize it wasn't easy. I had some difficult encounters with men and groups of men and felt very frightened. I was in Pittsburgh in 1978 working for the Steelworkers; I was one of very few women, and there were staff and elected people from all over the U.S. I was in a hotel bar talking to a black guy, and his friend looked at me and said, "Get up and go to your room and lock the door and stay there, because there's a whole thing happening here with these good old boys, and it's not safe. I want you to go, and I'll walk behind you to your room." I knew he was a good man so I did what he said. The whole night I was scared, because men were pounding on my door, and I couldn't leave my room. I was there for a week and faced a lot of difficult circumstances.

Another time I went out west to teach a course with a guy who was head of the Steelworkers in Canada, and the first thing he did was reach over and touch my breast. A guy heading up the Canadian labour movement, who I admired for his progressive ideas, and he tried to get me to go to bed with him. I was dumbfounded. I told very few people about it because of who he was.

I kept working in the labour movement, though, because, fuck them, it was my movement as well as theirs. I wish we'd stood up to them more. Women talked about it among themselves and found ways to protect each other. We could rarely get jobs on staff, and if we did, we were treated like shit. There were some men who were allies, but some of the stuff was awful, and you couldn't talk about it because you'd have to talk against the labour movement. It was the same on the left in general. Women just kept on going and fought it out and kept establishing our place. We were pretty brave, and we had each other. I established friendships I still have today. That's a wonderful thing.

The women in Organized Working Women included both union members and non-union members working on the left. One of the debates that happened was about moving into the labour movement. The Communist Party women didn't want to do that. We had a battle, and the organization separated over it. Some of us felt we needed an organized presence as women in the labour movement if we were going to make change. We didn't want to function like a lobby group on the outside. We decided to fight at the next Ontario Federation of Labour convention to set up a women's committee. So we left OWW, and OWW continued as an independent organization. It would have been better if the organization had stayed together, but that's not how it happened. It was the times.

The fight to set up the OFL women's committee was pretty heavy. We organized in all the different unions, Auto Workers, Steel and CUPE. Both Auto and Steel supported us, and so did Cliff Pilkey, who was the OFL president at the time. We put forward a motion, but it was blocked on the floor. So the issue had to be decided by the executive, which had only one woman, and she was anti-feminist. They had a huge showdown around it, but the motion finally passed by one vote, with Pilkey as the deciding vote.

Organizing on equal pay for work of equal value was very important. There were struggles around city hall workers and around nurses. There were specific campaigns on issues such as the right to work, getting women hired, allowing women to unionize, getting a voice for women in the labour movement. We were learning as we went along. We didn't have a vision, but one thing led to another. We invited women from outside the labour movement to speak on issues like daycare. There was lots of tension and struggle over what we were trying to do. We wanted to establish women's issues as an important part of the labour movement.

Frances Lankin

While I was working at the Don Jail in Toronto, I got involved in my union, the Ontario Public Service Employees Union (OPSEU). It was a way of finding a role and protection and becoming one of the guys. I became a steward, and from there I learned about the Region 5 women's caucus. At work I was one of the guys, so I didn't go to the women's caucus meeting, even though I wanted to. I felt I had to have a more solid footing at the jail first. But I connected with some of the women. By the time I was vice-president of my local at the Don, I had started to work on getting women settled in the workplace, and I had friendships with the guys I worked with. They knew who I was, and I was a respected leader in the union, so I had more latitude to let my thoughts develop. When I did start to attend women's caucus meetings and women's conferences and meet women at the Federation of Labour, I found both an avenue to do something about issues that mattered to me and women who had an analysis on these issues. This was a place where the dots in my life could be connected.

When I left the Don, I went to OPSEU as a women's equality issue worker, and I became a member of the OFL women's committee. All our energy went into encouraging women's involvement in their unions. The unions were male-dominated, and little wins like anti-harassment policies were what we focused on. We knew the leadership had to change too, but how did you change it from the bottom up? We needed to figure out how to do this without tokenism. We had to have allies, and the most significant one was Cliff Pilkey, who was OFL president from 1976 to 1986. He was amazing on a number of things, like the leadership he showed in supporting a woman's right to choose. He sat down and gave us a real school-of-hard-knocks lecture on how power worked and how, if we didn't approach it right, we would tokenize the women who came forward. It was a collective proposal, listening to Pilkey and talking back and forth to get it established.

It was a huge process, both organizing to get the concept of affirmative action in place, and then organizing to make sure that the women who got into those positions would bring a feminist perspective.

We didn't think we had it in the bag before the 1982 OFL convention, though we felt there was leadership support for it. Having Pilkey on side, and the leads in the key affiliates on side, and general OFL board support made us hopeful. A lot of work had been done in the various caucuses that met before the convention to try to prepare the way for the debate. But we still had to find the right symbolic leaders to be on our side; we knew that the leadership level had to be nailed down first. We had to know when the resolution was coming up and have people at the microphone and get the mechanics right.

The affirmative action resolution passed, and then we were going to the vote on electing. There were two women from Steel running. We had hopes that one of them would win, but there were some concerns about extra ballots around the Steel area and no real control. I remember being outraged that we had worked so hard and now were going to be sabotaged by the guys. I couldn't let that happen. I said, "We're going to monitor what's going on," and I walked into the middle of the Steel delegation and crossed my arms and watched what was going on. As an ex–jail guard, I could handle this. And the candidate we supported won.

Coalition of Black Trade Unionists

June Veecock

My first unionized job was in a hospital, where I looked after accounts. All the women there were junior or intermediate clerks, but only senior clerks got the raises. This was in the late 1970s. I was active in our union, CUPE, as part of the women's committee and on health and safety.

There were very few black women in the union at the time, and I wondered where the other women like me were. I was asked to organize a conference, even though the only thing I'd ever organized was a dinner party. It was out of that conference that the Coalition of Black Trade Unionists was conceived. I was organizing something that many people would have thought was divisive. Janis Sarra was the woman's director at the Ontario Federation of Labour at the time, and she would invite me to meetings. There was so much I wanted to learn, and eventually I got into the swing of things. I learned about organizing and used what I learned to organize women of colour and people of colour in general. I really valued that experience.

I started pushing around women of colour issues and made a lot of enemies. I ruffled a lot of feathers, because I was always reminding white women that we had to do things differently. You don't wait until the last minute to invite black women to speak; instead, you need to involve them throughout the struggle. I remember one women's conference with the Canadian Labour Congress where Nancy Riche was speaking.[3] I looked around the room, and of three hundred women, I saw about ten women of colour. I said I thought we should protest. I said we should all sit in the front, along with a woman who had a disability. We just sat quietly, all the women of colour in the front row. Later we made a speech at one of the plenaries. It was a silent protest, and it was effective.

Julie Davis, a strong feminist, was coming on as the executive vice-president of the OFL. Women were feeling great about that, but I had been asked to speak at the convention on anti-racism, and I talked about how only white women were making gains. I was very blunt. It was a dynamic speech, and people of colour were pleased that I had raised the issues of our realities. I was angry, so I wasn't scared. Carol Phillips and Sue Genge were always there to tell me I did well when I left the podium.[4] Some women weren't pleased, but too bad.

There were little incremental changes that we got through the Coalition of Black Trade Unionists. One of the most effective methods of organizing was the report card on the hiring practices of unions. We would look at hospitals and see that not one woman of colour had been hired. But after the report cards started being used, there was a significant improvement. Now there is visible minority affirmative action. Steel appointed a woman of colour to represent them on the OFL executive board, in the women's affirmative action seat, and that really pleased me. We wanted two seats on the CLC for visible minorities. We wore buttons and were organizing. They offered us two seats, one for a man and one for a woman. But we wanted to decide who should sit. If we got boxed into having one seat for a man and one for a woman, we would have no claim to some of the women's

---

3. Nancy Riche was executive vice-president and secretary-treasurer of the CLC from 1986 to 2002 and a powerful fighter for women.
4. Carol Phillips is a senior staff person with the Canadian Auto Workers and Sue Genge is women's director of the CLC. At the time, they were both members of the OFL women's committee.

affirmative action seats. I felt that wasn't a good thing. It caused a lot of confusion, and people didn't understand it. That was a struggle that made enemies for me, but sometimes I long for those days, because I don't see the same determination now.

Canadian Union of Public Employees

Judy Darcy

The role of women in the Canadian labour movement is recognized all over the world. The union women organizing around affirmative action and choice were women who saw themselves as feminists. They saw themselves as active in the women's movement.

It was the alliance with the women's movement that showed the first organizational commitment of the labour movement to social unionism. We were able to build recognition in the labour movement that the women's movement was a major ally. During the Eaton's strike, there was a rallying cry around women's issues. The Fleck strike, too, was an important landmark, where people in the labour movement came to understand that there was another movement out there that could be an ally.[5] It gave us a whole other perspective on the issues we were fighting for.

I served as president of the Canadian Union of Public Employees, CUPE, from 1991 to 2003. On a personal level, it's scary, exciting, lonely, empowering and discouraging to be the head of a major union. The reality that men are still incredibly sexist is very discouraging. I think things are slipping backward now, and that's ironic. It feels like contradictory trends, because there are more women in powerful positions now. When I stepped down there were five women presidents of major unions, so things are changing on one level. Some barriers have come down. But it's like you have two worlds colliding. There are still incredibly deep-seated attitudes, and male leaders seem oblivious to their own behaviour. In the same meeting you can be dealing with radical stuff on equality issues and women will feel like they're being dismissed and marginalized when they speak. We challenge the men, but it's only recently that we have a critical mass of women who can challenge collectively. A lot of stuff happens in a private,

---

5. The Eaton's strike and the Fleck strike were both first-contract struggles with a high proportion of women workers. Feminists did strike support such as walking the picket line.

personal way. Ways of being treated that diminish you and make you feel small. If you're a woman union leader, you're supposed to be powerful, and harassment and sexism are not supposed to happen to you. The first time I was a victim of harassment, I blocked it out. It was after I became president, and a member asked me for an autographed bra. I was completely humiliated, and I didn't know what to say. Harassment is a joy stealer. Sexist treatment is insidious, because if you stand up for yourself, it's seen as a sign of weakness. If you want to run with the tough guys, you have to be tough. It will be denied if you claim you're being treated differently. But you also feel like it's a sign of weakness if you *don't* get in and fight with them.

It's harder to fight for yourself. It takes a lot of guts to do it. You have to feel strong enough and confident enough to argue hard for your position. But now there's a mass of women in leadership who can challenge sexism together.

EIGHT

COMING OUT
Lesbians Organize

*Difference must be not merely tolerated, but seen as a fund
of necessary polarities between which our creativity can spark.*

—AUDRE LORDE, *SISTER OUTSIDER*

HOMOSEXUALITY WAS ILLEGAL in Canada until Prime Minister Pierre Trudeau's 1969 assertion that "the state has no place in the bedrooms of the nation." Lesbians were forced to remain in the closet, hiding their sexual orientation from their families, their employers and their communities. In big cities, there were often clubs where women could meet each other, but outside of that small world, lesbians were vilified. The emergence of the women's movement should have meant liberation for lesbians, but society's prejudice against them permeated the women's movement as well. The emergence of the gay liberation movement with the Stonewall riots in New York in 1969 began to change all this. In a 1982 essay entitled "Mothers, Sisters, Lovers, Listen," lesbian feminist Amy Gottlieb wrote:

The herstory of lesbians' struggle for self- and collective identity and against the barren and degrading experience of the closet is a long one. We are only beginning to uncover who we are—reclaiming a lost heritage of witches, women who lived together in friendship networks, spinsters—all women who have resisted the male right to possession of women.

Anti-feminist baiters often accused feminists of being a bunch of lesbians, and many women's groups responded with denial, pressuring the lesbians in their ranks to remain silent. The demand by lesbians to be recognized by their heterosexual sisters set the stage for a feminism that would be inclusive of all women. Politically active lesbians remained a core group within the women's movement, and many also continued to work for gay and lesbian liberation, sometimes alongside gay men and sometimes in the new lesbian organizations they created.

Ellen Woodsworth

I was aware of feeling attracted to women from the time I was quite young. I felt, I think, too ashamed of it and didn't know what to do with my feelings, even though my mother had lesbian friends, my father had gay friends. I was aware of homosexuality, but I was very afraid of my feelings, my passions. I stuffed them away and used them for the movement, I guess.

And then in 1969 I met a woman at a national YWCA retreat and got involved with her. It was a very exciting time; many, many things were happening. We felt that we were changing things. Men and women were on the move together. First Nations rights were getting stronger. And I realized that I needed to come out, so I did. I met some other women in Vancouver, where I was living, and we formed a house that we called New Morning. We formed a lesbian feminist collective in that house: Margo Dunn, D.J. O'Donnell, Sharon Ladd and I. We would go down to the clubs and talk to the women there about feminism. And we would go to the women's movement and talk to the women's movement about lesbianism.

In the fall of 1970, I went to Washington, D.C., for the Black Panthers' Revolutionary Constitutional Convention. We travelled in a bus full of women from all across the U.S., and I met some women who were talking about a conference with Indo-Chinese women that was going to be held in Vancouver the following year. When I got home, I decided to work on this conference, but at the same time I was talking about lesbian issues, and everyone was saying no, no, no, no, you can't talk about that at this conference, the Indo-Chinese women from Vietnam, Cambodia and Laos won't know what you're talking about. Lesbianism doesn't happen there.

Some lesbian feminists from Edmonton and Portland came to the conference, and a group of us kept pressuring and demanding that the conference include a fish bowl—an organizational tool where you sit in a circle and talk about your lives. So we had this fish bowl where we talked about being lesbian feminists at the conference. Some feminists there, the women's liberationists, were very angry at us for doing this. They said lesbianism was an American cultural import and that it was an imperialist act on our part to even be raising it. But we said no, we're women's liberationists, all of us have fought for the independence of Vietnam, we've fought in the student movements, fought against capitalism; we have a right to talk about what it means to be lesbian feminists.

It was very empowering for us, because we had found each other and we didn't feel so isolated. We understood the connectivity of the different liberation movements. It was a breakthrough that they had not been able to stop us, that they had been able to listen to us, even though the women from Vietnam and Cambodia said that lesbianism did not exist in their countries. That was the way they perceived it, though they were very courteous. So it was a big breakthrough. Our house, New Morning, became an incredible base from which we talked to women, and other women slowly started to come out.

I was doing some work for the *Georgia Straight,* Vancouver's weekly cultural paper, and I remember writing little feminist lines or quotes in the columns of the newspaper; that was as much content as I could get in. I tried to get some lesbian articles into the *Pedestal,* the women's liberation newspaper in Vancouver and the only one in Canada at the time, but they wouldn't print them. It was pretty terrible. While I was in Toronto for my brother's wedding in 1972, I met someone who worked for *Guerilla,* a biweekly newspaper there. She knew how to start a newspaper, technically how to do it, and I knew what I wanted to say—I knew I wanted an international newspaper that talked about liberation issues, and I wanted to be sure that it had lesbian content. So I moved to Toronto and Holly Devor and I started *The Other Woman.*

Those early years were difficult. It was as if you were afraid all the time of your feelings, of your desires. You were afraid that if you came out, you would give something that was really wonderful—the women's liberation movement—a bad name. You felt you were going to be shut down, and people would be afraid of you, afraid of touching you, afraid of you touching them.

There weren't other lesbians in the women's movement at that time. There were lesbians in the bars—at the Vanport, Champagne Charlie's, the Dufferin, at a number of different bars in Vancouver and in Toronto—but not in the women's movement. Things started to move fairly quickly at a certain point, but before that, the biggest way to keep the women's movement quiet was to call women lesbians. It was a way to shut women up and to discredit the women's movement. To some degree, I think that's still true; I think our oppression is still so strong that women can be shut up by being called lesbians.

We started *The Other Woman* and drew some more women into it. Then we approached the women at the Dupont Street Women's Centre and asked them if we could start a lesbian drop-in. We encountered fierce opposition, really fierce opposition, but finally they gave us the basement. From there we organized the first gay women's conference in Canada. We had a big argument over whether it should be called a gay women's conference or a lesbian conference. We held that at 21 McGill Street, which was a YWCA in 1973 and later became an expensive women's club.

Once we had started the newspaper, we had a vehicle that we could use to talk to people across Canada and throughout the U.S. Then a woman named Judith Quinlan and I started Cora, the women's liberation bookmobile.[1] We travelled all over Ontario and into Quebec selling feminist books and kids' books. That was another vehicle for reaching out and talking to people about things.

As a lesbian feminist, I was so angry at the world. I can't remember who said it first, but I really like the expression "Lesbianism is the rage of women condensed to the point of explosion." I think everything came together for me at that moment of realizing how unjust the world is for women. I didn't want anything to do with men, I didn't want anything to do with male left politics; they really didn't get it. We had to go forge a woman's world, women's organizations, women's campaigns. People were threatened by that; I can see that now. I was working very hard in a specific way for an independent women's movement, a really independent women's movement. As a lesbian, I could just say, that's it, I don't want anymore of this. So it was very new, and for some people it was like overturning a rock, revealing something that had always been considered slimy and dirty and illegal and disgraceful at so many levels. There were radical women in the women's liberation movements who understood our commonality, because they understood our analysis of capitalism, our understanding of race. We came out of the social movements; we came out of the left. In *The Other Woman*, we would talk about what was happening in Quebec, what was

---

1. Cora: The Feminist Bookmobile was named after suffragist E. Cora Hind. The bookmobile was established in 1973 and disbanded in 1975.

happening in Vietnam, about the anti-racist movements. So these radical women were allies in that way, but they still fought with us, still had fears of us at an intimate or a personal level. If we hadn't been feminists, if we hadn't had an analytical way of seeing our oppression, it would have been much worse. Now that I've lived in the world much longer, I've met so many lesbians, in so many circles, who went into therapy or were committed; the repulsion people had toward lesbians was so strong that many women broke.

In the 1970s you were either gay or straight. There was almost no talk of bisexuality. There was no talk of transgendered communities, almost no talk about transvestites. It was polarized. When people tried to talk about bisexual rights, we put them down as trying to have the best of both worlds. We also struggled as lesbian feminists with lesbians who considered themselves gay and were offended by us because we were so political. They just wanted to live their lives. They had created a possible but painful existence, using the bars. And here we were saying that on a queer day, you could see forever. We were wanting to throw the world open. We were young and brash, and we had no idea, emotionally, of how hard those lesbians' lives had been and what they had gone through in the 1950s. As we started to learn more, we realized that they had gone through hell. We learned that in the concentration camps, lesbians wore black triangles. All kinds of things that were hidden, we started to find out about.

Deb Parent

I came out when I was twelve and in grade eight. I went to a Catholic school, and when the priest mentioned the word homosexual, I realized who I was. I felt like I belonged for the first time in my life, and I was elated. I went to the guidance counsellor and yelled, "Guess what, I'm a homosexual." I was sent to a psychiatrist. I remember later seeing a video called *Still Sane,* about an art installation around a woman being incarcerated for being a dyke.[2] That could have been my story, but because of my age, I wasn't taken really seriously. I came out again when I was nineteen and found a bigger political community of lesbians. That confirmed my pride in being gay.

---

2. *Still Sane* was first an art show, then a book published by Press Gang in 1985. In it, visual artist Persimmon Blackbridge and writer Sheila Gilhooly tell Gilhooly's story of being committed to a psychiatric institution in Ontario in the 1970s for being a lesbian.

I was living in Ottawa at the time of the first national lesbian conference, in 1976. The idea of organizing as lesbians was new, and meeting hundreds of women from across the country was a powerful experience. When I got back from the conference, I became active in Lesbians of Ottawa. I did media because I was willing to speak publicly.

There were about three hundred women at the second national conference, held in Toronto in 1979. It was clear that lesbians were hungry to develop a political identity of our own. Lesbians were active in women's services and in gay and lesbian organizations, and we realized we had to do something for ourselves. There was talk of lesbians pulling out of the feminist movement. The issue was, how do we attend to and articulate the issues that are relevant to us? We had a commonality of oppression with gay men, but there were issues that affected us as women that gay men didn't share. Some lesbians felt we were diluting our energy if we worked with either gay men or heterosexual women. But for lesbians in small communities, there wasn't a choice.

As a working-class woman, I understood internalized and externalized oppression. When I came out as a lesbian, the family and community that I grew up in ended up on the other side of a chasm. I was split in a number of ways. I felt who I was as a lesbian and who I was as a working-class woman couldn't be integrated. It takes time to learn who your people are and what your history is. In smaller communities, it's even harder to find people like you. At the lesbian conferences, we felt the energy could live, but back in the communities, it was fragmented. Women had to work with gay men and heterosexual women.

After the first conference, women went back into their communities and realized what a huge struggle it was to organize as lesbians without resources. So the second conference had a different vision, a different focus. Was there a way to work with gay men and heterosexual women and still bring lesbian issues to the fore?

NINE

INDIAN RIGHTS FOR INDIAN WOMEN

Changing the Indian Act

*I never betrayed my nation, even though others said that I did.
I feel that my nation betrayed me. As Aboriginal people we should
be entitled to all the rights of Canadians but also to special rights
as Aboriginals. I insist that my nation treat people with equality.*

—GAIL STACEY-MOORE

I N 1971 MARY TWO-AXE EARLY, a Mohawk woman from Kahnawake, founded a group called Indian Rights for Indian Women to fight discrimination in Canada's Indian Act. That same year, the Supreme Court of Canada had narrowly ruled in the Jeannette Lavell case that section 121B of the Indian Act did not discriminate against women, despite that Indian women who married non-status men lost their Indian status, while Indian men conferred their status on non-status wives. The National Action Committee on the Status of Women organized a day of mourning to protest the decision. Aboriginal women received another setback when the Canadian Human Rights Act replaced the Bill of Rights in 1978 and the Indian Act was excluded from coverage.

It was not only the courts and the government that opposed their demands: Aboriginal women faced strong opposition from many Aboriginal men in their fight to change the Indian Act. The National Indian

Brotherhood argued that any tampering with the Indian Act ran the risk of encouraging the federal government to do away altogether with special Indian status. Some Indian leaders labelled the organizers "white-washed women's libbers."[1] But Indian women courageously continued their campaign, which would last almost twenty years. They used every tactic they could think of to gain support. The United Nations Human Rights Committee agreed in 1978 to hear the case of Sandra Lovelace, an Aboriginal woman from the Tobique Reserve in New Brunswick who charged that the Indian Act was discriminatory. In 1979 native women walked from Oka, near Montreal, to Parliament Hill to demand amendments to the act. Prime Minister Joe Clark promised the changes they sought, but his government was soon defeated. In 1981 the U.N. committee found Canada in breach of the Covenant on Civil and Political Rights. Indian women were finally victorious when the Canadian Charter of Rights and Freedoms was proclaimed in 1985. Mary Two-Axe Early was the first woman to regain her status.

QUEBEC NATIVE WOMEN'S ASSOCIATION

Gail Stacey-Moore

I'm Mohawk from Kahnawake. When I got married to a white man and was living on the reserve in a house we rented from a relative, I got a call from Mary Two-Axe Early. She asked me if I realized what I had done, and she started talking to me about the problems I'd be running into. Section 121B of the Indian Act said if I married a white man I would lose all my special rights. My children wouldn't be able to go to the reserve schools. My brother, who married a white woman, didn't lose his rights, and his wife received Indian rights. I didn't believe I would have the problems Mary told me about because my family was accepting of my husband. But when my daughter was three years old, I realized I would have to leave the reserve, because I didn't want her to be bussed off the reserve to school. By that time I'd also realized that there was a community pool where my children and I weren't allowed to swim because I had married a white person.

I decided to go to a meeting that Mary had called. There I heard a lot of stories about women who had been evicted. I saw pictures of a woman being taken out of her house and put on the back of a pickup truck and taken off

---

1. *Enough Is Enough: Aboriginal Women Speak Out,* as told to Janet Silman (Women's Press, 1987).

the reserve into town. The people on the reserve did this. Because we have been subjected to so much from the non-Aboriginal population, there is a lot of anger and hatred against people who have married outside. Many people have had to seek psychological help because of the stresses and obstacles put in their way. After that meeting, I became shocked by the way women were being forced to live. They were being denied water and electricity. We inherit land from our families, so if we want to build a house on the reserve, we can. But women who had married outside couldn't get the services.

I started having meetings at my home on the reserve. I had to call the meetings for after dark, because there was a bylaw that any gathering bigger than three people could be stopped by the council or the peacekeepers. Many women would only come after dark. We'd discuss issues and get a plan of action.

We travelled to Ottawa to meet with ministers and presented briefs. People in Ottawa were tolerant, but they didn't take us seriously. It was a new issue. That's when I started to think that I should know some more about the law. Some ministers were informed and others knew nothing. So I felt I would have to teach them to understand what was wrong.

I started by reading the Indian Act. It was not easily understandable, but I persisted. I started moving out to other organizations and joined the Quebec wing of the Native Council of Canada, because I wanted a more powerful lobby.[2] I became part of the executive and sat on the national board. I saw that the women's issues were put on the side. These were non-status Indians. They were trying to get recognition, but not from the women's point of view. We couldn't get anywhere with the status group.[3] That's when I started working on constitutional issues. I wrote a paper on the constitution for the Quebec organization of the Native Council of Canada. Later, during the repatriation debate in the early 1980s, I wrote their position on the constitution.[4] I received a lot of pressure to become a lawyer. I didn't want to do that, because I felt the law would keep me from being free to do what I had to do.

---

2. The Native Council of Canada was formed in 1971 to represent non-status Aboriginal people who mostly lived off reserve. The organization changed its name to the Congress of Aboriginal Peoples in 1994.
3. At that time, the National Indian Brotherhood. The group is now called the Assembly of First Nations.
4. Prime Minister Trudeau had proposed a series of amendments to the constitution, including a charter of rights and freedoms.

Soon after that, I became involved with the Quebec Native Women's Association. The organization had come to a standstill, but I got together with women and decided to help. I got a grant to hold an assembly and became vice-president. I travelled all around the province and explained to native women what the act was doing to them. I talked to them about constitutional issues as well, because they weren't getting the information. I knew we had to take a stand, and we had to have strong women's support behind us. I didn't want to make decisions for people who didn't know what was going on. I wanted to represent actual people who knew what I was doing. Sometimes I would be in communities where I'd speak English, someone spoke French and another spoke Montagnais. There are nine Aboriginal nations in Quebec, and I went all over. Sometimes I'd have to spend weeks somewhere because the weather stranded me.

I had contact with women's groups across the country, which had started when I was with Mary's group. Nellie Carlson was sitting at her kitchen window when someone drove by and shot a bullet at her. This happened in Alberta, where there was a great deal of resistance toward native women gaining rights among native men. These kinds of stories gave me the determination to work to change these injustices. Meeting women who had gone through so many horrific things gave me an unshakeable sense of commitment. I would go to Ottawa and lobby. The standing committee on the constitution was meeting and working things out clause by clause. We'd lobby wherever we could catch the ministers. Sometimes women would come in from across the country and have no place to stay. We slept on the floor of one room if we had to. Once, we were flown to Toronto on a chartered plane. You had to be ready to move and accept any kind of living conditions in order to get your work done.

Sometimes we drove out to Ottawa with Madeleine Parent. She would come with me because native women were afraid. Madeleine was from NAC, and Mary was looking for their support. By watching Madeleine, I learned what lobbying was and knew I could do it. NAC was incredibly supportive to Mary and her group. Their presence was already established, and we could take advantage of that. We were invited to every NAC meeting. I felt it was a solidarity thing rather than being part of the organization. Because we were raised in a different culture, there were too many differences. There are women's issues and cultural issues. You can only touch the surface. We've grown up with too much violence and so many differences. Even people who I thought were advanced in their thinking unintentionally said hurtful things. All of this doesn't mean you can't work together and treat each other with respect.

I did all my work voluntarily. Only my expenses were paid. My husband was employed all his life, and if it weren't for him, I wouldn't have been able to do it. He looked after the children, too. I often felt guilty for leaving the family, but I never doubted the work I had chosen to do. I was determined in a steely way. There were times when Aboriginal women in Quebec were afraid for their lives. There was such intensity in the lobby against us. Sometimes I'd walk into a room and all the native men would glare at me. I'd go because I knew we had to have a presence there. Once I walked in and across from me were about forty Aboriginal men from Alberta. They had a battery of high-paid lawyers, and they didn't want the women who had married out getting their rights back. They said they could be outvoted if the women got their rights back. They were all staring at me. I stopped and thought about it and thought, If I'm going to die, I'm going to make the biggest commotion possible. I was frightened, but I went right to the front. I wouldn't let fear stop me. I'd think about the elderly women back on the reserve, raising their children in poverty and not having the rights of a normal human being. I'd say to myself, who else is going to speak for them?

I asked for a session with the lawyers who were working with the Quebec Native Women. We discussed the issues and came up with the idea of the double majority vote, meaning that if there was an issue of land, there would have to be a majority vote from both the old members and the new members. This was rejected by the Native Council because it was put forward by a women's group, even though it was a reasonable solution. Then, in 1982, the constitution was repatriated. Because there was legislation that had to be cleaned up, the government asked for a three-year moratorium on section 121B. The Indian Act was one of the acts that had to be changed to accommodate the Charter. By 1985 the legislation was cleaned up, and we had won.

We went to Tobique to celebrate our 1985 victory. There was a reception at the reserve community hall, and we were their special guests because we had worked together for so long. It was nice to have a celebration. We didn't have one in Kahnawake, because it was more of a contentious issue there. The biggest resistance is still from Kahnawake. There is still a wall in my community against Aboriginal women marrying out. You can volunteer or donate your money to the community, but you're never a full member.

I still live outside the community. I don't want my husband exposed to the radical elements on the reserve. Today my daughter is living on land that I inherited from my grandmother and the band council continues to deny her services.

The Indian Act abolished the traditional matriarchal society for a patriarchal one. Our men turned to the Indian Act to get back into a position of strength, and they still use it today.

NATIVE WOMEN'S WALK

Caroline Ennis

In 1977 I was going to school in Fredericton. I had a best friend who was living on our reserve in Tobique, whose husband told her to leave the house. The way things were set out, the man owned the house, and he could kick the woman and her children out. Glenna Perley went to the provincial court, and they offered her a dollar a year for her and her children. She couldn't get the government to provide any support or get her husband to support her. It started happening to other women, and then one day a group of women marched into the band office and told the chief he had to do something. He put them down, and they said, "Okay, we're going to stay right here." My friend Glenna was one of them and her aunt was another.

The women occupied the band office. The chief sent the staff home, and the occupation went on for two or three months. The chief called Hydro and had the power shut off, and the women were in there with their children. Glenna's uncle brought in a stove made out of an old iron drum and some wood, and that's how they heated the place. Glenna called me and told me what was happening, and I got in touch with some women's groups in Fredericton.

I had been on a board with the singer Anne Murray to organize the first transition house in Fredericton. I called her as well, and we collected blankets and canned foods and sleeping bags to help them in the occupation. My husband and I were both in university, but we'd go up on weekends. The kids in the occupation had a difficult time, because they were harassed by other children, and Glenna had death threats and threats of having her home burned down. One night we were in the band office and people were partying next door. All we could hear was Glenna's name being sworn at and talk about killing the women or burning them out. After the next election, the women were blamed for the defeat of the chief, and someone did try to burn the place down.

My husband was on the New Brunswick Human Rights Commission as a student. He started talking with the head of the commission, and the idea of going to the United Nations came up. When Aboriginal women were turned down by the Supreme Court in 1973 in the Jeannette Lavell case, we had exhausted all domestic remedies, so the United Nations accepted the complaint. Sandra Lovelace, a woman from Tobique who had married off reserve, agreed to be the complainant. It was dangerous at that point.

Our complaint initially had nothing to do with loss of status but, rather, the lack of housing on the reserve. Prior to the Sandra Lovelace complaint, all women who were alone on the reserve were discriminated against. My mother wasn't allowed on the housing list. Single mothers weren't allowed on the housing list. You had to be married or living with a man. I was also amazed that if you married a white man you lost status, but if a white woman married an Aboriginal she gained status. The men felt it was their tradition to discriminate against women. Many times we would be out in a public place and Indian men would come up to us and argue about what we were doing. It was very threatening. They felt that I was trying to take the white women's status away. I would have if I could have. It was the injustice that motivated me. I don't think it's right to discriminate against anyone. Because it was so blatant, so open and accepted, it drove me crazy. It had happened to my mother and now it was happening to my friends. Everyone accepted it because the government had decided this was how it would happen.

I think what the government did was genocide. If you married outside and had children, you wouldn't be able to teach them what we value. If that happens for long enough, there will be no Indian culture. The government encouraged interracial marriage. Higher education would cost us our status, as would service in the military. If you voted in elections you would lose your status as well. It's racism, because they wanted us to assimilate and disappear.

The newspapers covered the occupation of the band office. We were attacked by crowds that threw rocks at the windows. I called the RCMP, but they were afraid to come. The next day, I called RCMP headquarters in Ottawa and told them, "If somebody gets killed here, I'm pointing the finger at the RCMP for not showing up." The next time I called, they pulled cops from all over the province to show up. The occupation ended for a short while, but Indian Affairs gave the new chief such a hard time that he resigned. The reserve was split down the middle. The women living there took the brunt of the tension. We had to walk around in groups because there were serious threats.

With the situation even worse on the reserve, Glenna came up with the idea for the Native Women's Walk to Ottawa. She got the idea from the Longest Walk, which was organized in 1978 by the American Indian Movement and went from California to Washington, D.C. I didn't realize the kind of work it would take to organize and run the march. But I was angry and stubborn enough to stick to it. The march was in 1979.

I was really poor, and I had no money to pay for anything, so I talked Noel Kinsella, the chairperson of the New Brunswick Human Rights Commission, into letting me use their offices. I felt I had come on earth to carry this out. Nobody else but me could have done it; I had the skills and the determination to do it. I don't look up to anyone because of who they are, because we're all human beings, exactly the same. I don't defer to anyone. I phoned women's groups in Canada and the U.S., all the churches and everybody. Eventually the United Church paid for three of us to go to Toronto for three weeks and use their resources to work on this project. The Catholic Church wouldn't do a thing. Gail Stacey-Moore was involved with the Quebec Native Women, and she and Mary Two-Axe Early would help us. They funded our hotel rooms.

In the five days it took us to march from Oka to Ottawa, the numbers changed each day. There were always a lot of people walking. I wanted only women and children walking, because I didn't want the RCMP to beat up on the men. I told the RCMP what I would tolerate from them and told them we wanted only women cops walking with us. I called the media because they offered us protection. We got a lot of media for the march. We fed people with money from the church, and one of the reporters from a Toronto paper found a way to get a plea for donations into the paper. Indian Affairs paid for the bus we used. They gave us $7000.

I was totally exhausted by the time we got to Ottawa. I remember getting to Parliament Hill and looking at all these women crying and wondering why I felt absolutely no emotion. I knew what I had to do, and I went up to Flora MacDonald's office. She was the minister of Indian affairs. I could see myself doing the things I did as if I was outside myself. I wondered if I was having a nervous breakdown.

Joe Clark promised he would make the changes we demanded to the Indian Act, but his government fell right after the march. So we had to wait several years until the Charter of Rights became the issue for the act to be changed. The U.N. complaint was settled during Trudeau's regime. Flora MacDonald remained an ally throughout the entire struggle. I spent some time on the NAC executive during those years, because I understood we needed mainstream support to change the Indian Act. Some of the native women opposed mainstream groups, but I convinced them it was necessary.

The women in Tobique had the courage to fight because they had nowhere else to go. To this day I'll speak up when I see injustice.

TEN

TAKING IT
TO THE STREETS
International Women's Day

For the people hear us singing
Bread and roses, bread and roses

—"BREAD AND ROSES," FEMINIST ANTHEM
BY JAMES OPPENHEIM

B Y 1977, FEMINISTS WERE EVERYWHERE: on campus, in the unions, in the professions. Services like rape crisis centres, women's centres and daycare centres had begun to spread beyond the big cities. A movement against violence against women was beginning to cohere. But much of this was invisible to the general public. The media, for the first of many times, was proclaiming that women's liberation was dead. And ideological differences within the movement became ever more present as socialist feminists, liberal feminists and radical feminists staked their claims to the various issues. In this milieu, a group of women in Toronto decided to organize the first International Women's Day celebration in English Canada.

International Women's Day had been celebrated across Europe and in Communist countries since the early twentieth century. The date of March 8 was fixed in 1977 by the United Nations. Its origins lay in the struggle of working-class women for bread and roses, a living wage and a better life. There are many myths about the specifics, including that it commemorates the Triangle Shirtwaist Factory fire in New York City on March 25, 1911, in which 140 immigrant women lost their lives because the bosses had locked them in, and the strike of Russian women for peace and bread at the end of February 1917, which kicked off the Russian Revolution. Quebec women had begun to organize their own IWD celebrations in 1973.

The organizing for International Women's Day in Toronto pulled together a cross-section of feminists active in women's groups and in various progressive organizations. As a grassroots coalition open to everyone, it embodied, sometimes quite painfully, the diverse voices in the women's movement and the changes these women were demanding. Depending on the time of year, organizing meetings were held monthly or weekly, with as many as a hundred women sitting in a circle discussing the issues.

IWD organizing continued in Toronto after that first year, and each annual demonstration was linked to a key issue. The event was quickly taken up right across the country, becoming a gathering point for feminist activists and their allies.

INTERNATIONAL WOMEN'S DAY COALITION

Carolyn Egan

In the fall of 1977, I was approached by Varda Burstyn, who was a member of the RMG, the Revolutionary Marxist Group. She was pulling together a meeting of women from a range of organizations to talk about the perception in the newspapers that the women's movement was dead. We were concerned because, since 1975, the International Women's Year, there had been no broad manifestation of the women's movement. During that meeting, we agreed to plan an action for March 8, 1978.

As the planning began, a very real political difference began to emerge. There were women who defined themselves as radical feminists and those of us who defined ourselves as socialist feminists, and no doubt many in between. To my mind, the question was about how to organize, how to be inclusive and build a broad mass movement, but it became focused on whether or not men should be allowed to participate in the march.

The debate became quite sharp, to the point that we had to organize some decision-making meetings. On our side, the argument was that we wanted the march to be broad and have trade unionists come out and women from the immigrant communities, and a lot of them worked side by side with men. There were two or three meetings debating this, with about eighty women at each meeting. When the final vote came, our position won three to one. Some of the women who took the other position felt they could no longer work with us. We were saddened by their withdrawal, but we decided we had to go on.

It was a big gamble, because we didn't know if we would be able to have an impact on the broader community. We had booked Convocation Hall at the University of Toronto. We had called it for 11 A.M., and at five minutes to eleven the hall was empty except for the organizers. My heart was sinking. And then someone who was outside came running in and said, "They're coming, they're coming," and within fifteen minutes the hall had filled right up. It was mainly women who came, but there were some men as well. It was a dramatic moment. The women's movement had really not been in the streets up until then. There was a march in '75 for the International Year of Women, but otherwise nothing. For the organizers in 1978, the turnout was a confirmation that the politic we were arguing really had impact. The march we went on through the streets of Toronto was a powerful thing, and it was picked up in the press.

The night before the march, the women who had left the group held a women-only event. It was maybe two hundred women and a small march. But the difference was dramatic. That night you had the women who functioned within the structure of the women's movement, but the next day you had a broad cross-section of women who believed they were struggling for women's equality.

Susan G. Cole

Lesbians were trying to get recognized inside feminism. Lesbianism was considered a liability. We were at the IWD meetings and sniffing these things out. We were coming at it from the point of view that this was a woman's event. All women should be welcome, and guys should stand to the side. The Trotskyist strategy was not to limit it in any way.[1] The lesbian point of view went against that. In those days we were loud, and we knew that we weren't dealing with popular opinions. But I still feel that a women-only expression was a reasonable thing to bring up. A woman's

---

1. The Trotskyists referred to here are the Revolutionary Marxist Group (RMG) and the League for Socialist Action. The RMG emerged from the breakup of the New Left and was led by a breakaway group in the left wing of the Waffle. It formed in 1973 and disbanded in 1977. The League for Socialist Action was an older group that had been active in the abortion movement.

dance was okay; the other side thought that was a compromise. But we wanted the demo for women only. It wasn't about having sex, it was a movement for social change, and we felt trivialized. We felt that there would be nothing more powerful for women to see than a large group of angry women asserting themselves. Politically speaking, we felt that even though the numbers might be smaller, the impact would be stronger. We were trying to articulate a different aesthetic.

This was the first time lesbians were demanding to be heard. Some of us were also members of WAVAW, Women against Violence against Women, and we were fighting for violence against women to be heard in the women's movement as well. Socialist feminists had been political longer, and their politics came from a different place. The movement against violence against women came from women who had had that experience. That dynamic is particularly Canadian. In the U.S., violence against women was part of the women's movement from the beginning. In Canada, the most sophisticated political people were socialist, which was different. The radical feminist view was that everything springs from gender difference. That was the politics I was working on.

These were hard things to talk about, and it was easy to dismiss us because of the lesbian issue. The Trots had a single-issue approach. They weren't interested in multiple issues. They saw lesbianism as bad for feminist organizing, especially at that time. Lesbian organizers were closeted because they were afraid of repercussions. People wanted a political movement that would draw people in, and homophobic straight women were afraid that the lesbians would turn people off. In some ways, we were the backbone of the movement, and yet we were invisible.

IWD was fundamentally democratic, meeting every month all through the year. It was a place to find out what was going on. I wanted to be part of it. The debate was intense, and then there was a vote. I remember the WAVAW women standing at the back of the room with our arms crossed. We walked out of the meeting when we lost. This was a time of confrontation politics, and we wanted to do something different.

We organized our own fair that year and got a permit and marched through the streets. It had a different feel. It was more of a celebration, but it was still political. Later we decided we would go back to working on the big demonstration, but it took a while. And then things started to heat up around the sex and pornography stuff. IWD was the first stage in the rumbling. I think the pornography debates took it further.

Varda Burstyn

The way it started in Toronto was that I had been a member of the Revolutionary Marxist Group for six years. We were a small group, and we were discussing joining another small group, and I was very concerned that their orientation to the women's movement would be destructive. Around us, tremendous things were happening. The women's liberation movement had started in the late 1960s, but in the late seventies, there was a huge crisis of political direction. A vital current of radical feminists associated with *Broadside* was launching their organization—WAVAW—and did important work. But they believed everything bad flowed from men, and this didn't represent the views of many other feminists. Increasingly, there were more liberal feminists too who believed women should get more of the pie, not rebake it. And then there were the women, also growing in numbers, in the NDP, the independent left and in the trade unions who had had extensive and lively discussions and had organized on women's issues for a long time as well. But this current didn't have structures to pull it together or any way to place itself in the political landscape. This concerned me deeply because neither the radical nor liberal feminists could provide the leadership that was necessary to growing a really representative women's movement. It seemed to me that a big public meeting and a vibrant demonstration in the streets of the city would allow the whole movement to see itself and make space for socialist feminists as a visible, coherent force in the world. It would also ensure that my little organization did decent work with the women's movement.

I contacted Caroyn Egan, and we identified ten women who we felt were particularly important in the movement, including several WAVAW women, and we called a meeting to launch the project. We organized from the very first meeting for every woman there to identify other individuals and organizations to bring to the next meeting. We chose people on the basis of their track records in organizing; people who were embedded in their milieu. To join our initial group, you had to commit to doing that. It was an unbelievable six months of organizing. Everybody went to the organizations they were involved with and brought them along. We formulated motions to support the project, which union locals passed; women in international solidarity groups and some political parties did the same thing. We wanted to show both organizational and individual support.

As our IWD organizing meetings proceeded, so did WAVAW's. But the unitary effort failed in January, and WAVAW broke away. They didn't want men involved in the demonstration. The other groups and individuals did. At that moment it felt like a failure, but I couldn't see the rightness of fighting for the idea of inclusion yet excluding men from a support role on the demo. That made no sense. The reason the event ultimately worked is that a lot of the women who were part of that original organizing committee really wanted to have some way to act. They didn't want to just go to the NDP, which wasn't feminist enough or socialist enough. They wanted to have a way to show themselves and the world the power of socialist feminism. Despite the variety of priorities among the remaining majority, there was a great will to work together and struggle through differences. So we were able to achieve balance and a large vibrant, fabulous set of events and actions within that. We demonstrated that feminism was an important part of a movement for social justice and vice versa. By the time we got to the rally and demo, a hundred organizations endorsed us.

Reflecting on the failure to link with WAVAW—it was painful and sad. But the majority of women didn't want violence against women to be the dominant theme, though no one thought it an unimportant issue, and WAVAW considered it cause enough for a split. The majority of the organizers were working hard on other issues of economic and social rights. We wanted them represented, in public and in the press. We listed twenty demands, and we had a debate about which would be *the* one to focus on. In the end, the event reflected many themes and issues—which is the glory of the movement.

Dionne Brand

In the late seventies, I belonged to a group called the Committee against the Deportation of Immigrant Women (CADIW), which had a lot of links with WAVAW. We thought that feminists needed to organize around this issue, which was mainly the deportation of Jamaican domestic workers. We were disillusioned with the black community organizations. So we leafleted and organized meetings. There were just three of us who comprised the organization in 1978, but, remember, only five guys started the Black Panther Party.

CADIW went to the IWD meetings to raise the issue of women being deported. We felt there would be support for our demands there. Since we were still organizing in the black community, our relationship with IWD at that time was a nervous one. We didn't know what the interests of those women were, nor did we see them as dovetailing with ours. So we went there in coalition mode, rather than to become part of the organization.

I went to Grenada in '83, and when I came back there was the beginning of the Black Women's Collective. We started to get involved in IWD to bring that element to it. We still worked in the black community, and wanted to embody the women's movement, to be part of it in a formal way that would also change it. We thought it should have a wider sense. In 1986, when IWD came up with the slogan "Women against Racism from Toronto to South Africa," we decided we would pick up on that. We heard that it was going to be a year about anti-racism, and we went to the meetings. We thought this was our issue and we could give some kind of direction.

We came into the room and said, "Wait a second. What do you mean, and how do you do this, and what kind of decisions are you making?" There were capable women who had run IWD for a long time, and the bureaucracy of it was well in hand. So we came in conflict with some of the ways they did things. Suddenly it was very charged. We also had connections with some Aboriginal women and the Native Women's group. We got in touch with them and invited them to join the meetings with IWD as well. At those meetings, when people started to vote on things like who should speak, what route the march would take, what the poster would look like, the writing of demands, we said, "Hold it." We held up the meeting and said we had to caucus on some things. It introduced into the coalition the possibility that how decisions got made wasn't necessarily democratic. Racism in the society means something about how power is distributed. You can't have the tyranny of the majority. That shook things up in the coalition that year.

We had discussions in our group about how to proceed in coalition with other people who might not have all interests intersecting with yours. We had a central issue about the liberation of women, but we had a different sense as black people about what knowledges people have in the world and who we were with in the world. From being involved in radical left politics, you learned about the exclusion of women in decision making. Then we came to the feminist movement and we dreamed about how to organize it. We talked about how to work it out, and we read a lot, too.

It was hot. The women's movement is where all this kind of stuff happens. It's very charged and angry, but it's where it happens. People from outside can look at it and see it as fighting, but we're fighting for something. It will look like it's in disarray, a mess, but that's what struggle looks like. You're fighting for ideas, you're fighting all the prejudices. It looks messy, and at the time you feel like, who do they think they are? I do think that the vision of us, ten or so black women walking into the room, was scary for people, and that played to our paranoia. Like, what the hell do you mean, scary? That's a racist concept about what black people represent, which is totally not what we are. We are in the weakest position, so how could we be scary? I think we had allies, and I don't think the women who were upset with us were against us. I also think there were women who admired us. It was ground we had to fight on and for. I don't think anyone coming into the room left as who they were before. It was a transformative time. Its effects were both good and bad. I think it spawned some radical changes, but also some not-so-good changes. Some white women threw their hands up in the air because they lost control and so felt they couldn't do anything. They withdrew their goodwill.

I also think there were people who interpreted those interventions as nationalist moments. In years after I would hear things like "Native women must always lead the march" and "These people must always do that." Well, some strategies are necessary for particular historical moments, but we hope for transformations that end those necessities.

When we went into IWD, we said that the racism thing is not like an issue that you can do and then go away. It's how some people live, and there needed to be radical change in thinking to figure that out. The general society was also going through this guilt thing. We hated the guilt. Guilt is petrifying. Guilt means you can do nothing. Guilt also means that you don't see how your life will change. Lots of decisions were made on guilt. I thought what the coalition needed to do was some workshops for white women about racism. Not where the black women and women of colour come in and say what racism is, but white women sitting down with each other and talking about how it works in their lives. We suggested that, and it was a no no. We all live in the same space, and racism affects white women. Not just as perpetrators of racism—it affects your life, too. Who you think you can be friends with, who you don't. It would have been a good, thoughtful way of going about things to have workshops about it.

We thought if white women could see racism as structuring their lives too, and not always to their benefit, as limiting their lives, though not in the same way it does for women of colour, then that's the moment in which they could embrace the experiences of women of colour. And that is the moment at which they could challenge some of those things. We had it right about what we felt, but not always about what to do. I always hope for that moment. It didn't happen in 1986, but I am sure it happened between two people somewhere. It's not impossible for you to figure out what I might be living.

After '86, there wasn't any organizing in the women's movement that wasn't inclusive. People really tried for inclusion. I think there wasn't another IWD where the speakers weren't varied. As much as it was difficult and rancorous, as much as people didn't speak to each other for years, for years, I don't think another discussion came up without attention to inclusiveness. That was good. What was bad was that we thought we couldn't speak to each other after the fight. Everyone learned from it.

PART III
The 1980s

Feminism is the political theory and practice that struggles to free all women: women of colour, working class women, poor women, disabled women, lesbians, old women—as well as white, economically privileged, heterosexual women.

—BARBARA SMITH, *BUT SOME OF US ARE BRAVE*

R EACTIONARY FORCES BEGAN to turn back the rights revolution in the 1980s. Calling for privatization, deregulation, increased military spending and deep cuts to both social services and taxes, neo-liberal leaders such as Margaret Thatcher in England and Ronald Reagan in the United States implemented a massive propaganda campaign that seriously altered public discourse and smashed all opposition. Within a few short years, the notion of government as a force for curbing the excesses of capitalism, in the interests of the people, changed to criticism of the so-called nanny or welfare state, which supposedly prevented good citizens from making money and contributing to the economy. Groups fighting for equal rights were labelled "special interests," with the dubious assertion that the public interest lay with that of the corporations. Thatcher defeated the powerful British miners' union after a year-long strike in 1984–85. Reagan signalled his hard line by firing traffic controllers during their strike in 1981.

In Canada, the decade opened with a fight against the economic policies of the Trudeau government. The labour movement's largest-ever demonstration took place in the middle of the 1981 recession, with more than one hundred thousand people on Parliament Hill protesting Prime Minister Trudeau's proposal for wage and price controls. Despite this massive opposition, the legislation was brought in the following year. Neo-liberalism began in earnest with the 1984 election of Brian Mulroney and his Progressive Conservatives. Mulroney had campaigned against free trade with the United States, but once in power he became an enthusiastic proponent. Both the Liberals and the NDP opposed the Free Trade Agreement, but the most visible opposition came from social movements in coalition with the labour movement. A cross-country coalition called the Pro-Canada Network took shape, and its key spokespeople, including Bob White from the Canadian

Labour Congress, Maude Barlow from the Council of Canadians, and Marjorie Griffin Cohen from the National Action Committee on the Status of Women, became familiar faces on the national news. On the provincial level, British Columbia's Social Credit government brought in a series of harsh measures that attacked the rights of workers and citizens and severely cut back social services. B.C. feminists joined with labour and community groups to create the Solidarity Coalition. Although the coalition organized a one-day general strike as a prelude to broader strike action, the labour leadership settled with the government in a move community activists saw as a betrayal. The founding of the Reform Party in 1987 gave a new national voice to both Western alienation and neo-conservative anti-feminist politics.

Yet, although the American women's movement declined after Ronald Reagan's election victory in 1980, Canadian feminism in the 1980s became a more potent force. Feminist organizing around economic issues escalated as it became clear that demanding equal pay for equal work was not enough; equality could not be achieved as long as women were ghettoized into low-paying "female" jobs. In the 1984 report from her Royal Commission on Equality in Employment, Judge Rosalie Abella coined the term "employment equity" and stimulated an alliance of women, "visible minorities," people with disabilities and Aboriginal people which would continue into the decades that followed. Child care also became a feminist issue on a national scale. Massive mobilizations of women demanding legal abortion across the country resulted in the establishment of free-standing abortion clinics in Winnipeg and Toronto and a court battle that led to the striking down of the abortion law in 1988.

When the Parti Québécois's May 20, 1980, referendum on sovereignty resulted in a decisive defeat for the independence movement, Trudeau moved on his promise to repatriate the constitution, initiating a decade-long fight in which the women's movement would play a central role. The first and only leaders' debate on women's issues, held during the 1984 election, signalled a higher profile for the National Action Committee on the Status of Women in national politics.

In addition, the proclamation of the equality section of the Charter of Rights and Freedoms in 1985 created a major new arm of struggle for Canadian feminism. Using the Charter protections that women had won, the Women's Legal Education and Action Fund intervened in multiple cases and helped establish landmark legal victories for women on everything from sexual harassment, pregnancy discrimination, and sex bias in employment standards to spousal support and reproductive freedom. Helping the Supreme Court develop a feminist interpretation of the Charter, LEAF successfully reversed several major legal setbacks of the 1970s. In 1981 Bertha Wilson had become the first woman appointed to the Supreme Court, and her judgments pushed the court toward a progressive interpretation of equality rights. Women also made some progress in mainstream politics. In 1980 in Nova Scotia, Alexa McDonough became the first women leader of a provincial political party—the provincial NDP—and in 1987 Audrey McLaughlin became the first woman leader of a federal political party, thanks to a campaign fought hard by feminists within the NDP.

In 1984, using statistics compiled by the Canadian Advisory Council on the Status of Women, NDP MP Margaret Mitchell raised the issue of wife battering during a speech in the House of Commons. Male MPs responded with laughter and catcalls. Nevertheless, the silence around violence against women was breaking down. Linda MacLeod's landmark report *Wife Battering in Canada: The Vicious Circle* estimated that one in ten women experienced this kind of violence, a finding shocking to people outside the anti-violence movement. By 1987 MacLeod could report that the number of women's shelters had tripled since 1982, from 85 shelters to 264.[1] In 1983 the Canadian Association of Sexual Assault Centres spearheaded the fight for a new rape shield law that defined rape as a form of violence, removed restrictions around a woman charging her husband and forbade the questioning of a victim about her sexual history. Feminist groups saw the law as a step forward, but they were rightfully concerned by the lack of definition of the term "sexual assault" and by the law's failure to remove the provision permitting the "honest belief" of consent as a defence. These problems would not be corrected until after the Supreme Court struck down the law in 1991.

By the mid-1980s, feminism had gone truly mainstream. A poll of *Chatelaine* readers revealed that 47 percent were willing to identify themselves as feminists. But there continued to be serious political differences among feminists themselves. The debate on pornography centred first on censorship, but issues of sexuality, representation and freedom of expression soon came to the fore. And the most influential feminist literature of the decade came from African American writers who challenged the idea that women had a common experience in the world. *Ain't I a Woman? Black Women and*

---

1. *The Politics of the Body in Canadian Women's Issues*, vol. 1, by Ruth Roach Pierson et al. (James Lorimer, 1993).

Feminism by bell hooks, *Sister Outsider* by Audre Lorde and *Women, Race and Class* by Angela Davis all gave good ammunition to feminists of colour struggling against white domination in the women's movement. The often painful struggles that ensued helped create the most multiracial women's movement in the world and, in so doing, sink the roots of feminism into every community in the country.

ELEVEN

IT'S NOT JUST ABOUT IDENTITY
Women of Colour Organize

*If we want a beloved community, we must stand for justice,
have recognition for difference without attaching difference to privilege.*

—BELL HOOKS

WOMEN OF COLOUR have always been involved in the Canadian women's movement, although their numbers were few at first. Rosemary Brown, Fleurette Osborne and others raised their voices early on in local and national status of women groups, but the majority of women of colour did not feel welcome in white-dominated women's groups.

Immigrant women, black women and other women of colour began founding their own groups in the 1970s and early 1980s. In the feminist tradition, these groups organized the services that were needed by women in their communities. The Congress of Black Women was founded at a conference of two hundred participants in 1973. Groups such as Toronto's Immigrant Women's Health Centre provided not only services but a base for consciousness-raising and advocacy. The oppressive immigration laws that discriminated against domestic workers were the focus of organizations such as Intercede in Toronto and the Philippine Women Centre in Vancouver. Groups such as Vancouver's South Asian Women's Centre pioneered advocacy around issues of violence against women. When the National Organization of Immigrant and Visible Minority Women of Canada was founded in 1986 in Winnipeg, issues of race and gender began to come to the fore in organizations that had until then concentrated on settlement and immigration issues. Some women of colour worked individually or in coalition with the mainstream movement, pushing for recognition of their issues. Their organizing challenged the movement's structure and priorities.

Dionne Brand

The 1960s and the civil rights movement were very exciting, and when I came to Toronto from Trinidad in 1970 I wanted to be involved in radical politics. I got involved in anti-racist politics early on, with the Black Education Project and *Spear* magazine. My left politics were honed and developed in the community. There were a lot of black organizations in the city fighting for civil and human rights. In 1973 there was a huge black people's conference at Harbord Collegiate, and my feminism was influenced by the radical politics of the movement. Being involved in African liberation support committees and other initiatives in the city developed for me into feminism as a philosophy. I wanted to know how to move the politics that way.

In the black liberation movement in Toronto there was a group that was aware of gender inequality. There were very forthright women who would call down guys on certain questions. The black movement was a cultural movement as well, and we took on the question of figuring out what the roles of men and women would be. There were cultural nationalist debates about the restoration of the roles of women as maternal and obedient, walking three paces behind as the mother of the community and so on. There was also the idea that the revolution had to come first and then they'd deal with women's issues. We discussed what was more important, black struggle or black woman's struggle. It was similar to the white left movement. I began to read Shulamith Firestone and Angela Davis and Selma James,[1] and I started to think that my role wasn't to support black men to establish a black patriarchy. How would I formulate a theory in which I could live? I read and thought about it, and that's how I decided how to conduct myself. I continued to be involved in black organizations, but my place changed.

The urgency of work in the black community was pressing. There were kids in schools who were really suffering. There was urgency to African

---

1. Selma James was a British feminist who led the group Wages for Housework.

liberation work. My own work as a writer was very pressing as well. In the late 1970s I started going to International Women's Day organizing meetings. Sherona Hall had organized a women's group around the issue of unfair deportations, and we thought that feminists needed to organize around this issue too.

Back in the seventies, there used to be a Miss Black Ontario pageant. The whole community thought this was an uplifting event, but we organized a protest at the Sheraton Hotel. We got about three other women to come with us and we made a huge banner and put out a manifesto. Our leaflet said we didn't have to imitate the degradation of white women. The community was aghast, but we had so much fun.

There was a move toward "middle-classing" in the 1980s. There was an opening for blacks during that era with the rise of multiculturalism, and there was a sense of arriving. What that got translated into was this middle-classing of the black community politics, and some of us who considered ourselves feminists and leftists distrusted that.

Then too, most of the issues the women's movement took up were representative of middle-class white women, and we didn't feel part of that either, but we also needed to respond to the black community organizing. This is when we formed the Black Women's Collective as a radical black feminist group. We had lots of discussions about politics and decided to work within the women's movement as well as others.

Winnie Ng

I got involved in women's issues through organizing with the International Ladies Garment Workers Union (ILGWU) from 1977 to 1979.[2] We were organizing immigrant women who were sewing-machine operators and finishers. The job segregation by gender was noticeable; the men were cutters, with higher-paying jobs and their own union. The ILGWU work was hard and lonely.

From there I went to the Toronto Immigrant Women's Health Centre as the counsellor for the Chinese community. We had counsellors from the Italian, Portuguese, Spanish and West Indian communities. We operated as a collective, and it was a revelation. We started the day with women gathering and talking about the night before. We shared a big room, which

2. The ILGWU was organized in 1900 and joined UNITE, the Union of Needletrades, Textiles and Industrial Employees, in 1995.

was nurturing. After the more hierarchical organizations I'd been in, the women's collective was a breath of fresh air.

The Immigrant Women's Health Centre had started in 1976. We did advocacy, and we were the only group doing therapeutic abortion counselling with immigrant women in their own languages. We met with resistance from the churches and the communities and from the husbands. There were a lot of wife-abuse scenarios that came out through the counselling. We lined women up with shelters and rape crisis centres and recommended marital counselling. Sometimes the husbands made threats and stomped out of our offices.

In 1979 we were able to respond to the influx of the Vietnamese boat people; we were the first organization to get a Vietnamese-speaking counsellor. We also linked the workplace with women's health issues. We applied to Health Canada for a pilot project where we learned preventive health care and had a screening program at women's worksites. We targeted the garment factories. We had a mobile unit to do Pap tests and a lot of other good stuff. Our hidden agenda was to look at the whole area of occupational health and safety.

Back in 1975 I had gotten involved with a group called Women Working with Immigrant Women. There was a campaign to fund ESL classes, and we started women's groups for new immigrant women. Ours was like a Chinese consciousness-raising group for women. We talked about finance, family and abuse, and set up prenatal classes. WWIW was doing things we felt were needed. There was so little social support that it was easy to do outreach and get a lot of participants. We weren't competing with other organizations. We were the only ones in the city taking a stand on women's bodies and their health.

I attended the first IWD march in Toronto in 1978 with my daughter. Our whole collective went. But I didn't feel part of the women's movement at the time. We saw it as separate, because there was never any effort to include us. I saw myself more as part of the immigrant women's community. I would have called myself a feminist, I guess, but that wasn't the label I used. I called myself an organizer. There was a sense in the immigrant women's group that we wanted our own voice, even though there were others who wanted to do good and speak for us. Some of the ESL teachers took a missionary approach. That's what motivated us to push the group forward. The collective gave us strength. There was a comfort level among the women, and we felt free to talk about things.

The Immigrant Working Women's Centre was a hub of activity. We worked closely with the Immigrant Women's Job Centre and the Working Women's Community Centre, and we provided links to the other communities. We all participated in the marches against the shooting of Albert Johnson and of Michael Wade Lawson.[3] As the circle began to expand, we worked closely with black women and with women of other racial backgrounds, which led to us creating the Coalition of Visible Minority Women in 1983, and to the formation of the National Organization of Immigrant and Visible Minority Women (NOIVM) in 1986. We linked with the whole anti-racist thing. I remember us talking over a number of dinners, maybe ten, fifteen women. There was a sense of vibrancy and fearlessness. We structured it so that at each monthly meeting, one community would share its stories and we'd discuss them. We had an honest, upfront discussion with the native women, who didn't see themselves as part of the group. They were supportive, but they didn't want to be seen as visible minority women.

The Coalition of Visible Minority Women found a lot of common ground, and one of the projects we took on was identifying foreign-trained women and the lack of access they had in Canada to their former occupations. We applied for funding and piloted a retraining and entry to nursing project, setting up an office and hiring a coordinator. The project turned our volunteer activism into a job. The funding was beneficial, but it took away the independence and vibrancy of a group of women coming together.

The coalition kept meeting, and we got very involved in employment equity legislation. There was no tension among the different groups, and I found it to be a growing experience, both politically and workwise.

Salome Lukas

I came to Canada in September 1969 from Cyprus, when I was twenty. I didn't bring a lot of political experience with me. A lot of things were new to me, but I'm a fast learner. I was involved with the organizing campaign at Puretex, where I was working. It was a significant organizing campaign and strike. The importance was that the workers there were immigrant

---

3. The black community was highly mobilized in protest of these police shootings. Albert Johnson was killed by police in 1979 and Michael Wade Lawson in 1988.

women, with a majority of Italian, Portuguese and Greek, 250 of us. There was support on the picket lines, and I remember a number of women coming. This was in 1978, and that's how I got involved in the organized movement. We weren't successful in saving our jobs, and the plant was closed down, so I applied for a job at Women Working with Immigrant Women (WWIW).

WWIW set the standard across the country for years. It was a Toronto organization established as a network of community-based agencies of women who were immigrants or worked with immigrants. There were people in social services, like teachers and nurses, who didn't have the language skills and so couldn't serve the different communities. Some of these people asked the YWCA to organize workshops to sensitize them to the needs of newcomers. The people who attended decided to stay together and support each other. That's how WWIW was established.

We did research on the needs of immigrant women who experienced domestic violence and established Shirley Sameroo House in 1984 as a shelter to meet the needs of immigrant women. Those women wouldn't use other shelters because they didn't have staff who were culturally sensitive. I didn't see immigration issues as separate from racism at that point. I thought I was fighting for both.

A provincial network for WWIW was established at the same time as the Coalition of Visible Minority Women. WWIW was very grassroots, working with more working-class people, whereas the women in the coalition were academics. We went from there to organize NOIVM, the national organization. We had a conference in Winnipeg where we were snowed in, and there were jokes about how we were forced to debate and work out our issues. When the second conference was organized, no visible minority women were involved in organizing it. Black women were furious with the national committee, which had excluded them from the planning. The NOIVM members were not all immigrant women; there were many who were Canadian born, but the issue of racism had not been put on the agenda.

We had fights in the provincial coalition and the national organization in which WWIW took the position that we should be making links with movements like NAC, the National Action Committee on the Status of Women. The attacks during those years sent me home crying. I remember women saying, "Why should we work with NAC?" I would hear that at every convention. Women wanted to organize in their own communities, and they wanted ownership of the issues and of how they chose to fight.

I felt, once you organize within your own communities, where do you go
next? We had to make links, and no matter how bad you felt, you still had
to make the links and put your issues on the national agenda. We had to
put the issue of racism on the agenda.

Akua Benjamin

The Congress of Black Women was started by Kay Livingstone in 1973. It
also had links with the Negro Women's Association.[4] Primarily, the
congress was a national organization of indigenous African Canadian
women. It seemed to me to be older women, certainly by the time we got
to know them. The organization wasn't as well known or vibrant in the late
1970s and early 1980s as it once had been, but it got revitalized in 1983
when I was hired by the Ontario Women's Directorate to do a conference
on visible minority women. Now, this wasn't just OWD's idea. Visible
minority women had been pushing for it. I did outreach to women of
colour in about thirteen communities. The conference took place, and
there were two reports that came out of it. One was the decision to form an
organization. In the literature you'll find there's been some criticism about
that. Some black women have said that the Coalition of Visible Minority
Women was developed by the government, but that's not true. It came out
of a conference sponsored by the government, but the government did not
start it. The conference included First Nations women, but soon after that,
the First Nations women said their issues were different. They went off in
their own organization, but we have always had a strong link.

So the congress got revitalized, and the coalition also formed that year.
The coalition included Korean, Chinese, Filipina, Vietnamese, Laotian,
South Asian and Japanese women. We had a large gathering of women
from all these different communities. At one point, the congress and the
coalition were so close that we were supporting each others' activities. It
was a good example of being separate but at the same time coming
together.

Prior to this period in the 1980s, there was absolutely no focus on visible
minorities or racialized women. You would hear talk about immigrant
women, but even that was very limited. We felt that immigration was a

---

4. The first National Congress of Black Women, which was held in Toronto in April
1973, brought together two hundred women from across Canada. The Negro
Women's Association was created in 1951 and disbanded in 1976.

temporary status issue, dealing with settlement and adaptation. Issues of gender, colour, race and sexuality were not being addressed at all. No government policy existed to deal with these kinds of issues. At the time, we were on the heels of second-wave feminism, so women had a heightened consciousness of themselves as facing difficulties because of gender issues. The coalition seemed like a natural kind of progression. The '83 conference was supposed to be for two hundred women. About five hundred women showed up, overwhelmingly saying that we needed a voice.

As we got together, we began to see that we had a lot in common, but we had a lot of differences as well. With differences, you begin to see conflict in terms of language, in terms of who has access to employment and what kind. You have one group of women who are professional and have education. You have another group of women who are domestics. The issues do cut across, but we also have a lot of differences in how we experience sexism, racism or ageism.

And it wasn't only about difference. Korean women wanted to get in touch with other Korean women, because they felt isolated. One of the issues in a lot of communities was wife abuse. It was such a hidden issue at the time, even among us as women of colour. Women felt they needed a space to talk about the issues in their own community. They needed a space where they could talk in their own language.

The coalition did a lot of good work at the federal and provincial government levels around the issue of domestics. This was a huge issue. These women couldn't be unionized. They were abused, and so on. We also galvanized women across the country. Before that there had been a body of immigrant women pulled together by the Secretary of State that met once a year. When I realized what was going on, I said no, we're not having it. We refused to do it, and instead we consolidated around this organization. But the organization was very weak, and it was not doing what it was meant to be doing. So the Coalition of Visible Minority Women in Toronto called for a national organization. We met with women across the country. The coalition was strong and had strident and militant voices, but NOIVM, the National Organization of Immigrant and Visible Minority Women, which was created in 1986, was never as militant.

One of the things that happened in the Congress of Black Women, and our chapter in particular, was the issue of lesbian women. Lesbian women took us to task, and rightly so. It became a lesson for me. We had women in the black community who were lesbians and had always worked in these heterosexual organizations. We took heterosexism as the norm, but it had absolutely no meaning for us until the lesbian women raised the issue that this was very oppressive. They said, "We've put up with this for a long time, but you've got to change now. You guys have to do something. Do your homework, learn, but you have to change." It became a huge, huge issue in the congress, because the heterosexual women in their dominance and their privilege—and I include myself in that—felt this was an imposition. This was the way we'd always been, and we'd worked well together, so what was this all of a sudden saying we had to be more inclusive?

We began to make some changes, but they were not far-reaching enough, and we continued to make serious errors. For example, putting on events with flyers not saying lesbian women were part of us. Or we would hold book readings, and unless it was drawn to our attention for the hundredth time, we would not include lesbian writers. We weren't looking at our own heterosexism. As a result of those issues primarily, we began to fracture.

Every year, the congress had a conference for women from around the country. One year a lesbian woman put her name forward for president. Ontario had the most chapters, thirteen out of twenty, so a group of us went around and canvassed the other chapters. We had the majority, so we knew the woman was in. But when we actually got to the vote, she lost. And she lost by a landslide. I think we were the only chapter that voted for this woman. I hit the roof. I went and told every caucus at the conference, we need to get together before we leave this room. I just laid into everyone. "You're very dishonest," I said to them. "If you knew you weren't going to vote for her, you should have said so from the beginning."

Well, that was the demise, because the lesbian woman felt that after all the work she had done there was no place for her. It gave a signal to lesbians from across the country that no matter how hard you work, you will never be accepted. When it opened up as a discussion in our own chapter, it was an attack on everybody. "What happened at the conference happens on a daily basis in the organization," this woman said. I felt so hurt by that. The person said, "I feel this is a hateful organization." I said, "How can you say that?" I explained that I had called people on their heterosexism. But I saw a parallel. Like white women might say to women of colour, "Your voices are too difficult, it's too hard. You want us to change. You want us to take up the issue." We hear white women say, "We championed your cause, what more do you want?" And I said that to lesbian women: We have championed your cause, we have embraced you. We later had a forum that was jam-packed with lesbian women denouncing us. I remember Faith Nolan calling us "the Congress of Bleak Women."[5] That dispute killed the congress.

When I think about the white women's movement, I think about who the women were and what kind of organizing they were doing. They did a lot of consciousness-raising, sitting around and bonding and then starting services or whatever. Then you had a movement that was a radical feminist movement, mostly lesbian women. They began to challenge this other movement. Their voice got very strong and strident. Then you had these black women and women of colour. We began with the questions about how to unseat white dominance in the movement. Women of colour went in first to see what it was, but the minute you got there, if you didn't bow to that kind of organizing, you were marginalized. All of this began to clash. There was a cauldron then, and communication became really unsettling. And as women came to question their feminism, they did it in a way that became so embattled in the movement itself. We were all moving forward but not paying sufficient attention to each other. It was a real battleground. You know you have the same goal as these white women, but you are going into a battle.

Why did white women give up that consciousness-changing, personal stuff? They couldn't maintain themselves without women of colour, and that pushed white women more into more state-focused demands. I read some time ago about how collectives changed into hierarchal organizations when they started to serve poor women. As soon as an organization started dealing with other than middle-class women, it had to move poor women and women of colour onto the board, and the minute it did that, crises started. These poor women wanted healing, but they also wanted change on bread-and-butter issues.

It's like different streams are converging in a movement, and so there's a lot of conflict and a lot of turmoil, like a whirlpool, until we get past that stage. If you can swim, if you can hang in there for that whirlpool, you are fine, but that whirlpool could suck you under as well. There were women who stayed the course, women who struggled, like Winnie Ng, Carmencita

---

5. Faith Nolan is a singer and musician well known as an activist in the women's movement.

Hermandez, Barbara Isaac, Salome Lukas, Fleurette Osborne. We would say to them, yes, we will be part of NAC and IWD, but you go, because if I go there, I will have a fit. So there were women who were working in that cauldron. But then I saw another group of women who came in from our community. I did not see them pull their weight in that. I saw them being more destructive than positive.

One of the things I learned coming out of the U.N. Conference on Racism in Durban in 2001 was that you cannot take up the issues of difference, whether it be race, gender or poverty, without a process of healing. A lot of work in activism is about structural change. It's about getting a policy change. It is about putting in place a program. Of course, we did consciousness-raising, but we were focused externally on state apparatus. So we never recognized sufficiently how we ourselves need to heal from all the history of difference that has divided us. First Nations women brought that to our attention.

I think we have to recognize how similar we are, but also how very different we are in the way we see each other: how we come at the issue, how we speak to the issue, what we leave in, what we leave out, what we attempt, what we don't attempt. And each of us has to be on a journey of healing. We understand the negative side of the differences, but we don't understand how to heal those differences as we work together. We take it for granted that we are doing that, that you are healing in your own way in the process and so am I, and sometimes we connect. But as we work together, all kinds of issues that we didn't know were there can crop up. I wouldn't join an organization now without a process of healing, because that's our undoing.

Let me use the example of a mixed black and white group. Say you are in a group and you have had personal experience with an issue. But instead of dealing with how that issue has affected you internally, you spew it out into the room and start taking it out on a white ally. And the ally becomes almost the perpetrator of your experience. This is what I think happens. This person symbolizes all the shit that you've been through, especially if the person has said something that is not sensitive. So how do you and this person heal yourselves in that? By recognizing what it is you are doing. To recognize that what I just said is more about me than about you. I have to claim responsibility for that. I have to see that it has an impact on you. But the white person has to understand, "Hey, that wasn't about me. It was about her. But she's also calling attention to something that I symbolize."

So there's an interrogation on both sides. The people who join activism, I feel, they're not just wide-eyed idealists. They've been hurt, they've been victimized.

The bad thing about all this is that it adds hours to the task. This is what happened in our groups. We didn't have time to sit around and do the processing of stuff. We were about carrying out a task. With this stuff, you'd better build time into it. There is a lot of time simply deconstructing what you just said, why it impacted on me. But at the end of it, it is remarkable to see what happens. People come away with a clearer sense that we can really work together and push the boundaries of this stuff. It becomes a shared problem, it becomes a shared responsibility, which I feel was missing in a lot of our work together. There was shared responsibility for the tasks, but not for our healing.

TWELVE

NOTWITHSTANDING
Women and the Constitution

Whatever women do, they must do it twice as well as men to be half as good.
Luckily this is not that difficult.

—CHARLOTTE WHITTON[1]

I N THE WAKE of the May 1980 Quebec referendum, in which 40 percent of Quebeckers voted yes to sovereignty association with Canada, Prime Minister Pierre Trudeau decided it was a priority to renew federalism. He called together the provincial premiers for their regular constitutional conference and announced with typical flair that the federal government was going to repatriate the constitution, which was still based in British law, with the British Privy Council as the ultimate authority. Thus began a process that would define Canadian politics over the next decade and bring the women's movement into mainstream political debates with an impact that no one ever imagined.

At the time Trudeau made his announcement, Doris Anderson was president of the Canadian Advisory Council on the Status of Women, a government-appointed body that reported to the minister responsible for the status of women. The Advisory Council had published some excellent research, particularly on violence against women, but it was mistrusted by the women's movement. Although the council was at arm's length from the government, most of its appointees were loyal Liberals unlikely to make any waves.

---

1. Charlotte Whitton served as mayor of Ottawa for several terms in the 1950s and 1960s.

Women had begun to realize the relevance of constitutional issues in 1978, when Trudeau gave power over divorce to the provinces. Prairie feminists, who had fought for equality in marital property laws, led a women's rebellion in English Canada, persuading Trudeau to reverse the changes. At Doris Anderson's instigation, the Advisory Council published a primer on women and the constitution just as the debate on repatriating the constitution was getting underway. During the National Action Committee's midyear meeting in October 1980, Doris and Parti Québécois vice-president Louise Harel led a seminar on the constitutional changes Trudeau was proposing. As Penny Kome writes in her book *The Taking of Twenty-Eight*, "By the end of the day, women were exhausted and thoroughly alarmed: The Charter of Rights, as it stood, seemed to jeopardize women's legal rights rather than protect them." Feminist lawyers were troubled by section 1 of the Charter, which guaranteed rights and freedoms "subject only to such reasonable limits prescribed by law as can be demonstrably justified in a free and democratic society."

A month later, NAC president Lynn MacDonald made a presentation to the special joint committee on the constitution, recommending changes that included the modification of what was then called the anti-discrimination clause, section 15. In January 1981, Justice Minister Jean Chrétien announced changes that met some of women's concerns. Section 15 had become the equality clause, and the clause now offered four kinds of protection: "equality before and under the law" and "equal benefit and protection of the law." The new wording provided for an interpretation of equal results as well as equal treatment. In the language of rights, the clause guaranteed substantive rather than formal equality: If the impact of a law or a practice was discriminatory, then the law or practice was discriminatory. Equality rights were still subject to the limits of section 1 of the Charter, however, and women wanted these rights to be absolute. Feminists developed section 28 in order to address the limits.

Soon afterward, Lloyd Axworthy, the minister responsible for the status of women, cancelled a women's conference on the constitution that the Advisory Council had been planning. The explosion that followed is legend in the women's movement. Doris Anderson resigned as Advisory Council president, and in a spontaneous rebellion, feminists undertook an extraordinary flurry of activity that resulted in more than a thousand women meeting on Parliament Hill on Valentine's Day, 1981. Some differences emerged at the conference. NAC was divided on the constitution, primarily because women in Quebec did not support Trudeau's unilateral repatriation of the constitution. Some Progressive Conservative and NDP women, including NAC president Lynn MacDonald, were also concerned that an entrenched charter would give too much power to unelected judges, and thus Americanize the Canadian system. Another group of women that argued in favour of pushing for women's equality within the proposed charter formed an ad hoc committee.

The Ad Hoc Committee won many of its demands, but Quebec never signed the constitution. In 1984 Progressive Conservative prime minister Brian Mulroney began the process of persuading Quebec to sign. His 1987 amendment, the Meech Lake Accord, divided both the country and the women's movement over its proposed "distinct society" clause for Quebec. The Ad Hoc Committee opposed Meech Lake, concerned that the distinct society clause would jeopardize what they had worked so hard to achieve and had thought were iron-clad equality rights in the constitution. Their position brought to a head the division between feminists in Quebec and the rest of Canada on other constitutional matters.

THE EQUALITY CLAUSE

Doris Anderson

The Advisory Council on the Status of Women was a bipartisan group of women set up in 1973 to advise the government. Initially, the government put Katie Cooke in as president. She was a skilled bureaucrat, and the council turned out excellent research for ten years, including the first paper on battered women. After Katie's tenure, the government realized what it had done, and it started appointing political hacks to the council, women who had worked for the major political parties, rather than being activists. Those women quickly became politicized, but they stayed loyal to the parties that had appointed them. When I was appointed as president in 1979, I wanted the council to do a lot more than advise the government. We did a lot of research, and the government started to come and ask us about legislation before it got started. Because I was a journalist, we also put out factual pamphlets on things like abortion and occupational hazards and distributed them widely. We held a conference on violence against women and brought in groups from women's shelters. Women's groups looked on the council's appointments as patronage, which they were, but we did as much as we could.

Then the constitutional issue happened, and it seemed to me that if anyone was going to bring women's groups together to talk about how this would affect women, the Advisory Council should do it. I thought it was going to be important work, but boring. We got eleven papers produced for a conference to be held in the fall of 1980, and then there was a strike among the interpreters. There were a lot of problems inside the council at the time. I had people on staff who were working against me and leaking information to the Status of Women like moles.[2] The Status of Women didn't want us to get too radical. I was persuaded by the council's executive that we couldn't cross the interpreters' picket line and that I should cancel the conference. We rescheduled it for February.

When I look back on it now, I don't think the government wanted us to hold that conference. The minister responsible for the status of women, Lloyd Axworthy, had decided it should be cancelled. I pointed out how bad cancelling it would be for the Advisory Council; we would look like a bunch of patsies and we'd be destroyed. But they only paid lip service to me. So I decided that I would go to the press, quit as president of the council and tell them why. It was marvellous. The story was on the front page for a whole week.

I always ran my life a certain way. I always had enough money in the bank so I could quit my job if I had to. But I needed another job then. I had kids who were still in high school, and I was a single mother earning a reasonable salary. I did some freelance work and got by, and once I got back to Toronto, I started writing for the *Toronto Star*. It was a big sacrifice leaving my job at the council, but I wanted the world to know that what had happened was wrong. Women got together anyway, of course, and put on a conference that the Liberals have regretted ever since. It was a triumph of the women's movement.

Nancy Ruth

I had been active in the women's movement in Toronto since 1979, when Kay Macpherson called to invite me to a meeting, organized by Linda Ryan Nye at the Cow Café on John Street in Toronto. The Advisory Council conference had been cancelled, and we all thought, They can't do this to us;

---

2. The Status of Women was the name of the government department under the control of the minister.

we'll put on our own conference. We kept meeting after that. Someone knew Pat Hacker in Ottawa, who could organize. We developed a list of French and English speakers and notified all the women's groups. MPs Margaret Mitchell, Flora MacDonald and Judy Erola helped, as did a number of women civil servants. We had no money, but everyone phoned everyone they knew, and we got thirteen hundred women to Ottawa. Joe Clark and Maureen McTeer held a reception for us at Stornaway. Pauline Jewett was there.[3] The National Film Board's Studio D came and filmed us that Saturday. We were in the West Block, in the same room where all the constitutional negotiations had gone on before ours. It was some Valentine's conference. Maude Barlow was working at City Hall for Ottawa's mayor, Marion Dewar, and she arranged for us to hold the second day of the conference, on Sunday, at City Hall. That's where our resolutions were laid out and voted on.

Pat Hacker

It was the Cow Café meetings in Toronto that pulled things together. I was in Ottawa working for Women's Career Counselling Service, a place where women came for various kinds of help. Our office was across the hall from the first rape crisis centre in Ontario. I was already involved with a nest of women, so I set up a meeting and the women from Toronto flew in. Things happened very quickly. Women started organizing on January 27 and the conference was set for February 14. About thirty women showed up at the first Ottawa meeting, and some money was put up, and a woman no one knew took the money and set up a bank account. Everybody continued doing things because we had a shared vision. We were mad as hell at Axworthy cancelling the conference and we weren't going to take it. That was the common goal. Sometimes that kind of magic and energy and connection can just happen. Nancy Ruth bankrolled the conference, and a number of organizations handled money for us. The Federation of Women Teachers of Ontario was generous. They put forward money quickly and extended the awareness through their links.

All kinds of women worked through their organizations to help us mobilize. Women who worked in government would go from floor to floor so they wouldn't be seen doing too much photocopying at one machine. Secretaries and women who worked at lower management levels helped us. Maureen O'Neil at Status of Women Canada made her office

---

3. Pauline Jewett was an NDP Member of Parliament. She was first elected in 1963 as a Liberal and moved to the NDP in 1979.

and equipment available to us, even though the minister was against us. Women took risks and let us use their offices when they weren't there. Even signatures were forged to get things done. Women lied to the RCMP when they questioned our use of government phone lines. We had a lot of access to the Parliament Buildings. We could go in and say we were going to see whomever, and the security guards would almost always say okay. There wasn't much security in those days.

The physical aspects of things had to be arranged, and ultimately that was taken care of. We would call and meet people and persuade the political parties to pay for coffee and tea. The Liberal Party didn't want to be seen as hindering us too much. It paid a price for cancelling the conference. The interpreters agreed to work at the conference for free.

Women from all the different provinces and concerns were included, though there were disputes over Quebec.[4] More than a thousand women came to the conference from across the country. They paid their own way and were billeted in people's homes. Both individuals and representatives from organizations came, but it was largely individual women who felt strongly and wanted to work in their regions. A lot of women knitted during the conference, and Studio D filmed it all.

The result of the conference was a sense of triumph and accomplishment, a demonstration to women and men and political parties and government of what women could do. We wanted women's rights entrenched in the Charter. Before the women's movement, we'd seen ourselves as wives and mothers who stood by and helped. As feminists we had started dealing with issues of child care and the abuse of women, but this constitutional issue was more political. It affected the laws, and we were engaging debate and having an influence on matters beyond what we would generally tackle.

Marilou McPhedran

I happened to be in Ottawa in November 1980 at the time of the joint Senate–House of Commons hearings on the constitution. The evening before the National Action Committee presentation was scheduled to present, I got this phone call. The NAC woman said, "We need you to come down to the hotel and help us." They needed a lawyer, and if I could be helpful on this constitutional stuff, that was cool.

---

4. The Fédération des femmes du Québec did not want to support an event that condoned the new constitution, because Quebec disagreed with Trudeau's proposals. This was one major reason why NAC did not initially support the conference.

So I ended up being with NAC the next morning when they gave the presentation. Senator Harry Hayes, as co-chair of the committee, said to them, "Well, it is all fine and good for you girls to be here, but who is home looking after the kids?" We were all back and forth with this look of complete shock. Lynn MacDonald, the president of NAC at the time, was sitting at the front, and her mouth was sort of wide open. His comment became a significant news item, and it was an important pivot point in raising the awareness of women across the country. Largely as a result of Hayes's insulting behaviour, I ended up saying, okay, I'm going to get involved now; where do we go from here?

There are many different perspectives on what happened between the Ad Hoc Committee and NAC. The leaders of NAC at the time did not support an entrenched charter of rights. In an ideal situation, the Ad Hoc Committee might not have chosen an entrenched charter either, but there was going to be one, and if we sat out the process of amending it, we were going to get screwed, the same way we'd been screwed by Diefenbaker's Bill of Rights, under which we'd lost every single legal challenge on the basis of either women or Aboriginal equality.[5] The Ad Hoc Committee came into being in order to address these issues and these issues alone—women's equality in the constitution.

A small number of us were out of Ottawa coordinating the thing. I had a government job by this point, and I did absolutely nothing of my job during this time. I mean nothing. I think the wonderful man who had hired me knew what I was doing. I showed up at work, but I used the government phone lines for long-distance calling across the country all day long, organizing the conference and doing the follow-up. I left my office in Hull easily four times a day to go to Ottawa to lobby. There probably weren't too many rules that I didn't break. I organized the legal part of it. And when we finished the conference, we had this amazing set of resolutions. I look back twenty years later and I think, damn, what we pulled together was astonishing.

There was a lot of dissension in the room during the conference. Lynn MacDonald completely disagreed with the direction we were taking. Maureen McTeer was there, and she too was strongly against an entrenched charter. Many speakers came to the microphone, and many of them disagreed with

5. One example was the Stella Bliss case, in which the Supreme Court ruled Bliss was discriminated against not because of gender but because of her pregnancy.

each other. It was challenging finding a way to reach consensus and to have voices heard and not have breakaways. I remember, for example, being in the hallway with a group of Aboriginal women, trying to work out how the resolutions could be changed to include the amendments that they wanted. We then had to go back into the meeting and they went to the mike and addressed the assembly. After the conference, many of us from the Ad Hoc Committee—Nancy Ruth, Pat Hacker, Linda Ryan-Nye, Kay Macpherson, Doris Anderson, Kay Sigurjonsson—went on together to be the founders of LEAF, the Women's Legal Education and Action Fund.

After the conference, there was a sort of interregnum where the Charter was before the Supreme Court of Canada. The political stuff settled down, the status of women minister changed and the Opposition members of Parliament played a very important role. After a lot of lobbying and discussion, with the justice minister insisting that he would not change one more word in section 15, the equality rights section of the Charter, we said, "Okay, if we can't do 15, then how do we guarantee gender equality?" This is where section 28 came in. We ended up in a last-minute telephone conversation with lawyer Morris Manning, who was not noted for his feminism but whose wife was a feminist doctor very involved in the pro-choice movement. "If you could have only one thing," is the way I remember framing it, "what are the single most important words that we have to get in? What has to be the deal breaker for us? What do I have to absolutely stand firm on?" And he said, "'Notwithstanding.' You can do a lot with wording, but you've got to come out of there with 'notwithstanding' as the first word in that amendment. If you don't do that, then it will just be words. But if you get 'notwithstanding,' then you will create something that is potentially a tool that can be used in litigation. It might not be elegant wording, but that is the critical word." The wording of section 28 of the Charter became "Notwithstanding anything in this Charter, all the rights and freedoms in it are guaranteed equally to male and female persons."

THE MEECH LAKE ACCORD

Mary Eberts

Doris Anderson and the Advisory Council commissioned Bev Baines and me to write a primer on women and the constitution in 1980.[6] I stayed

---

6. Bev Baines is another feminist lawyer who was active on constitutional issues.

involved until it became clear that there was going to be a parting of the ways between the Advisory Council and Minister Axworthy. I bowed out because I was doing some important work for Lloyd Axworthy on domestic workers, and I didn't want to get iced. After the ad hoc conference, I got actively involved again.

The Meech deal was announced on a Saturday in 1987 in *The Globe and Mail*. I can remember getting a call from Bev. My house was being renovated; I was sitting on a crate and saying, "Oh, my god!" What disturbed me was that the guarantees of the Charter, like the equality clause, were being made subject to the new distinct society clause. We weren't against distinct society, but we thought the distinct society clause would trump women's rights to equality. It wasn't desirable that different rights would be given to women depending on their place of residence.

The Ad Hoc Committee resurrected itself to fight Meech, and they retained me to do an opinion on how bad the subjugation of equality and other rights was. I got John B. Laskin, my law partner, to co-author the opinion with me. We went to the parliamentary committee that was considering the issue. This was one of the opening shots in the deplorable and sleazy battle of opinions on Meech. People were purchased all over the country to give legal opinions saying that Meech didn't interfere with equality rights.

The opposition to Meech by women in English Canada set off a serious counter-reaction among Quebec women, and a rift that may never have healed came about. The Quebec women were speaking out of their own concerns, and I respect that. But the Quebec women wanted us to stay silent, and I don't think that's appropriate in a democracy. If it's important to the country, you should have the right to speak on it. When the price of amity is silence, I think we're in a bad situation.

I felt good about Meech being defeated at the time. But since then just about everything that was in Meech has been implemented as an administrative matter. And over the years, I've had a number of discussions with francophone Québécois in which they've told me about their grief at the defeat of the accord. I feel badly about that. The power politics of the Mulroney government fomented dissent and rupture and a legacy of ill will that we're still living with. The federal government was using every dirty trick in the book to stop resistance to Meech. The idea was that twelve men in a room and their bureaucrats knew best, and the rest of us should shut up. It was an explosive issue because it was handled in a thuggish way.

Ginette Drouin Busque

I was president of the Fédération des femmes du Québec from 1985 to 1989, the period of Meech Lake. We attended NAC's annual general meeting in June 1987 in Ottawa, and a resolution came from the floor to denounce the Meech Lake Accord as a threat to women's rights. So there were questions: Why was it a threat to women's rights? What we heard was that the women of Quebec were threatened, and that if women's rights were set back in Quebec, it would affect the rest of Canada. But the women's groups in Quebec had never been consulted about this, so we got up and walked out. For me, it was a powerful gesture. Then we had a discussion among ourselves. Would we stay or go back home? Women from the NAC executive came to ask that we stay, and we did.

Later we had a meeting in Montreal with NAC women, and we discussed this with them. A representative from Newfoundland said she was in Montreal for an abortion because there was no access to abortion in Newfoundland. I always thought that was ironic.[7]

The position that we took on Meech was at the same time legalist and emotional. We didn't believe Meech was an attack on women's rights, because the best defender of women's rights were women themselves, the Québécoises. We believed that the women of Quebec were capable of mounting the barricades if our rights were attacked. But we also believed NAC's legal arguments were wrong. It's not that we thought the gains of women were guaranteed in Meech. We knew it was possible to go backward, but what would save us was our vigilance.

All of this brought us to a position of being very upset with the women of English Canada. It brought us to a point of a split. In general there was good feeling between the FFQ and NAC, but it was very difficult for English Canada to accept the perspective of Quebec. If the threat was to us, we couldn't understand why it was such a drama in English Canada. Let us be with our misery. It's not your misery.

We kept links with NAC, but the differences on Meech were profound. We also discussed with NAC whether the FFQ should be seen as special, because we represented 110 organizations in Quebec. We are very representative of

---

7. One of the arguments made by women in English Canada was that the distinct society clause would permit Quebec to ban abortions in order to permit larger families. Quebec women were offended by this because abortion had been essentially legal in Quebec a decade before the rest of Canada.

Quebec. Shouldn't that give us a different status within NAC? We tried to do in the women's movement what Quebec was never able to do in Canada. In all the constitutional dossiers the provinces are equal, and that is the culture in Canada. I think this debate moved NAC forward on the constitutional issues.

In 1988 we reached a compromise on Meech. That was the fruit of a year of discussion. But NAC's fundamental position never really changed. We felt a malaise about NAC because of Meech. We were treated once again as one group like the others, so we decided to leave the organization in 1989.

Barbara Cameron

The president of NAC, Louise Dulude, wanted to pass a motion criticizing the Meech Lake Accord at NAC's annual general meeting in 1987. I didn't like the accord at all myself, but it was clear that the Quebec women were going to leave if we did condemn it. The angle of criticism was that recognizing Quebec as a distinct society was going to diminish protections for women under the Charter of Rights and Freedoms. So there was a counterposing of the recognition of Quebec and the rights of women. At the AGM we got the issue off the floor and into a discussion. Unity Johnson, who was with the National Organization of Immigrant and Visible Minority Women, played a really good role in that discussion, because it had the potential to be a gang-up of women of English Canada against the Quebec women. Even though she didn't agree with the Quebec position, Unity wouldn't let that happen. We ended up setting up a committee that was half Quebec women and half women from the rest of the country. Then there was quite a debate on the NAC executive. The president was actually forbidden to speak for NAC on the accord. So that meant NAC didn't split on the issue. It also meant that NAC was silent, though, so certainly the impression in Quebec was that the whole women's movement in English Canada had an individual rights position and was against distinct society.

Françoise David

I was with the women's centres in Quebec when I went to three or four meetings of NAC. It was like being in another world. People say about Quebec that we are Latin, meaning spontaneous and a bit disorganized. But for me, the NAC meetings were the most disorganized I had ever seen. I couldn't make out the procedure at all. They talked about everything, and all of a sudden there was an amendment. I had a terrible time following it, despite the translation, because I didn't understand the process. In addition, I went to a couple of workshops, and in the workshops there were always women crying. I asked myself, "What in the world is this?" I felt like I was with extraterrestrials at NAC. Most of my energy at the AGMs was spent trying to understand the culture. I was incapable of participating in the actual discussion. They were talking about all kinds of things that did not correspond to my experience.

Meech didn't aid in the comprehension of the two peoples. Up until the time that the people in English Canada said no to Meech, if you had asked the person on the street in Quebec what Meech Lake was, nine out of ten people wouldn't know. It wasn't really important to the people of Quebec until English Canada said no. Then, hello, we woke up. In the women's movement it was the same thing. It was the feminists in English Canada being against Meech that made us for Meech, even if we were bored by it.

Marilou McPhedran

What the Ad Hoc Committee was trying to do during the Meech period was consolidate the position among women. We wanted to put the onus on government to make changes in the accord so that it would not impinge on equality rights by responding to the needs of our distinct society. We believed that the government was fully responsible for resolving that, and that we had to keep the pressure on it to do so and not fight among ourselves.

At NAC's annual general meeting in 1987, we had a coalition of Aboriginal women, disabled women, francophone women living outside Quebec and women from different parts of the country taking the position that we weren't prepared to risk the equality guarantees in the Charter. It wasn't that we opposed distinct society, but we felt that it was possible to respond to both. That is where we got the Ad Hoc slogan, "We can afford a better accord."

We were in a pitched political battle to get the Ad Hoc position on the agenda at NAC. It was very difficult. Meech ran right to its deadline for approval by the provinces, and it wasn't killed until literally the day of its deadline in June of 1990, which was when Elijah Harper held up the eagle feather.

Judy Rebick

When I was elected president of NAC in June 1990, it was right at the
end of the Meech Lake stuff. Sandra DeLaronde, one of three Aboriginal
women on the executive that year, got me invited to a big rally in
Manitoba to support Elijah Harper. That was my first public activity as
president. I was the one who said, "Ten white men meeting behind closed
doors can't decide the fate of the country." That was the quote of the day in
The Globe and Mail. But I was in just at the tail end of Meech, so I didn't
play much of a role.

After Meech, Barb Cameron and I decided to try to reverse the anti-
Quebec thing in the women's movement that had happened over the
accord. With the Aboriginal women in NAC, we developed a three-nations
position, which was pretty far-seeing, I think. Through lots of debate and
discussion on the executive, we developed the position that Canada is
composed of three nations, each of which is multicultural and multiracial,
and each of which has the right to self-determination. At first we didn't see
the issue of women of colour as part of this. For me, this was a national
issue; racism was a different question. Salome Lukas fought us hard on
that, and she had to walk out of an executive meeting before we understood
that we had to integrate the inclusion of racial minorities into our position
as well.

We took the position that both Quebec and Aboriginal people should
decide for themselves what kind of relationship they wanted with the
federal state; then we could negotiate what the relationship was among
all three. I travelled across the country trying to convince women of this
position. It was a huge debate, but we won it at the 1991 AGM.

Sandra DeLaronde

In 1990 I had just been elected to the NAC executive from Manitoba. There
were very strong women with very strong positions in this debate. When
you work with people who are oppressed on many levels, or who have a
sense of oppression in the larger society, it is necessary to know that you are
dealing with institutions that have a power over mentality. Was it Quebec's
right over Aboriginal rights? That's what Meech Lake was about. That's
what the repatriation of the constitution was about, the rights of English
and French Canada over Aboriginal people. Monique Simard, who was the
Quebec vice-president of NAC, and I had some interesting discussions over

Quebec. In the end we had a better understanding of each other's position. That involved a lot of talking and understanding and trying to present a three-nations position that was new to people.

In the women's struggle, we could not afford not to give equality to the three-nations position. The struggle of Aboriginal people shouldn't be seen as an add-on. The sovereign issues of Quebec had to be real in that, but each position had to be respected in its own right and seen as equal.

Salome Lukas

The position on Quebec and Aboriginal self-government was being discussed at the time I was elected to the NAC executive in 1990. NAC wanted a francophone woman, a native woman and an English-speaking woman to go on tour to discuss this. I said in response, "How about having a woman of colour as part of the tour?" Priscilla Settee, who was the treasurer of NAC at the time, said because there was going to be a native woman on the tour, we should rest assured that the issue of racism would be dealt with. And I said, you will be dealing with racism as it affects native people, but other communities experience racism differently. I think it was Madeleine Parent who said that equality issues or human rights issues were not part of the constitutional debate. I responded, "The country I am a citizen of is amending its constitution, and you are telling me that my life is not part of this discussion." I was furious.

I don't remember what changed my mind, but I remember Madeleine admitting she was wrong. That meant a lot to me. It meant we could broaden the discussion and the debate and deal with all of those issues. I stayed on the constitution committee in developing the position. We never did the tour, but that discussion did broaden NAC's position to include other constituencies and issues. The three national communities included all these other communities.

THIRTEEN

FREEDOM
OF CHOICE
The Morgentaler Clinics

When I dare to be powerful—to use my strength in the service of my vision,
then it becomes less and less important whether I am afraid.

—AUDRE LORDE

A BORTION WAS THE FIRST ISSUE to unite the women's movement, and it was the issue that put the greatest numbers of women into the streets in protest. As in the United States, feminists in Canada had to battle a powerful anti-choice movement as well as the federal and provincial governments, the cops and the courts. Dr. Henry Morgentaler, who had started doing abortions in Montreal in 1968, was willing to go to jail not once but twice to defend a woman's right to choose.

Quebec essentially legalized abortion in 1976, after three juries had acquitted Dr. Morgentaler, but the restrictive 1969 abortion law remained in effect in the rest of Canada. After the 1973 *Rowe* v. *Wade* decision in the United States made first-trimester abortions legal, many Canadian women's liberation groups set up a kind of underground railroad to ferry women to abortion clinics in the United States. The Canadian Association for Repeal of the Abortion Law was founded in the same year. CARAL, which later changed its name to the Canadian Abortion Rights Action League, supported Dr. Morgentaler by raising funds, but the group also lobbied provincial governments to improve access, pressured hospitals to provide services and educated the public.

Consistent organizing and lobbying by feminists resulted in the *Report of the Committee on the Operation of the Abortion Law,* more commonly known as the Badgley Report, in 1977, which told the government what many Canadian women knew first-hand: "The procedure provided in the Criminal Code for obtaining therapeutic abortion is illusory for many Canadian women." Only one in five hospitals had actually set up the therapeutic abortion committees required under the law, and one in six women left the country to obtain an abortion. Federal Health and Welfare minister Marc Lalonde suggested that the provinces set up women's clinics, but opposition from anti-abortionists was so immediate that he made no further effort to improve access. In 1979 two doctors at the Health Sciences Centre in Winnipeg proposed a new reproductive health centre, including a hospital-affiliated clinic for abortions. Feminists rallied around the proposal, but once the doctors received the money, there was no further mention of the abortion clinic.

In 1982 a group of women's health workers decided to do something about deteriorating access to abortion in Ontario. They invited Dr. Morgentaler to help them challenge the law. Morgentaler opened clinics in both Winnipeg and Toronto. Both were raided by the police, setting off a massive struggle in the courts and in the streets. Women mobilized to support Morgentaler and demand reproductive rights. The popular slogan changed from "Free abortion on demand" to "A woman's right to choose." The debate continued at all levels of society, led by pro-choice and feminist activists. It was a highly polarized debate with opposition from a fanatical anti-choice faction that was sometimes violent and always very aggressive and confrontational. By the time it was over, there were abortion clinics in almost every province. The Supreme Court struck down the abortion law as unconstitutional in 1988, and a profound support for a woman's right to choose was expressed by almost 80 percent of the population in a 1998 Environics poll.

Toronto

Carolyn Egan

Early on, I started working at the Toronto Birth Control and VD Information Centre, which was formed in 1972, and I was also involved with the Immigrant Women's Health Centre. We dealt every day with women looking for abortions, so we were well aware of the problems of access. Throughout the 1970s we got involved in coalitions to try to expand access, but we weren't getting anywhere. The women we were seeing were having a heck of a time. If you could pay extra to a gynecologist or could afford to go to the U.S., you had access to abortion. If you were a low-income woman, an immigrant woman, a woman of colour who was not well connected or a woman who lived in the North, you couldn't. To get an appointment at Toronto General Hospital, for example, we would start calling at 8:30 A.M. and then call and call and call to get through. After forty-five minutes of this, the hospital would answer and tell us to call back the next day. That was the situation for us, working in clinics, so you can imagine the circumstance of a young woman or a woman working in a factory somewhere. We decided we had to do something about it.

We got together in the Committee for the Establishment of Abortion Clinics. In Europe, and even in Quebec, things were better than what we were facing in Ontario. We figured we needed both a doctor willing to challenge the law and a broad-based movement for change. We approached Henry Morgentaler, but at first he wasn't interested. He had done his thing, he felt. Then he was mugged in New York, and when he woke up and found out he was still alive, he decided he would do it.

First we felt we had to test the water. We were going to be challenging the state in a fundamental way, and we needed to know if the support was there. So we called a meeting for September 28, 1982, telling people that we were floating the idea of establishing a clinic in Toronto with Henry Morgentaler.

That was a dynamic meeting. A lot of people came out, and there was enthusiasm from many quarters. We had picked the right moment, it seemed. Out of that meeting we formed an organization, the Ontario Coalition for Abortion Clinics (OCAC), to fight for free-standing abortion clinics providing medically insured abortions and also for the repeal of the abortion law. We got an office, and different committees worked on a newspaper ad, outreach to different organizations and a large public meeting.

The public meeting was a huge success. People were lined up all the way around the block. They couldn't get into the hall. The anti-choice people tried to disrupt the meeting, but we had a strong group of marshals to keep them out. The media was very good on covering the event. And that, coupled with the huge success we had in getting signatories for the newspaper ad, made it clear there was a movement out there.

So we then began to develop strategies. A lot of women instrumental in OCAC came from a socialist feminist perspective. We didn't define OCAC as socialist; how could you? But we were in a power struggle with the state. We were going up against the federal government and the provincial government, and we had an organized right wing that was out to defeat us. In our view, the only way we could change the balance of power was to have a huge movement. We determined that the support of the Ontario Federation of Labour (OFL) was very important in that. It was our first step beyond the women's movement.

We planned our strategy for the next OFL convention. Women involved in Organized Working Women (OWW) took resolutions to the floor. In some ways, this was a big risk for us. I remember some union women saying this was a potentially divisive issue. But we felt it was better to have it debated. We talked in advance to people like Cliff Pilkey, president of the OFL at the time, and Wally Majesky, who was president of the Toronto Labour Council. We prepared union packages, and the OFL women's committee let us share their table. We had the best-organized intervention of any labour union convention that I've ever seen.

We also went to Women Working with Immigrant Women and put forward the argument about why this issue was so important to communities of colour. There was a debate, but generally, people were on side. Those two alliances were critical. Then there was CARAL, the Canadian Abortion Rights Action League, which was actively involved on the coordinating committee. So we had a real mix of communities and sectors. We didn't want to lobby politicians unless we could show we had a base. We had a pretty good idea that if we opened a clinic, it would be raided, and we would probably face a long court challenge. Our feeling was that Supreme Court justices do not function in a vacuum. They would want to uphold the law, but if the country was alive with people saying that this law was anachronistic, they would have to look at that. When there is no more respect for a law, how can you uphold it?

We did a tremendous amount of work going out to organizations, meetings, picnics, student groups, churches, etcetera. We had terrific media coverage, too. OCAC had open meetings and lots of demonstrations in the street. That allowed ordinary women and men to feel that this was their struggle. I think that was the difference between this movement and some others. People felt they owned it.

Judy Darcy

I was at the 1982 Ontario Federation of Labour convention when women came to discuss the abortion issue. I was a rank-and-file shit disturber from CUPE. In our own conventions, we had brought forward resolutions on choice that were hotly debated. I was also on the executive of the CUPE District Council of Toronto, and the other women on the executive were staunch Catholics who didn't support choice. It was difficult to stick to your guns, because it meant you parted company with women you worked with. Some people argued that unions shouldn't take a position on things like this, that we should focus on bread-and-butter issues. I held firm because it was a fundamental part of my politics. How could women control their lives if they couldn't control their bodies? I knew there were women who had access and women who didn't. Poor, working-class and native women didn't.

It was a deep, fundamental, emotional issue. We needed key male labour leaders who would stand up and speak. Cliff Pilkey, then president of the OFL, took a courageous position. He had bags of fake gold coins sent to him, as if he had committed the ultimate betrayal. He was vilified and got hate mail. I saw Cliff as a middle-of-the-road labour leader, but on affirmative action and choice he showed guts and gave a lot of leadership. The women's caucus at the OFL worked hard to persuade their union locals to support choice. Even in progressive locals there was still hot debate, but it was one of those moments where you had to stand up and be counted.

Judy Rebick

I was active in the Ontario Coalition for Abortion Clinics and chaired the big public meeting, where I met Dr. Morgentaler. He asked me to be spokesperson for the Toronto clinic, and OCAC agreed to it. The media was very sympathetic, and one reporter even taught me how to do a clip for television. There were hundreds of media and supporters the day we opened, June 15, 1983, and this was in a very small street. About 3 P.M., Henry arrived in a car, and another woman and I were supposed to escort him across the street to the clinic. This guy came out of nowhere into the street and attacked Henry, grabbing his arm. I felt such rage that I pushed the guy away and kept backing him up, and then he pulled out a pair of garden shears and made a move to stab me. I was so mad, I started to chase him. There were no police there at that point. Our people couldn't see what was happening, because the media was blocking their view, so no one moved to help me. The camera guys were getting their shot, but the print reporters could have helped. Afterward, I went behind the clinic and fell apart.

Three weeks later, when the police came to bust the clinic, I was at work at the Canadian Hearing Society, about ten blocks away. By the time I got to the clinic, the police were taking out files. We activated our phone tree, and people came down. We had already had to exercise a lot of tactical creativity because of the police behaviour. The police were following women who left the clinic and harassing women who were getting abortions, so we organized people to take the women to safe houses. The escorts became a corps of support. At that time the anti-choice groups were not picketing the clinic. They said they would leave it to the government to shut down.

Then the trial happened. Henry and Bob Scott, the other doctor working at the clinic, had been charged. Morris Manning was their lawyer, and a bunch of us met regularly with him. He knew that what went on outside would affect the trial. After the jury acquittal of Henry and Bob, Henry decided to reopen the clinic, and that's when the Right to Lifers decided to get involved. At a certain point, the Catholic Church called out their people, too. They had demonstrations Monday to Thursday, starting with about a thousand people and building to more than two thousand each day. But women kept coming to the clinic, no matter who harassed them.

The largest pro-choice demonstration up until then was two thousand people. CARAL was against organizing another one, because they feared we wouldn't be able to out-mobilize the Church. But we knew we had a lot of support from the media and the public. I never had a meal with Morgentaler in a restaurant when someone else eating there or a staff person didn't pay for it. Cameramen slipped me support money outside the clinic. OCAC felt we had to fight back, and even if we couldn't out-mobilize the anti-choice people, we had to stand up for ourselves. Once we decided to hold the demonstration, CARAL worked like crazy to build it. They were principled and dedicated to the cause. The media helped build the demonstration for us, by reporting every day on the anti-choice demonstrations in front of the clinic. Twelve to fifteen thousand people came out for our event. I think that demonstration was the turning point in public support for a woman's right to choose, because it demoralized the anti-choice people. Until that day, they really believed that they represented the majority.

The Court of Appeals overturned the jury decision, and then the case went to the Supreme Court. Morgentaler always said that the judges were against him but the people were with him. This was true until that case got to the Supreme Court. It took eight years from the day we opened the clinic, and it was a phenomenal struggle. But the day we won in the Supreme Court decision I remember people celebrating on the streetcar. People saw Henry as a hero—the little guy up against the system. Our eventual victory was a combination of his courage and peculiar form of charisma with our own great organization and a good lawyer, Morris Manning. By this point, we had ten years of experience in organizing, and the women's movement was at its height in Canada. The collective experience paid off.

Norma Scarborough

I was president of CARAL at the time the Toronto clinic opened. OCAC was much more involved in the clinic than CARAL was, but we thought it was a good idea. CARAL didn't have the savvy needed for that kind of an action, although there was no way we were going to admit that at the time.

I think CARAL did a good job. When feminist groups like NAC weren't paying enough attention to abortion, we would do what we did best, which was education. Then, when the issue came to public attention, a lot of people knew what they were talking about. Our work didn't have the pizzazz of what the left was doing. I understood that at the time, but I didn't like it. We were working very hard and not getting much credit. In retrospect I understand why. The basic quiet stuff needed to be done, but making the noise was what really got things going.

The shocking thing to me was the attitude of the anti-choice people. I personally got a letter that appeared to have human feces in it, at the CARAL office. That was horrifying, and there were a few of them. Someone sent letters with a thread coming out the end, making us think they were bombs. On the subway, a man and woman who looked straight out of a Norman Rockwell painting blocked me from getting off at my station and said, "Baby killer, baby killer, baby killer." Finally a couple of people noticed what was happening and pulled the alarm, and a security person came and got me out.

I was generally surprised at how well I was received in my own building, a seniors' residence, when they found out that I worked for the pro-choice movement. The day Henry won the trial, there was a group of people out in front of my building, and I got a standing ovation. There were some funny things, too. I was resting on my bed one Saturday afternoon, reading a book, when the phone rang. A man said, "You are a lesbian, cock-sucking bitch." And I said something like, I think you better come to the meetings to see what lesbians are about.

I think I was too much of a lady in those days. I did go to demonstrations and loved them, and over time I learned to appreciate them. I had a difficult time with CARAL's attitude toward OCAC. CARAL women felt we were the nice people and OCAC were the ruffians. Some people in OCAC put down people in CARAL, and I didn't like that, either. OCAC was having more fun than we were. I would much rather have been with OCAC, but I didn't think I knew enough. When it came to a counter-demonstration to the demonstrations organized by the Catholic Church, CARAL's view was that we couldn't pull off a big demonstration, and it was not a good idea to fail. But we had the sense to support OCAC when they decided to go ahead with it.

CARAL did raise a lot of money for Henry's court cases. We raised it almost entirely through direct mail to our membership. After Henry won the jury trial, Selma Edelstone, a close friend of his, took over organizing the fundraising for him. Henry would come to a board meeting and say he needed more money. Many people wouldn't talk about abortion publicly, but they were in favour of it, so they would send us money.

The women in my suburban neighbourhood had nothing to do with feminism. When I got involved in CARAL, I was isolating myself from that group. So I brought some of them to meetings. I would take four or five people from my bridge club, and they were really interested and excited by the idea. But women at the meetings, the Trotskyists, would get up with a tiny book in their hand where they had written notes and they would read the notes and always say the same kind of thing, and they scared the shit out of these people. Some of them thought they would be arrested just for being there. I used to get really pissed off about it, because I would get ten people to come to a meeting, and the left would scare these people off and they would never come back.

I was scared to death to talk to the OCAC women myself when I first met them. Once I got to know them, I realized it was just a difference in the way we looked at the world. I began to realize very quickly that the way they looked at the world was more realistic than the way I looked at the world. It was a huge experience for me. It helped to wreck my marriage. My husband married me thinking that I would be like his mother. I completely changed in midstream, and he didn't know what the hell to do about it. I am sure there were thousands of men who got hit the same way with women who went into the women's movement. I had been in the army, and life in the suburbs was boring. Being part of a group that was getting coverage in the newspaper was exciting. If I had been called a shit disturber, that would have thrilled me to the bone.

WINNIPEG

Ellen Kruger

I had formed a CARAL group in Manitoba, and Henry called me in 1983 about setting up a clinic in Winnipeg. We had tried to set up a clinic in the late 1970s and been shot down and betrayed. But he said he wanted to do it. He had the money and we had the organizational power. Henry came here because we had an NDP government. Initially, we had groups in Winnipeg that said no way, we support women's abortion rights but we don't support Henry Morgentaler. So we had all those things to iron out, and we weren't always successful.

In Manitoba we had learned well that political movements don't happen with one or two people. Any government, but especially an NDP government, has way more trouble turning you down when you've got a list of thirty organizations saying this is the right thing to do. Our coalition kept growing over the years. We had labour people, health people, women's movement people, academics; you name the sector, we had a group. There was a group of women working inside the NDP, too, and they thought everything was going to be fine.

From the time the clinic opened on May 5, 1983, all of us were blown away by how that movement grew. I've never seen anything like it, and I don't know whether I ever will again. Women we'd never seen before came with their homemade placards to stand outside and counter the anti-choice people. People were phoning, sending money. It was the early days of direct mail fundraising campaigns. Over a year, I think we raised nearly $100,000, and that wasn't counting the Morgentaler Defence Fund.

The media women in our group became our communications committee. We had a coordinated, professional pamphlet, a bus ads campaign and huge billboards. It was magnificent. One day I was riding the bus past the Morgentaler clinic, and some man made a derogatory comment about the clinic. A woman behind him, a woman in her fifties or sixties, said, "You leave women's business to women. That clinic needs to be there." Those kinds of things were happening.

Roland Penner, the Attorney General at the time, had previously been a member of the Communist Party. Howard Pawley, the premier, was sort of a good guy. He wasn't really strong on abortion rights, but we thought we could count on him. We had the highest number of women we'd ever had in the cabinet. Muriel Smith, a feminist, was the minister of community services. But Penner turned out to be a by-the-book guy. As we heard it, the Attorney General's department did not have a good working relationship with the police, and the police were going to enforce the law.

Henry opened the clinic anyway. The police let him know when they were going to raid, and they did. There was the horror of them parading seven women out and arresting them, women who had just had abortions, three of them still in recovery. It was horrible, horrible. The staff were all arrested. The clinic opened again, and there would be another raid. There were three raids within a short period. They'd confiscate the equipment, and Henry would order more. Re-equip. We were expecting Penner to put a stop to the raids, but he didn't. He said the Attorney General could not interfere with the role of the police. The women inside the NDP were trying to lobby and getting nowhere.

People were outraged. We had prepared notices that said, if the police raid, show up at the legislature at such and such a time, and hundreds of people showed up like that. For a while we were having rallies every week. People who had never gone to demonstrations were there. You'd see people who held high-profile positions there, too.

Prior to the raids, we had heard that the Manitoba Federation of Labour (MFL) wasn't going to be on side. But we went to the women's committee of the MFL and they voted yes and joined the coalition. The MFL board ordered the women to withdraw, because they said this was endangering their relationship with government. The women were outraged. I remember we had a rally sometime after that. As a good leftist you are not supposed to bad-mouth labour, but I thought, fuck this. So in my speech I attacked the head of the MFL, saying we in the women's movement had always been out there at labour rallies, because it was the right thing to do. Where were they? Some of the MFL women started an independent group, Labour Women for Choice. We had Lawyers for Choice, we had Doctors for Choice. People formed their own little groups.

We held a rally where Muriel Smith was booed. There were about eight hundred people out there screaming for the government to do something, and Muriel came out and started by saying there was nothing the government could do. People started booing, catcalling. I was weeping. Other people were weeping. Muriel was weeping, saying this. She was weeping in public as the minister of community services. We thought, how can she have ended up in a position like this? We knew she didn't support what the government was doing, but she was a member of the team. It was an awful moment. She ended up not being able to complete her speech. The government wanted to send somebody out to placate the crowd. They thought Muriel could do it. Send a woman out. In the end it was the Supreme Court decision in 1988 that allowed our clinic, not the NDP.

Muriel Smith

By the early 1980s, a lot of us women were making headway into the male world, making some gains. The gains weren't dramatic, but we were there and able to have some impact on the decision making. What we wanted was for more women to come along. We didn't always call it feminism.

Morgentaler came to Winnipeg, and a lot of us met with him and sympathized with what he was trying to do. We had five women in the NDP, three in the cabinet. The three of us in cabinet were all urban. The other two were a bit younger than I was. Politically, each party was split on the issue of abortion. The NDP were prepared to move a little, but they ran into the feeling that it was morally wrong. The most we could get them to do was expand the service in hospitals. We kept arguing that for women who were young, Aboriginal, less well educated, rural, it was still terribly difficult. We had made a little headway on it, but we had a very strong Catholic lobby throughout the 1980s. One of our high officials in the justice department wore the little feet thing, which was the symbol of respect for fetal life. It was a hot issue everywhere. On the health side, the NDP didn't believe in funding private clinics, so that was part of it.

A demo was coming up, and none of the guys would go out and speak on the steps in the front of the legislature. One of my beliefs about being elected is that you owe it to the people to explain what you are doing and why. So I agreed to go, even though some people felt I was setting myself up.

I told the crowd, I support what you are doing on a personal level, but you have a government that comes from all parts of the province, all ages, different religions, different beliefs. I got through that okay, and then I went over to the side. Someone came up and hugged me, and then the tears came. The media was saying, "Why are you crying? Because this entire crowd is out there booing you?" I said no, it is just such a complicated, difficult issue.

I had elected to stay in government because I thought it was better to have people on the inside pushing these things. To me, the political process is a collective process. You can still think your own thoughts, and argue for them, but some things require organization in order to get them done. If you pull out, then there is no chance. So I was sort of comfortable staying where I was, even though I was heartsick about it.

FOURTEEN

NOT A LOVE STORY
The Pornography Wars

Pornography is the theory, rape is the practice.

—ROBIN MORGAN, *THEORY AND PRACTICE:*
PORNOGRAPHY AND RAPE[1]

Sexist pornography is a product of the economic
and social conditions of our society—not vice versa.

—VARDA BURSTYN, *WOMEN AGAINST CENSORSHIP*

T HERE HAS NEVER BEEN a more polarized debate within the women's movement than the debate over pornography. While there had always been some discussion on the issue among women in Canada, intense organizing began in the late 1970s against snuff films, which portrayed women being killed as a sexual turn-on. Radical feminists held militant protests against porn theatres in Toronto and outside the Red Hot Video store in Vancouver.

Theory developed by American radical feminists such as Andrea Dworkin and Catharine MacKinnon saw pornography as leading to violence against women, and those who embraced this view called for censorship. Other

---

1. Robin Morgan was editor-in-chief of *Ms.* magazine from 1989 to 1993 and is the author and/or editor of fourteen books, including *Sisterhood Is Powerful* (Random House, 1970) and *Sisterhood Is Global* (Doubleday, 1984).

feminists argued that the state would use anti-pornography laws against those on the sexual margins of society, not against the billion-dollar porn industry. But the debate went well beyond censorship to encompass fundamentally different analyses of sexuality and women's oppression. Some feminists posited that all intercourse was rape, a discussion many heterosexual women found difficult even to engage in. Lesbians were divided among themselves on the issue. Some lesbians led the fight against pornography; others resisted what they saw as interference in their sex lives. *Pleasure and Danger,* a collection of conference papers compiled by American academic Carole Vance, revealed a women's movement deeply divided on pornography and on issues of sexuality and sexual expression. Some feminists argued that the women's movement was moving away from its roots in female sexual liberation toward a new prudery.

With the release in 1981 of the National Film Board's *Not a Love Story: A Film about Pornography,* pornography became a major issue across Canada. The 1984 report of the Fraser Commission on Pornography and Prostitution instigated a mainstream debate. Three years later, the federal government introduced Bill C-54, which defined pornography as including depictions of intercourse between consenting adults. After widespread protest, much of it from feminists who wanted only degrading or violent sex to be censored, the bill died on the order paper. But the pornography debate raged on. In several highly publicized incidents, Canada Customs seized sexually explicit materials bound for the Toronto Women's Bookstore and Vancouver's gay and lesbian bookstore Little Sisters.

LEAF, the Women's Legal Education and Action Fund, with the assistance of anti-porn activist Catharine MacKinnon, intervened in a Supreme Court case concerning a video store owner in Winnipeg. In the 1992 Butler decision, the court ruled that simple explicit sex was not obscene and accepted LEAF's argument of what harm violent and degrading pornography causes:

> *There has been a growing recognition in recent cases that material which may be said to exploit sex in a "degrading or dehumanizing" manner will necessarily fail the community standards test, not because it offends against morals but because it is perceived by public opinion to be harmful to society, particularly women.*

The Butler decision was initially seen as a victory for feminists. But support for it faded as mainstream pornography continued to flood into the country and gay and lesbian materials continued to be targeted by Canada Customs. Activists mobilized against the strategy that resulted in Butler, and LEAF backed away from their original position. Today, despite the proliferation of pornography on the internet, as well as through the more traditional channels, feminists who oppose censorship are probably in the majority.

NOT A LOVE STORY

Bonnie Sherr Klein

I worked at the National Film Board in Montreal from 1967 to 1970, then went to Rochester, New York, where my husband, Michael, was doing a fellowship. In 1975 Kathleen Shannon invited me back to join Studio D, the women's studio she had started at the NFB during International Women's Year. She had two producers, but there were no senior women filmmakers, and I took on that role.

Studio D was always the orphan at the National Film Board and had little production money. But there was an administrative glitch, and all of a sudden there was money that had to be spent before an April 1, 1979, fiscal deadline. We were all scrambling for an idea that could be done quickly. One day I went to a convenience store with my daughter, Naomi, then nine years old, and saw the usual "tits and ass" magazines. I wondered what kind of sense they would make to her. I knew nothing about pornography, but I had a hunch that it had something to tell us. When I mentioned it at work, it turned out all the women had stories about pornography that they had never formulated. It was obvious there was something here, a window in which to see sexism undressed. I didn't start out hating pornography and wanting to get rid of it, as things were later interpreted. I was thinking of it as one way to understand what was going on between men and women. I was anti-sexism, not anti-sex. Nor was I advocating censorship. I thought, perhaps naively, that once we brought an issue to light and it was seen and analyzed, everything would change.

I recruited Dorothy Henaut, a fierce civil libertarian, as producer. Our proposal barely squeaked through the NFB's program committee. Then none of the feminists in Canada wanted to talk to me about it. They all said it wasn't an issue. So we had to go to the U.S. I was later criticized for filming Americans, but nobody in Canada had wanted to deal with it. Pornography was thought of as a frill, peripheral to the meat-and-potato issues of the day like abortion, the constitution and equal pay.

We approached the research as a kind of Alice in Porno Land. We were asking questions and not out to prove a thesis at the beginning. Ironically, a small group of us women filmmakers had been meeting to make an erotic women's sex film, and I thought pornography might be a way in, or at least something to deal with so we could go on to explore a truly women's eroticism. We did research on lesbian eroticism; Kate Millett, a well-known American radical feminist writer and artist, had created some wonderful images. And there was some photographic work by men that we found erotic. We were anything but anti-sex, as later accused; our motivation was sexy. Part of me was open to the fact that maybe pornography had something in it for us, that it might be a turn-on and feed our sexuality.

Early on in the research, I knew I didn't want to be a voyeur, looking at women in the industry as objects. A journalist friend had interviewed Lindalee Tracey, a stripper who had started Tits for Tots, a strip-a-thon to raise money for a children's hospital. I met Lindalee and fell in love with her. She'd begun a feminist investigation of pornography before me. She had met women from the U.S. group Women against Pornography, but she felt they were anti-sex. She came to trust me and agreed to be in the film. Dorothy urged that if I was going to use Lindalee as my guide through pornography, I had to be on camera as well, to speak in the first person and not try to put words in Lindalee's mouth. I thought I stank on camera. Some critics later felt that I was proselytizing Lindalee. In fact, our relationship was very sisterly. Lindalee wrote a poem for my birthday saying that we were sisters, the Madonna-whore dichotomy. We filmed a scene that we didn't use where I bought crotchless underwear under her tutelage.

I changed my thinking about pornography by being exposed to it. It wasn't all cheap strip shows. There was hard-core stuff where most of the women were strung out on heroin. It was sad, pathetic and awful. There were snuff films, girls in poor countries who were killed in films. I went from wide-eyed innocence to seeing how violent and sick pornography could be. One accurate criticism of Not a Love Story is that it doesn't make a distinction between soft core and snuff films. It became a continuum for us, a consistent and coherent line. This was explained by poet Kenneth Pitchford in the film. People get desensitized. If the industry is dependent on greater and greater stimuli to create sensation, then there is no end.

There is some criticism that the film has a "male gaze." The director of photography was Pierre Letarte, since there was not yet a female cinematographer at the Film Board. Pierre was supportive and terrific, but there is one moment that makes me cringe. Lindalee insisted on posing for *Hustler*'s Suze Randall, and the film zooms in on her vulva.

We did test screenings as the film was being made. The big editing challenge was deciding how much actual pornography to show. I wanted to use the minimum, but we had to use enough for women to know what was out there. Women's reactions to the film were highly visceral. We learned to go to the women's room after the screenings because some women became ill or withdrawn. Men, on the other hand, usually felt incredibly attacked and uncomfortable. A lot of good men didn't want to be tarred with the same brush. It touched them somewhere primeval, where their masculinity was involved, and some reactions were really hostile.

At first, the Film Board said the film couldn't be released because it was too explicit. I think the male managers thought the film was too insulting to men. The ban made it all the way to the commissioner of film, François Macerola, who said that it had to be seen. He was willing to be courageous and was maybe smart, too, because the notoriety and popularity of *Not a Love Story* helped put the Film Board back on the map.

The first big public showing was the premiere at the Toronto Film Festival in the fall of 1981. It was terribly scary. It was a huge event. Jay Scott, the highly respected film critic for *The Globe and Mail,* called me a "bourgeois, feminist fascist." He gave everyone permission to yell and scream and go crazy. The audience reaction broke down along gender lines. Most women were incredibly moved, disturbed, grateful and often relieved. Some said it was a litmus test for their relationships, in terms of how the men in their lives reacted to the film. Some men were fine. Some thought Studio D hated all men. Lots of men hated the film with a passion. The way we survived this was that we had screened the film enough with women to know it resonated with their experiences. We were grounded as a studio. I give Kathleen enormous credit for her leadership. Journalist Michele Landsberg said Jay Scott's reaction was so off the wall that she knew something good was happening. She gathered ordinary people off the street to come to a screening and wrote a newspaper column about their reactions.

The New York opening of the film almost a year later was fabulous. The first night was for industry people, and that was very gratifying. The second night was sponsored by *Ms.* magazine. You could really see that the film was part of the women's movement there. It was important and embedded in the culture.

I was haunted during the editing and release of the film by whether there was a way of having it speak as strongly to women and not be as threatening to men. I would like to have succeeded in both. Kathleen felt that in speaking to women, it probably wasn't possible not to alienate men. My exposure to the world of pornography ultimately made the film come from a place of anger. Of the five or six of us involved with the film, everybody's relationships failed except mine. Living with pornography had made us all very vulnerable.

Issues of pornography helped open the door to the issues of violence against women. It was never my aim or illusion to stop the porn industry because I saw pornography not as a cause but a reflection. I resented for a while being known for *Not a Love Story* because I didn't feel it was my best work. Today, I am proud of it. I still meet women who say that film opened their eyes and changed their lives. Lots of men say that to me, too. How many things do we do in our lives that have that effect?

WAVAW

Susan G. Cole

Not a Love Story very quickly set off the sense that something was really wrong. That is the wonderful thing about the film in one way, and the thing that's wrong with it in another. The film got people going on the censorship issue because they were startled by their reactions. It got them to talk about something that wasn't visible before. The people who don't use pornography don't know what's out there. Women looked at that film and were freaked by it.

In 1976 we organized a demonstration in Toronto against a film called *Snuff.* It was made in Latin America, where it said "life was cheap," and the ads said that a woman was actually killed in the film. Killing women for entertainment was horrible enough, but to think that people were getting sexual pleasure from it was something that had to be spoken against.

The movie was at a sex theatre and was advertised in the mainstream newspapers. I made a speech at the Toronto Eaton Centre and then we walked down Yonge Street and shut them down. The killing in the film was very obviously a hoax, but it didn't matter. It was making money off the backs of dead women, or there was the implication that it was. We went every night for at least a week, and the opposition just grew and grew. Women had a gut reaction to it. It was a good, smart, grassroots demonstration. We took pictures of guys going into the theatre.

WAVAW, Women against Violence against Women, formed in Toronto after this. There were between thirty and fifty of us. WAVAW did a variety of things. We did an action on Remembrance Day about the women who are raped during war. The work started to coalesce with a development of the theory about violence against women. It changed the way we were organizing. When you're dealing with violence against women, it brings up the issue of how you feel about men. It created a really interesting discussion about men and where they fit into our practice of living and culture. It isn't fair to say that WAVAW was lesbian driven, but it was lesbian led. Lesbians were willing to look harder at things. Heterosexual women had more at stake. They would say they could separate out the violence and the sex. But if it's about getting off, it is about sex—sex and power.

The sex breakup, the split in the women's movement over pornography, is a more personal story. Because my feelings were so strong and I was so convinced of my beliefs, I was truly astonished when not everyone agreed with me. I met with incredible hostility from women I would have had harmony with on many other issues. It was a hard time in my life.

I went to a conference called Canadian Images in 1981 to talk about film and gave a rip-roaring speech asking people to rethink certain liberal values. It had a big impact, and Carole Corbeil, a Toronto journalist, made me the quote of the day in *The Globe and Mail:* "Pornographers do whatever they can to take away my civil rights, so why shouldn't I take away theirs?"

Some of the reaction I got was about censorship, but I also wanted to do analysis about patriarchy and sex. I was talking about it and writing about it, and then American writer Carole Vance published her book *Pleasure and Danger,* about female sexuality. There was a growing movement to see anti-pornography politics as anti-sex. The movement brought together both lesbians and straight women. There were conferences, and conversations about things like sado-masochism were brought to the table. There were serious differences among feminists. Orgasm was seen by some women as the most important thing, because sexual expression of any kind was considered a value.

Carole Vance came to town, and there was a meeting at Hart House at the University of Toronto. She gave a presentation, and I was supposed to respond. This had been promoted as an anti-censorship meeting, but that wasn't communicated to me. By the time I got up to speak, women were screaming at me. I was demonized. I was the embodiment of that politic. This was when I realized that the split was official.

Up until then I thought there was a way for me to make people see that what I was talking about wasn't against them. But our politics were too different. I thought politics like "Rape is the theory, pornography is the practice" and "All intercourse is rape" were positions that should be debated in a strong way. People were horrified by that discussion. I think there's a liberal strain that says sexuality is the last expression of individualism. But people have to look at their own sexual practice. I thought that was okay, that feminism should go into every nook and cranny. People used to come to me after I spoke about pornography and tell me they were turned on by porn. I would say, "You're not a bad person; it's how you've been socialized." I resented the misperception that I was in the "all women are victims" category of thinking. Women wanted to be empowered, but to assume that they were in every situation is not right. If feminists participate in S&M, it's not life changing; it's still the same habit as in the patriarchal model.

I didn't back away from the fight, because I was doing workshops with women working in women's shelters, and every time I got out of the city and out on the road, it was reinforced that women were touched by what I was doing. I stopped thinking that censorship was the answer, though, because I could see that it would be poorly administered under the Canadian Criminal Code.

Women against Censorship

Varda Burstyn

The first thing I ever wrote about pornography was in 1978, after a march by WAVAW on Yonge Street in Toronto in front of one of those so-called porn palaces. That a theatre would show something that encouraged some kind of sexual experience from watching a woman being murdered demanded protest, but should it call for censorship? If the woman was actually being killed, then the film should be confiscated as evidence of a crime, rather than calling for laws that said you couldn't show it. I didn't want the theatre owners to show it, but that was different from calling for state censorship. If this wasn't acting, then it should be treated as a crime. That's when I began theorizing about what approach to take to pornography and censorship. I was seen as a traitor by a lot of feminists in '78 because I differed over pornography. It was a hideous experience, and I didn't want to be involved in the issue ever again.

Unfortunately, I was not to be free of it. I was doing some film studies, and I ended up teaching courses on gender and film. Because of that, I was invited to serve on the board of directors for a wonderful film festival in Peterborough called Canadian Images, run by Susan Ditta. I believe it was the only feminist film festival in Canada, and Su involved other feminists to help her program. In 1981 the festival screened a short film from B.C. called *A Message from Our Sponsor*. It showed images of a man and woman having sex, and also images of women in ads. It asked viewers which was the greater obscenity: the way women were treated in the ads or the sexual images? Which was more offensive? I thought that was a good point. But the festival was busted by the Ontario Board of Censors and the festival's director went to trial. Her defence cost tens of thousands of dollars. This happened because she critiqued pornography. Suddenly I was on the board of an organization that was facing the full legal wrath of the Ontario government.

The next summer we programmed a day on pornography, and we showed *Not a Love Story*, which had been censored in Ontario. Irony of ironies, many of the women who eventually became part of the group Women against Censorship didn't like *Not a Love Story*, because they felt it lacked depth and led to conclusions that would be harmful to feminists. It was a film that showed sex workers as victims, which many are, but that's not all they are. A lot of women felt the film talked about pornography as a tremendous evil, without making room for shared fantasy between men and women. There was a lot of bad feeling about it.

Picture a beautiful evening in Peterborough and everyone gathered on Saturday night for the big event of the festival. *Not a Love Story* had been shown during the day, and I was moderating the evening discussion. Reporter Carole Corbeil arrived late to cover the event for *The Globe and Mail*. I was trying very hard to explain that there was a feminist position that was not pro-censorship, one that was critical of sexism but was not for censorship. But she left early and wrote me up as a pro-censorship feminist. "Here are a bunch of feminazis," she said, and she included me. Over the six or seven years that I worked on this, the mainstream press almost never understood that there was a feminist position against censorship.

It was a very painful debate. I did an interview for *Penthouse Forum* after my research showed that 60 percent of its readers were women, and I was attacked viciously for that by Catharine MacKinnon in *Broadside*, the Toronto feminist newspaper. *Broadside* then censored my piece defending myself. I was attacked as a pornographer, as an agent for pornographers and as someone who justified violence against women. I went across the country three times in the space of six years. Typically it would be me against three other people, and I had to stick up for the side that said censorship is dangerous and what we have to do is address the conditions that victimize women, otherwise, we will wind up in trouble. It was hard always being in the tiny minority. At the end of every one of my speeches, women would come up and say they agreed with me but were afraid to say so because they'd be kicked out of their groups.

To me, it seemed that all sexual representation got thrown in with pornography. To suggest women can't represent our sexuality is insane. That penetration is rape and that all men are rapists were important ideas in the current that I worked against. I thought there were more important things to address; for example, putting out our own media so that we could put out our own versions of sexuality and erotica. In 1987 I stopped and said I would no longer have my life taken over by the issue. We all stopped. At that point, librarians had mobilized against censorship, and a piece of legislation, Bill C-54, that had been put forward in the House of Commons was pulled back. So we thought we had won, and that we had enough legislation to cover what needed to be covered. But the anti-pornography women didn't quit. I remember hearing on the radio that the Supreme Court had passed the Butler decision that LEAF had been working in favour of, and that suddenly the laws of Canada contained language that American feminists had rejected and we were saddled with it. Even though I had worked for years to stop this, I couldn't continue, so I did not go back. By then I was working on reproductive and genetic technologies, which I think are much greater threats.

Sex is about our most intimate selves. One of the earliest things the women's movement said was that women were not sex objects. Of course we don't want to be objects, but we all want to be sexually attractive. And sex is biological; when we experience arousal, we experience it in our bodies, and our bodies and our minds are one. So we feel that our identity and our sexuality are closely linked. All of these things were fiercely provoked by this debate. There was also a crisis of political leadership in the radical feminist movement, in my view. To have an analysis that basically says men are the problem, I think brings you to a number of dead ends. If men are the enemy, then sleeping with the enemy became the worst thing. Women who were attracted to the censorship current and were heterosexual felt conflicted about that. We got viciously attacked as a result, and maybe we viciously attacked back, I don't know.

We brought these very private things out in public, and it was upsetting. We said over and over again that it was easy to see that *Hustler* and *Penthouse* were getting across the border and the authorities would never bust the kind of pornography feminists were concerned about. We have to empower women and change the way that communication happens. By censorship, all we are doing is empowering governments to have more power over people considered marginal or deviant or different: gays, lesbians, artists. The only thing that will work is to change how people feel and relate to each other, and the whole economics of sexuality, and that the women's movement failed to do.

FIFTEEN

FEDERAL POLITICS
NAC Becomes a Player

The thing I loved about NAC was that all these women got on the executive because they burned with a white flame about one particular issue.

—DORIS ANDERSON

B Y 1980 the National Action Committee on the Status of Women was a major voice for feminism and a truly national organization. Early debates on regional representation had been resolved, and there was significant representation from every province on the NAC executive. Almost every women's group in the country was a member, from the Imperial Order of Daughters of the Empire and the Women's Temperance League to rape crisis centres and the women's committee of the Communist Party of Canada. During an NAC debate on women in the military, women officers came to the mike to defend their role. When NAC took a position on prostitution, prostitutes themselves participated in the committee making the proposals.

NAC's annual general meetings in Ottawa, with as many as five hundred delegates voting on resolutions, often looked like chaos. The meetings were run using Robert's Rules of Order, but few of the delegates were familiar with the procedures, and the chair was as sisterly as possible in allowing for errors. More than once, something would be decided on the floor only to be reversed the next day after some backroom brow beating. But NAC's AGM was an extraordinarily open and democratic space. As in other large organizations, AGM resolutions were policy, but it was the NAC executive who determined priorities. In her book *Politics as if Women Mattered,* Jill Vickers calls NAC "a parliament for women."

The annual NAC lobby, held on the Monday following the AGM, was legendary. Members of each political party, including cabinet ministers and opposition leaders, were invited to meet with NAC delegates in an often raucous session. It was a tremendous media event, with delegates heckling and booing in response to answers they didn't like. Members of Parliament, especially ministers, were unused to such public disrespect, and they saw the yearly lobby as a trial. But the women's movement was so powerful at the time that governments did not want to risk boycotting the event. Brian Mulroney attended the year he was elected prime minister.

Despite serious internal debates in the early 1980s on the issues of pensions for homemakers, government funding for the organization and whether the NAC office should be in Toronto or Ottawa, NAC continued as a formidable force on the national scene. In 1984 it successfully sponsored the first and only leaders' debate on women's issues during a federal election. Two years later, NAC organized a broad opposition to the Mulroney government's proposed free trade agreement with the United States. And when Mulroney initiated the so-called Canada Round of constitutional negotiations in 1992, NAC took a highly controversial position against the proposed Charlottetown Accord, working alongside Aboriginal women from across the country to orchestrate its defeat.

THE FEDERAL LEADERS' DEBATE

Chaviva Hošek

In the late 1970s, when I was a professor at the University of Toronto, I joined the Ontario Committee on the Status of Women. Lots of impressive women were involved, and it was an interesting group. When I first arrived, they were trying to articulate equal pay for work of equal value. Child care was an issue. That committee was where I learned that you could write a brief to your government. I started learning what you could actually do as a citizen.

My first year on the NAC executive was '79 or '80. The organization was a shock coming from the committee on the status of women. NAC was riven with factions. There were old hatreds and new ones being formed before my eyes. So a lot of my learning at NAC was about conflict.

Basically, the problems in the women's movement reflected the struggles in the rest of the country. I learned about labour issues, pensions and pension reform, social policy issues, federal-provincial problems. I learned that the social comes before the economic.

I ran for president of NAC and was elected in 1984. The leaders' debate wasn't my idea; it was Valerie Preston's. Trudeau wasn't interested in women's issues, although he was the first to name a minister in charge of women's issues—Marc Lalonde, who was very supportive. Trudeau would never have agreed to a leaders' debate on women's issues, but because there was a new Liberal leader, John Turner, who had something to prove, and a new Tory leader, Brian Mulroney, who people thought might win the election, we thought they might go for it. Ed Broadbent and the NDP had nothing to lose. I didn't talk to the NAC executive but just started to organize it. I used the occasion of my media interviews as president to get stories about the gender gap out.[1] I was on the phone for three weeks and followed my nose to find a way to these guys. The last bit of the deal with Turner was done through Judy Erola, who had been in Trudeau's cabinet. I argued that this was an incredible opportunity and there were a lot of women's votes out there up for grabs. Somebody in Mulroney's camp had said, if Turner says yes, we'll do it. At some point, Turner said yes, and that was it.

Then the struggle to control the damn thing began. When I proposed the idea, the media treated me with complete contempt. After I got agreement, they descended on me like friends. I realized I was in trouble, because I didn't know how to organize the debate. The executive was angry at me for not talking to them first and also for putting us into the mainstream. But I wanted us to be paid attention to. I wanted us to have an impact. I thought the NAC lobby was good for getting women's feelings out, but not for making change. I had a fundamental disagreement with others about what NAC was. I thought it should be an instrument for change. Some NAC leaders used to say that we were going to get millions of women out on the street. I said, what if you can't? I thought people were giving their power away. So a lot of people were mad at me and thought I was doing the leaders' debate to enhance my glory.

The debate was held at the Royal York Hotel in Toronto, and hundreds of people came. It was broadcast during prime time. I had already negotiated

---

1. In the 1981 U.S. election, a gender gap was identified for the first time: Fewer women than men voted for Ronald Reagan.

with the three parties and all the media guys about who was going to be in the room and how they would behave. Suddenly the boys from the parties arrived and wanted us to do what they said. But we weren't going to respond with a "yes, master" attitude. It was an eye-opening experience. It was hard, but we got it done on our own terms. We managed to put women in political space as a legitimate group. We were responsible citizens talking about things that a lot of people cared about. It was a credible event, and it was perceived that way. Some of the Mulroney government's later reluctance to do the deep cutting we feared on women's issues may have come from that debate.

Most of the debates within NAC were on economic issues, and they were between the women in the labour movement and those who weren't. The union women were struggling for a voice in the labour movement and wanted the women's movement to support them. I found their styles harsh, punitive and personal. They assumed that if someone disagreed with them, that person was evil. I would say one of the reasons I'm a Liberal is that I know I can be wrong. I want to live and work with people who might countenance that they're wrong. The labour movement women couldn't deal with that. NAC was the harshest political experience I ever had. One of the big surprises for me was that the conflicts didn't drive me away. Fighting isn't my style, but I was shocked by the divisiveness and became angry about it. When the nice ladies in NAC gave way on the issues they believed in, I was shocked. I stayed because I cared about the issues and learned so much. My view is that you only change the world in the streets at revolutionary moments, and I didn't feel we were going to make the revolution. I wanted NAC to become a player on the national scene, and I have a sense of satisfaction that I achieved it.

Kay Sigurjonsson

Chaviva phoned to tell me that the parties had approved in principle a debate on women's issues. She was looking for somewhere to hold it, as I recall. I was assistant executive director of the Federation of Women Teachers of Ontario, and we had about a thousand people coming to the Royal York Hotel that same week, for our annual general meeting. So the debate ended up being there. That was a stumbling block for the Conservatives. I think they thought, quite rightly, that they would not be popular with an audience of teachers. But they came around. They didn't want to be the party that refused to debate women's issues.

The energy in that room was absolutely terrific. The leaders were really tuned in to every question. We had worked for days devising the questions. It was very laborious. Since nobody else was asking those kinds of questions, we had to explain the issues first. So the questions were endless. They were longer than the answers. It was an amazing opportunity to educate the public, if anybody kept watching after the first ten minutes.

I think that debate was the high point of NAC's existence. NAC developed some clout and had some strong leaders after Chaviva, but I don't think it was as political or as important ever again. Partly I attribute that to Chaviva herself. A lot of people were critical of her because she was in the backrooms of the Liberal Party. Some people thought she was too moderate; you know, all the sorts of criticism that the women's movement goes in for. We eat each other alive. But I thought her approach to the political parties was powerful. Because she seemed moderate, they listened to her. I think she had a real impact. NAC has tended to be antagonistic to government. There are lots of times it has to be, but that isn't the only way for an organization to behave. Chaviva had a different way, more collaborative. Yet on issues, she was as tough as anybody else. She was very, very smart politically.

THE NAC EXECUTIVE

Doris Anderson

What I loved about NAC was that, on the executive, you had women from traditional organizations, like church groups and the Y, and you had radical feminists, from rape crisis centres and women's centres and organizations that were about as far left as you can get. All those women weren't exactly great pals; I don't think I can say that. There was an awful lot to be done at our executive meetings, which were always on a weekend. We had to make progress on all kinds of policy, and plan what we were going to attack, and what we were going to go to Ottawa about, and everything else. The meetings were tense, and there was a lot of disagreement, but it was never about the main issue. It was about how we should do it. I always tried to get people together on the Saturday night for dinner, usually at my place, and get them talking. One night it was about how each of us had lost our virginity, and another night it was about how we got married, just ordinary things that happen in a woman's life. That broke down a lot of barriers.

I was brought into NAC as a peacemaker at a time of crisis. It seemed to me the organization went through a crisis every three to five years. NAC had an office and a secretary and a staff in Toronto, and it had been run by a Toronto group for a long time. At one point, another group of women came in, some of them from the union movement and some from organizations that felt NAC needed to be pushed on things like abortion and child care. These women wanted to move the office to Ottawa, have better representation across the country and get rid of government funding for NAC. Lynn MacDonald, the president at the time, was trying to push through these radical changes. They were greatly resisted by what I'll call the old guard. The dispute coalesced around an argument about pensions.

I ran for president that year. I got the job, and everybody thought I was crazy, because I was taking over this organization that was at loggerheads. I sat down at the first executive meeting and listened to both sides, and then I said, "Okay, I want this pension thing taken aside in a little committee with the two sides represented and I want it resolved. When it's resolved, come on back. If you can't resolve it, that's okay too. But it's off this table. We're not going to argue about it at every meeting." And that got rid of the fight, because when women got in a little group and they didn't have an audience, things were resolved very quickly.

I didn't think getting rid of funding from Ottawa was sensible, because then we would be spending all our time raising money. Since the government was already giving lots of organizations money, I thought, why not us? I found a middle road, and I stopped the nonsense that had been going on at the annual meetings, where women were getting at one another from the floor. A wonderful group of women headed by Jill Vickers and a couple of other academics chaired the meetings and we neutralized things. But the organization had to change. It was like a Toronto club, and it couldn't be run that way.

In the early 1980s, the government used to bring in groups like NAC to respond to legislation when it was still in committee after the first reading. We often made real changes there; for example, in the sexual assault legislation.[2] It was 1982, and Jean Chrétien was minister of justice. The government did an almost 180-degree turn, and that was because of the women who had been dealing with this issue for years and

---

2. The 1983 legislation implemented "rape shield" provisions to prevent victims from being questioned on their sexual history.

what they were able to tell the committee. I've always said that any money the government put into the women's movement they got back a thousandfold in good advice, if they listened to it.

FREE TRADE

Despite running against free trade in the 1984 election, Canada's new prime minister, Brian Mulroney, started to negotiate an agreement with the United States in May of 1986. The United States wanted the agreement to include all trade in services and intellectual property; unhindered access to investment in Canadian industries, particularly the energy sector; and limits on Canadian government policies that might reduce U.S. exports.

The labour movement and the left opposed free trade. Their initial concern was that Canadian jobs in the manufacturing sector would be lost. As feminist researchers got involved, it became clear that women in the textile industries would be the workers hit hardest, and that service workers would also suffer. Opponents worried that free trade with the United States would pressure Canada into creating a level playing field in social services. And the Council of Canadians warned that a broad trade agreement with the elephant to the south would be a risk to Canadian sovereignty. NAC's employment committee, always a site of left-wing activism, decided that opposition to free trade should be a priority for the organization.

Marjorie Griffin Cohen

I was a full-time mother teaching part time at York University when I joined the Ontario Committee on the Status of Women. After the Royal Commission's report on the status of women came out, I started this whole organizing of women workers in banks. I didn't know anything about organizing, so someone said call Madeleine Parent, and that's how I got pulled into NAC.

Usually there were not huge fights in NAC, and the organization would let people do what they were doing on their issues. The major tensions came with Chaviva Hošek, because she supported the Liberals. Because of that, we had to pass a resolution that no one from NAC could meet with the government by herself. There was a big change when Chaviva became president. Suddenly, all of NAC's literature said that we were a lobby group. But we didn't present briefs to Parliament thinking we would convince them through lobbying; we did it to get press coverage and to raise public opinion to force changes.

Every time there was a major policy issue—for example, on unemployment insurance—NAC would try to have a brief, so that we could understand what it was going to mean for women. The federal budget was an obvious opportunity to criticize the government for what it was doing. And in those days, we would have individual consultations with the finance minister. We were always outraged when the budget came out, since the finance minister would never talk about child care. Speaking out on all these issues added to our credibility.

I was on the NAC executive off and on for about fifteen years. I was on the board of *Canadian Forum* magazine during the Tokyo round of the GATT (General Agreement on Tariffs and Trade) talks in the late 1970s, and the magazine asked me to comment. I was interested in the issue because I wanted to establish a language and trades training centre for Latin American and Portuguese women, and we were interviewing these women to see what kinds of work they were doing. What occurred to me was that the industries those women were working in would be affected in a devastating way by the GATT. So I wrote an editorial in the *Forum* on this. Then there was the Macdonald Commission report in support of free trade.[3] Doris Anderson was on the editorial board of *Policy Options,* the publication of the Institute for Research on Public Policy, and she asked if I would review the report from a feminist perspective. So I did. I read the whole bloody thousand-page report and was outraged. I took it to NAC and said, "We have to deal with this issue."

At that time, 1985, I had just finished my Ph.D. My marriage had just ended, I was teaching full time at York University and I had two kids, ages eleven and fifteen. So I didn't have time for anything. Laurell Ritchie, who was on the employment committee, called and said, "A bunch of people want to get together on trade, and we want you to chair the meeting." I told her that I couldn't do it, and she said, yeah, yeah, yeah. But she was great. Later on, she did things like read the page proofs of my book to help me when I had to go out speaking. Doris asking me to do that article and Laurell getting me to chair that meeting really changed my life.

3. In 1982 the Macdonald Commission held hearings across Canada to determine a "consensus on Canada's future." Their report recommended free trade with the United States.

We had a meeting at the NAC office to see if we could put together a coalition. We held it there because NAC was considered a neutral organization. All the other organizations were suspicious of each other. After a great discussion in which everyone was very wary of everyone else, Abe Rothstein[4] said the main thing we needed was some letterhead. That was absolutely brilliant. It wasn't "What should we call ourselves?"; it was "What should we put on the letterhead?" So we said, "Let's be the Coalition against Free Trade."

Initially, we did a brief to go to some government commission, and at first we concentrated on industry. Louise Dulude, who became president of NAC the following year and was never a fan of mine, said to me, "I understand what you are saying in the brief about manufacturing, but you have not made a case about services. I think you need some research there." I was offended. I did not react well, but when I thought about it, I realized she was absolutely right. So this set me off to do research on the service sector. I ended up writing a book called *Free Trade and the Future of Women's Work: Manufacturing and Service Industries*. What was really important was that the discussion of the service sector came only from us, that is, NAC and me. You have to remember this was before we had seen the free trade agreements and their impact on services.

We had a tremendous effect across the country. We did amazing work on educating the NAC membership. We sent out briefs and pamphlets. I would go in sync with the Coalition against Free Trade, but I would speak on NAC's behalf almost every weekend. The main thing was to speak to women's groups, so that they could figure out what free trade meant for them. I didn't know what it would mean for women nurses or women farmers, but I would go and talk to them and tell them what I knew, and then they would go and do their own research.

I worked closely with the Steelworkers on trade, and also with CAW, the Canadian Auto Workers Union. NAC was central in initiating these coalitions against free trade. I don't think they would have happened otherwise. We had one hell of a time with the Canadian Labour Congress. They wanted the women's movement to be there, but they wanted to run the show. I am not the kind of person to agree to that. Let me just say that it was a steep learning curve. We eventually had showdowns. The CLC didn't do the work, but they wanted to control it. We learned to work together,

---

4. Abe Rothstein was a well-known Canadian nationalist.

but it was not easy. At the national level, Louise Dulude was the person responsible for starting the Pro-Canada Network. The other important thing was the research that was being done. We had good relationships with lots of academics, and they would come to our meetings. That was extremely important, because much of this stuff was quite technical.

I remember being out in Vancouver on a panel with Bishop Remi de Roo, who was representing the Canadian Conference of Catholic Bishops. We agreed to focus only on where we agreed and kept away from the issue of abortion. We were smart on both sides. The Conference of Catholic Bishops had very intelligent people, and at that time Tony Clarke was working with them.[5] Almost every other group would have been a natural ally for us, but that one was unusual. We held meetings in a convent in Quebec. I remember speaking to farm women in a convent in Bruno, Saskatchewan.

One of the most important things that happened around free trade was our communications. NAC had 650 member women's groups, and there was no email then, remember. That was the strength of the anti–free trade coalitions in general: our networks. We went from 75 percent of the population favouring free trade when the debate started to a time after the 1988 election when 75 percent of people were *against* free trade. We were able to change public opinion that much, because we had tremendous communication.

The federal government has been successful since then in taking away the money from these groups, so that they can't communicate. I always felt that NAC's funding was a problem. My major issue was that we should get away from relying on government funding. We could have financed the organization easily through individual membership. Your average women's group didn't have the money to contribute to NAC, but individual women could have.

THE CHARLOTTETOWN ACCORD

After the defeat of the Meech Lake Accord in 1990, Brian Mulroney was determined to find another way to get Quebec to buy into the constitution. In 1992 he initiated the Canada Round of constitutional negotiations.

---

5. Tony Clarke is now the director of the Polaris Institute and a key player in the anti-globalization movement.

Refusing to heed the warning of the 1991 Spicer Commission, the Citizens' Forum on Canada's Future, that there was a "fury in the land," Mulroney pressed ahead on constitutional changes dealing with Aboriginal issues, Western alienation, and Quebec. When his parliamentary committee failed to attract much attention, he opted for a series of people's constitutional conferences, which were organized by independent policy organizations and held in five cities. The conferences, televised live on CBC *Newsworld*, provided a democratic forum for debate. Delegates included politicians, academics, representatives from advocacy groups, unions and industry, and ordinary citizens chosen by lottery. All participants had access to the same information, and all of the discussion was public.

Based on its three-nation position, NAC argued in the first conference, held in Halifax, that Quebec should have different powers from the other provinces so that it could control its social programs, but strong federal protection for social programs should be maintained in the rest of Canada. The government called it asymmetrical federalism. A general devolution of power to the provinces on social programs, NAC argued, would not only weaken standards on existing programs like health care but also mean that no new national program, such as child care, would ever come about. NAC won that position in Halifax, and then again in Vancouver. In Montreal, unions defeated the idea of an economic union—free trade among the provinces—which would lead in labour's view to a race to the bottom. In Toronto, the Assembly of First Nations won the debate on the issue of Aboriginal self-government. In Calgary, the issue was a Triple E Senate: Elected, Equal and Efficient. NAC proposed male/female parity and made a successful alliance with the Triple E group to support proportional representation in the election of senators. By the close of the last conference, in Vancouver, it appeared that Canadians would get a constitution that women across the country could support, with protection for social programs and equality rights, a breakthrough in political representation for women, and Aboriginal self-government.

Judy Rebick

I was president of NAC during this time, and after the constitutional conferences we felt pretty good about where the accord seemed to be going. Then the premiers went behind closed doors with the Aboriginal leaders, and we started to hear from the Native Council of Canada, a group that represented non-status Aboriginal people, that things were going badly on our issues. Everything we had won, the premiers were doing away with. And not only were the premiers turning back almost everything we had supported, they had come up with this crazy Canada clause, which set up a hierarchy of rights and was a disaster. It was way worse than the distinct society clause ever was for women's rights. We asked for a meeting with the premiers. We met with all the people we could, to try to convince them to change the things we thought were important: changes to the Canada clause, Charter protection for Aboriginal women and no devolution of power to the provinces on social programs. But they weren't really interested in listening to us. It was power politics, and they didn't think we had any power.

Before the premiers went to Charlottetown for their final meeting, NAC held a women's conference in Ottawa. Then we went to Charlottetown and demonstrated outside the meeting. The Aboriginal women's groups were there, too. The premiers came out of the meeting with the Charlottetown Accord, and it was true: We had lost pretty much everything we thought we had won. The only exception was parity in the Senate. Bob Rae, the premier of Ontario, and Donald Cameron, the premier of Nova Scotia, said their provinces would support 50 percent women in the Senate. This was a significant victory for us, and it put us back on the media map.

NAC worked closely with the Aboriginal women's groups, but they were autonomous from us. We also had Aboriginal women on the NAC executive, Sandra DeLaronde and Reanna Erasmus. We always met with NWAC, the Native Women's Association of Canada, and talked with them about what they were demanding: a seat at the negotiating table and Charter protection for self-government. It was their position that they wanted the Charter of Rights and Freedoms to cover self-government, and NAC supported them in that. That was the hardest part of the fight. Obviously, Aboriginal self-government would have been a huge gain, but if the native women felt threatened without Charter protection as well, it was essential that NAC support them.

When a national referendum was called on the Charlottetown Accord, we had to decide what to do. Both the NDP and Canadian Labour Congress were supporting the yes side. They felt that with Aboriginal self-government and the defeat of the economic union included, it was the best deal we were going to get. In addition, there were four NDP premiers involved in the negotiations. NAC had never organized an electoral campaign, which was basically what organizing around a referendum was. NAC's constitution committee decided to present three options to the NAC executive without arguing for any of them, because it was such a big decision. At this point, Mulroney was saying that anyone who opposed Charlottetown was a traitor.

We went around the table at the NAC meeting. The thing about NAC is that it represents grassroots women's groups. Almost every woman at the meeting—trade union women, immigrant women, women from every province including Quebec, Aboriginal women—said, I've talked to the women in my community and they are against it. So it became clear that most of us were against the accord. Then the question became: Are we going to say no? If we do, are we going to lose our funding? Are we going to lose our organization? I remember Jackie Larkin saying, "It's true, we might lose our organization. But if we decide to say yes because we're afraid we'll lose our organization, then how are we any different from them? It is just opportunism. If we lose our organization, we'll build another one." And the Aboriginal women were telling us that the people in their communities, not just the Aboriginal women who were organizers, were against it.

I was the one least convinced we could carry off an electoral campaign. But again, the strength of the women's movement really came in. The night before the NAC executive meeting, Joe Clark, who was the minister responsible for constitutional affairs, called me to try to convince me that NAC should support the accord. I said to him, it is a little late; if you thought we were important, you should have negotiated something with us earlier. By that point the polls showed that the government was in trouble in B.C., and the government thought our position might influence the B.C. vote enough to make it a no.

We held a press conference, and we said no. The headlines everywhere were "NAC says no." Publicly, everybody denounced us. Not Bob White, who was president of the CLC—he never did. But Audrey McLaughlin (then head of the NDP), Bob Rae, all the Aboriginal chiefs, every ally we had ever had: Everybody denounced us. In the NAC office that first day, however, 80 percent of the calls were positive. The next day, 90 percent were. We got hundreds and hundreds of phone calls supporting us.

The Charlottetown Accord was agreed to by the First Ministers on August 28, and the referendum was scheduled for October 26. How we did our campaign, I just don't know. Email was just coming in then, so we were using that. Every night I would send out questions and answers, because we had women across the country who were debating cabinet ministers, who were debating politicians. We got invited everywhere to debate. It was really only Preston Manning, the leader of the Reform Party, and NAC who were high profile on the no side in English Canada, and the Reform Party was quite marginal then. We had every member of the NAC executive speaking and debating. It was incredible.

It was the most engaged I've ever seen the Canadian public be in politics. It completely changed my politics, that experience. People had a vote and they took it really, really seriously. They studied up.

The referendum happened, and we won. It was defeated. But that was one of the worst nights of my life. The CBC had a big panel, and I was on it. I saw one premier after another speak, and I thought, they don't get it. They don't understand what has just happened, and nothing is going to change. Ovide Mercredi, head of the Assembly of First Nations at the time, and Ron George, the head of the Native Council of Canada, were so upset. That was heartbreaking.

If you read anything on Charlottetown now, it says that the Reform Party was the opposition. People ignore NAC's opposition. Even academics ignore it. It was such a trauma for the elites to be defeated by a grassroots, populist campaign that they went into denial about it. On the tenth anniversary of Charlottetown's defeat, there wasn't one word in the media about it, even though it was one of the most profound political experiences this country has ever had.

So they wiped out what we did. And what did we gain out of doing it? Nothing. The government managed to bring in everything it wanted to bring in anyway, through administrative changes, and of course native self-government didn't happen. So even though we won the referendum, it was a defeat in a way. The one thing we did gain was that women from Quebec, women from English Canada and Aboriginal women were united for the first time on a constitutional issue.

The impact of the referendum on NAC was quite negative in some ways. Beginning around 1988, NAC had started to move left around the free trade stuff, and many liberal women left then. There was a debate about self-determination in the Palestinian territories, and a lot of the Jewish groups left over that. During the Gulf War, military women and Tory women left. Then there was a whole "NAC doesn't speak for me" mobilization during Charlottetown from white, liberal women who no longer identified with the organization. That campaign was very powerful symbolically. Governments felt much freer to attack the women's movement. A lot of the media decided they had given us too much power through our profile. And, of course, the federal and provincial governments were absolutely furious with us.

Sandra DeLaronde

A lot of the time in NAC I felt really out of my element because the issues were so different and the personalities were so different. But I always had the elders in the community. Before I left, when I would go back, or even when I was away, I could talk or phone up and get guidance. On this occasion, with the Charlottetown Accord, there were some very real fears in NAC about what would happen if they said no. I didn't think of it at the time, but that really had an impact on people's individual career paths, the personal costs that we were faced with during that campaign and after. It wasn't all roses.

I remember we talked about what our positions were, and then I phoned back home, up north to Le Pas, Manitoba, and talked to some women there. One of them, my grandmother, she said, "Well, whatever you decide, you know we will support you," so it was kind of like that. We talked about the spirit and about prayer. If it is the right decision, things will work out. We went back to the meeting with NAC, and I just happened to have my grandmother's shawl. I didn't always travel with it, but I happened to have it with me, so I brought it in and talked about our conversation. That shawl was over eighty years old, so it carried for me a lot of strength, a lot of the struggles that the women who had worn it had gone through and their strength to come through those struggles. So I wore it. People cried when I told them the story. It was like we had all achieved, or recognized that we would be achieving, a new level of growth personally. It also meant that we would have the strength of ordinary women who wouldn't normally be involved in this kind of activity. And it turned out that we did. So it was quite an amazing experience.

To me, that is what the women's movement is about. We may be talking about a three-nations policy, but who does it affect? That old woman living in a one-bedroom house or a two-room house in northern Manitoba who can't afford her hydro or her water, or doesn't even have water. Those are the people who make a difference. When the vote counts, their votes count too. About eight years after this, I went to a meeting, and there were some Metis leaders there, men, of course. One of them pulled me off to the side and said, "You know, I'm still angry with you." I said, "What for?" "Well, because you got up on national TV and said that as an Aboriginal woman you were saying no." And why did I do that when all of the rest of the leadership was voting yes? Well, it was the right thing to do. So I said, "Good for you. You've had a chance after all these years to talk about your anger. Now I hope you can let it go."

That is how passionate people were who were involved in the fight on the ground. Sometimes it brings to mind images of sword fighting or hand-to-hand combat, because that is what it felt like. It is one thing when you are fighting for issues with the mainstream community, because you've been socialized to think that they are the enemy. Aboriginal men and Aboriginal women fight together in the struggle. Then to be in a situation where you are the only one, and other people are really mad at you … it was difficult. There were a lot of tears and a lot of anger. I lost friends and relationships because of how intense the fight was. Meech Lake was more of a political debate. But Charlottetown was fought on the ground, and the anti-Charlottetown fight was led by women in every community.

THE NATIVE WOMEN'S ASSOCIATION of Canada, under the leadership of Gail Stacey-Moore, also waged a major battle on the Charlottetown Accord. NAC supported NWAC, but NWAC worked quite independently on their issues. First and foremost, they were demanding a seat at the negotiating table. The male-dominated Aboriginal groups, including the Assembly of First Nations, the Native Council of Canada and the Inuit Tapirisat, were all involved in the negotiations with the First Ministers.

Gail Stacey-Moore

I was president of the Native Women's Association of Canada during the Charlottetown Accord. What we were trying to establish was that Aboriginal women be given a seat at the constitutional table. We went all the way to the Supreme Court. The judgment came down, and it said that we were being discriminated against by our own men, but we still couldn't get a seat at the table. Every place into the negotiations where we could get an invitation, we had to go through a native group. Sometimes we could only sit at the back and not make any statements. The province of Quebec let us in, and we were allowed to speak there. The issue we raised first was that section 35, which recognized self-government, also had to recognize equality between men and women. We wanted to make sure that any future decision would cover equality. Section 28, the equality clause, covered those issues under the charter of individual rights. But section 35 was outside the Charter. Aboriginal women wanted to make sure that if section 28 didn't cover us, then section 35 would. The Aboriginal chiefs were against it. They didn't want to recognize the Charter. But we needed a legal mechanism for us to appeal to. After living a life of discrimination, we decided we couldn't trust the men. We had no laws or protection, because the Indian Act superseded the Human Rights Act. We knew that without legislation to protect us, we couldn't trust anyone.

We went to Charlottetown, and we found that we were locked out. Everything was shut down. The premiers and the Aboriginal leaders were having this private meeting and trying to get a deal before we got in to hear what was going on. I wondered whether I should crash the doors or sit and be quiet. I decided to wait and see what was happening. All the groups trying to get a say were locked out. Then all of a sudden the meetings were over.

We participated in the demonstration that the other women's groups held. I didn't have any problems with NAC over Charlottetown. Madeleine Parent encouraged me to get involved with NAC, but I was too overloaded with all the things I was doing with Aboriginal women. I found that it was a waste of my time to do anything but actively work on the issue. So many lives depended on it. I felt that NAC totally supported the Aboriginal women. We were closest with NAC over this issue. But when we tried to do a joint press conference, the media focused on NAC. I didn't get in a word. I knew then that we had to be on our own.

We made a video, and we got $10,000 to encourage Aboriginal people to vote no during the referendum. We got it broadcast because they had to give equal time to the no and the yes sides. Later, women told me they voted no because of the film we did. We had a lot of coverage. The Aboriginal men's councils continued to ignore us. In the end there was a big lobby to get me out of office, because the men saw me as too dangerous.

I felt we had a victory with the defeat of Charlottetown. It was short-lived, though, because we still had the issues to deal with. It had been a long hard struggle, and we still didn't achieve anything. Asking women to stand up against their brothers, sisters and fathers—that's no celebration as such.

I'm not a bra burner. I don't perceive myself as a feminist but as a strong matriarchal woman. When I met up with feminists, I thought I was one, but I started to see that because Aboriginal women are not part of the larger society, we're treated differently and have different issues. If there's anyone who's looking after their nations, it's been the Aboriginal women. I know that I am a true Aboriginal and 100 percent for nationhood. I see it as inclusive and not exclusive.

SIXTEEN

CLOSING THE WAGE GAP
Employment and Pay Equity

*Our struggle is not to have a female Einstein get appointed
as an assistant professor. It is for a woman schlemiel
to get as quickly promoted as a male schlemiel.*

—BELLA ABZUG

E CONOMIC EQUALITY was a key demand of the women's movement
from the beginning. The demand at first was equal pay for equal work,
but it soon became clear that the problem went beyond wage discrimination.
Women were ghettoized into a small number of low-paying "female" jobs.
During the 1970s and 1980s, many women fought for access to jobs traditionally held by men. Writing in 1982, union activist Deirdre Gallagher
reflected the enthusiasm of the time:

> *Women in the Canadian labour movement are proud of the many
> victories we have won in the last ten years. There are so many firsts it is
> difficult to count them all. The first women pilots, miners, the first women
> working on the green chain in the B.C. logging industry, the first
> women to climb telephone poles on line crews, the first women to work on
> the coke ovens at the Steel Co. of Canada—and, since the Second World
> War, the first woman electrician, carpenter, and tool and die maker.*[1]

---

1. "Getting Organized in the CLC," in *Still Ain't Satisfied*, Women's Press, 1982.

In 1979 Action travail des femmes launched a human rights complaint against Canadian National Railway in Quebec for discriminating against women. Eight years later, the Supreme Court ordered CNR to hire a woman for one in every four unskilled blue-collar jobs. In management and the professions, women hit what was dubbed the "glass ceiling," a male culture that restricted their climb up the corporate or organizational ladder. Feminist organizing made some inroads here as well, and women moved into law and medicine in larger and larger numbers. Journalists like Doris Anderson, Michele Landsberg and June Callwood inspired many young women to follow in their footsteps.

All this organizing led in 1984 to Ontario family court judge Rosalie Abella heading up the Royal Commission on Equality in Employment. The commission began by focusing on women in the public sector but expanded to include three others groups that faced discrimination: visible minorities, Aboriginal people and people with disabilities. The struggle for what Abella called "employment equity" broadened considerably as people with disabilities and people of colour took on a major role both federally and provincially.

One solution to the undervaluing of female jobs was what the women's movement called "equal pay for work of equal value" and the government called "pay equity." A sophisticated method was developed for evaluating jobs according to a number of criteria, including skill, effort, level of responsibility and working conditions. In 1977 the federal government adopted pay equity for workers under its jurisdiction—those employed by the federal government, Crown corporations and the 10 percent of the private sector that is federally regulated—through an amendment to the Canadian Human Rights Act. This was a step forward, although women still had to lodge complaints to get the process underway. Quebec passed pay equity legislation covering both the public and private sector in 1976, but the other provinces lagged far behind. The government of Manitoba adopted pay equity in the public sector in 1985. In Ontario, the Pay Equity Coalition successfully lobbied for a public and private sector law that was passed in 1987. As a result in part of these measures, the wage gap between women and men working full time shrank. In 1970 women made 60 percent of male wages; in 1994, 72 percent.

Women into Steel

Debbie Field

In the women's movement in the 1970s, we were preoccupied with moving from equal pay for equal work to equal pay for work of equal value. At that

time I was the equal opportunities officer for OPSEU, the Ontario Public
Service Employees Union, and the first equal opportunities coordinator
for a union in Canada. We were part of something called the Equal Pay
Coalition, and in all our work we were asking why women made 60 percent
of what men made. In the beginning we thought it was simply discrimination:
that women were being paid less for doing the same job. But quickly we
came to realize that this was simplistic. There were women's jobs and men's
jobs. So we realized that women's and men's wages would only be equal
when women went, in some measure, into men's jobs. We understood this
at one level in terms of doctors and lawyers, and at another in terms of
working-class jobs. When we started to think about how women could get
into non-traditional higher-paying jobs, storming the bastions of industry
seemed like a good idea. In OPSEU we didn't have industrial jobs, but we
had jobs like janitors, so we started looking at re-evaluating work. I felt
we needed women to go into these jobs. Some women were upset with me;
they thought I was sending a message to women in white-collar jobs that
we didn't value their jobs but wanted them to jump into men's jobs. I think
there was a certain romantic notion, a Rosie the Riveter kind of idea, of
women going into men's jobs at the time.[2] I was twenty-eight and relatively
naïve about the physical differences between men and women. This was the
kind of macho side of the women's movement: We could do this stuff; we
were going to do this stuff.

When we started the campaign around Stelco, a large steel plant in
Hamilton, I didn't visualize that I would actually wind up getting a job
there. I thought I was waging a political campaign to raise the issue of
women working there. Working-class women in Hamilton were coming to
the conclusion that their brothers and fathers were able to get better-paid
jobs than they were. So the objective reason for this campaign was that
the sisters, daughters, wives and girlfriends of men who were working
at Stelco wanted in. One of my good friends in this process was Joanne
Santucci. Her father and all her brothers worked at Stelco. So why couldn't
Joanne work at Stelco? The real reason for the campaign was not ideological
but economic.

It was also a nice moment in terms of union history. A guy name Cec
Taylor was the president of Local 1005 of the United Steelworkers of

---

2. Rosie the Riveter was the image used to encourage women to work in factories
during World War II. The graphic of Rosie was quite common on feminist posters at
this time.

America at Stelco. He was getting educated about women's equality and he was wondering, why are there no women in my local? A few women had started working there during the war, but there had been no women hired since then. In 1978 he gave an interview to the *Hamilton Spectator* in which he said, "My mother worked in the glassworks in England when I was growing up, and I know that there are lots of jobs here in the plant that women can do. I encourage any women who are interested to come on down to the union hall." So in fact, Cec Taylor started the campaign.

A bunch of us went down there. At the first meeting there were about eight of us. The fact that I was an organizer really helped, because it meant there were a lot of things I could do with Cec in that situation. We decided to have a campaign and call it "Women Back into Stelco." We worked on it for maybe six months. It's astounding what we achieved.

By the time of that first meeting, we had all applied to Stelco for work. When you went in and filled out an application, you noticed that men's applications went into the top drawer and yours went into the bottom drawer. We had all had the same experience. So someone said, "Let's file a human rights case."

I moved to Hamilton from Toronto. We started to have public meetings and hand out leaflets down at the main Stelco office. I enrolled in a machine shop course and learned how to use—badly—a hammer. We held press conferences and even had NDP leader Ed Broadbent at one of them. We were a women's group, but not like the groups I had known in Toronto. Most people weren't members of groups, but they believed that Stelco should not discriminate against women. Nobody did polling in those days, but I think if we had walked down the streets of Hamilton, 70 to 80 percent of the people we asked would have supported us. One of the best moments in my political life was the day I walked into my Royal Bank branch and the teller, who had seen my picture in the newspaper, said, "Way to go. We are all behind you."

Stelco argued that they already had too many qualified men and that it wouldn't work out in terms of women and men getting along and that they'd have to build separate washrooms. But their tactic was mostly to keep quiet. They knew we had a lot of community support.

Social movements are like rivers. They either flow or they don't flow. As a political leader, you can change the direction, but you can never start the river flowing. The Stelco campaign was a lovely process. There was a belief that women could work in non-traditional jobs. The river was there and we placed ourselves in a particular spot and changed a little bit how it flowed.

A relatively small number of us had laid the human rights case, and there was a larger group that functioned like a solidarity committee. We'd get together once a week and come up with ideas. We didn't have any structure. It was done on a consensus model. People would suggest things and we would either do them or not. We came up with a slogan saying Stelco should hire 10 percent women.

At that time, human rights cases usually took two or three years to be resolved. But in this case, there were key decision makers at the union, plant and government levels who were ready for the change. Someone at the Human Rights Commission fast-tracked this thing. We started in October 1978 and won our case against Stelco by March of the following year. I don't think that kind of class-action complaint had been accepted before, either. The commission said Stelco had to hire 180 women. And we got a settlement of $3000 each as backpay for the period of time from the date we had applied. We were stunned. We didn't expect that.

Five of us from the committee were hired, along with 174 other women. They divided all the women up. We believed that Stelco made a lot of shrewd and calculating decisions to ensure that it would fail. The woman I worked with was totally hostile to feminist politics. She was there for the job. Even though the union wanted us there, no one had really thought through what it would mean. Washrooms and showers were a huge issue. The women had a trailer in which to change their clothes and take a shower, and we had to walk huge distances to it. We had to share a washroom with the men. They put up dividers so we couldn't see the urinals. So you would walk into the washroom and there would be an older immigrant man who was totally mortified because he had just finish peeing. Stelco should have put us all together on the floor so we could create a culture around women. That would have worked better.

Things started really well, with a hundred guys on a bridge overlooking Hamilton Bay clapping as we walked in. By the end it was pretty bad. In my area, we got into a lot of stuff around sexual harassment, in terms of pin-ups and graffiti and that kind of thing. Not all of us could do the work. I was put into the coke ovens, and a lot of the other agitators were put into tough jobs. The primary process was like hell—heat and fire and all this kind of stuff. The whole plant was rough and dirty, but there were lots of jobs in the mill that weren't that tough. There were lots of health and safety violations where we were, too. In the first month I was there, one guy died of stomach cancer and another of lung cancer, and everyone was concerned that their illnesses were job related. This was the beginning of the health and safety movement.

I had been a leader in the union movement, and I expected to be a leader coming in to Stelco. In retrospect, I wasn't patient enough. I should have spent a lot more time listening and not imagine that I could lead this thing. I was a middle-class woman; I had been a college teacher and a union organizer. The workers could not figure out who I was or why I was there. And we were very earnest in the work we did in those days. We were there for about a year and a half. There was a strike then, and after the strike all the women were laid off: last hired, first fired. The only women there now are professional women. Stelco still has a hiring policy for women, but because of the continual downsizing, it hasn't meant anything.

From the little bit that I've read about women who have gone into mining or lumber, I think we were naïve about what it takes to go into a male workplace. One needs some understanding of the difference between male and female. Part of what goes on in a brutalized, unsafe working environment is that guys survive by developing a macho culture. When you bring women in, men feel awkward. They are on their best behaviour for a period of time, and then something happens, like a woman can't quite carry the same load. In our case, Stelco had hired some summer students, and one of the guys wrote graffiti about one female student in the washroom that I took offence to. I got into an escalating graffiti war with them, which in retrospect I shouldn't have.

But it was a fantastic experience, because one of the things I learned is that the men I worked with understood everything more than I did. They understood the labour theory of value.[3] They understood how the system worked. They didn't disagree that they should have better working conditions; they just didn't agree that something like a random work stoppage would work. After a few months at Stelco, I realized that my entire vision of how the revolution would happen was wrong. No amount of my talking to these guys or leading actions against injustices in the workplace as I saw them was the proper solution. It was a tremendously humbling experience in terms of understanding the complexity of

---

3. A Marxist theory that explains that the value of an object is dependent on the work that has gone into producing it.

working-class consciousness and how sophisticated these guys are. They're wonderful. I had a fabulous time. I played cards and became a great euchre player. I still believe that the majority of guys wanted this to work. If we had been less naïve, we would have met with the shop stewards and the management to discuss an entry plan and how conflicts and differences of culture would be resolved as they emerged. So it was a fantastic experience, but not as good as it could have been. I wish we could have developed a strategy that would have stuck for generations.

Employment Equity

Flora MacDonald

In 1984 I was in the toughest cabinet post anyone could have, minister of employment and immigration. When I came in as minister, Canada had a 12 percent unemployment rate, and immigration was being, as usual, immigration, with myriad problems. It was the heaviest caseload department by far. But I always felt there was change needed within the public service. My predecessor had appointed a one-person Royal Commission to look into limited aspects of equity in the public service. The commissioner, Rosalie Abella, came to me shortly after I was made minister and said, "I would like to have my mandate enlarged." I said, "Rosie, take the whole thing, whatever you want." It was on that basis that she wrote her report, using the term "employment equity." She did not want to follow what the Americans had done in affirmative action, which had greatly congested the courts. It was the autumn of 1984 when she first approached me, and she gave me her report six months later, or less. And within six months I had legislation before the House.

The legislation took a while to get through the various committee stages, because so many organizations wanted to appear before the committee at second reading. There were those who were violently opposed to the object of employment equity, and those who were supporting it in a very moderate way. Generally, there wasn't a great deal of support. The opposition came both from those who felt there should be nothing and those who felt there should be much more. I had a lot of difficulty with women's groups, who were saying, "Why haven't you done this, this, this and this?" To me, they didn't understand the reality of the House. They didn't grasp the strength of the opposition to anything like this or the need to get it through so that, once enacted, you could build on it. That has always been my way: If you

can't get everything you want at the outset, get at least the basis that will
allow you to build.

The women's groups suggested any number of modifications, some of
which we adopted. I did a fairly good selling job on the caucus. When I
started talking to them particularly about the rights of their daughters
and granddaughters to have equal opportunities in developing careers and
getting jobs and so on, eventually most of them came around. Some of
them were outspokenly supportive.

So, there was sufficient support in the House to get it passed. Then I had
to get it past the Senate, which was more difficult. There were four categories
of people in the legislation: women, native people, disabled people and
people of colour. The greatest opposition came from those who were
disabled. They didn't think the legislation went far enough. They flooded
the galleries and stood up and shouted at me, because they wanted things
much, much more open for disabled people. And in the end, the people
who have worked hardest at taking advantage of that legislation are people
with disabilities. You will see that as you go through the public service.

Judy Rebick

I got involved in employment equity because my boss at the Canadian
Hearing Society was co-chair of the Coalition for Employment Equity for
People with Disabilities, and he asked me to act for him. The group was full
of amazing activists with remarkable spirit and energy. We didn't like the
federal bill that Flora MacDonald had introduced in 1986. It was weak,
because employer compliance was voluntary, not mandatory.

We organized a demonstration of disabled people on Parliament Hill
when the bill was being debated. We got the CNIB to provide buses and
drivers. There must have been two hundred of us. Almost everyone had a
disability of some sort—deaf, blind, in wheelchairs … I'm sure they never
saw anything like that before on Parliament Hill. We asked permission for
wheelchairs to go on the floor of the House, but the Speaker said no. Beryl
Potter, the co-chair of the coalition, was a triple amputee, and there was no
room for her wheelchair in the gallery. So she demanded that a security
guard put her in a regular chair. She wasn't going to miss that debate, even
if it meant her falling onto the floor. Needless to say, the security guard
found room for her wheelchair. Once the debate was over, people were
pretty upset, because they weren't going to change anything in the bill.

Beryl called to Mulroney in the corridor, saying, "I voted for you, Prime Minister, and you betrayed me." That clip was on every TV newscast.

The disabled people led that struggle and later led it again in Ontario. Our coalition of equality-seeking groups at the federal level set the stage for the equality-seeking coalitions that played a big role in the court challenges program later. The idea of the four groups came from Rosalie Abella's commission, but it ended up being a long-term coalition.

The Alliance for Employment Equity in Ontario, initiated in 1987, was mostly a coalition of people with disabilities and what we called at the time visible minorities. The labour movement played a role later on. But the white women's movement never played much of a role, although NAC did some key research. I worked with a young graduate student named Phebe-Jane Poole. She did some amazing research into the hiring and promotion practices of federally regulated employers, using the employment equity reports they were required to file under the legislation. She even managed to get stats on the situation of doubly oppressed women: women of colour, disabled and Aboriginal women. It was a terrific piece of work. I think it did have an impact, especially on some of the banks.

In Ontario, the Alliance met with labour and the NDP, and we drafted a model bill that was fed into the NDP's law once they formed the next government. I wasn't keen on the strategy, because employment equity is quite complex to implement. The big issue was quotas, which we called "targets and timetables." Our draft bill insisted that employers meet certain targets and timetables as a way of measuring their progress.

One of the interesting things about the Alliance for Employment Equity was that there were almost no tensions along racial lines. That was striking to me, because the women's movement was going through such a tough struggle on race issues at the time. I think two things made the difference: first, that white, able-bodied people were a small minority in the Alliance, and second, that we had all formed the group together. The women's movement was founded mostly by white women, and then women of colour had to fight for their place. I think that's what made the difference.

The NDP was elected in Ontario in 1990. We had already worked with them on drafting a bill, but getting it into legislation was a whole other issue. The NDP was pretty gutless on this issue, in my view. They brought in legislation that was stronger than the federal law but still didn't require employers to meet targets and timetables. And the NDP never really defended the bill. It *did* require positive action by employers to hire and promote groups that faced discrimination in the workplace, but the minister in charge kept denying that that was true, instead of explaining why positive action was important. The backlash against equality rights was getting pretty fierce by this time, and the first thing Mike Harris did when his Conservative government got elected was to repeal what he called "the quota bill."

Winnie Ng

The Coalition of Visible Minority Women got involved early on in the Alliance for Employment Equity. Sexism and racism are wings of the same bird of oppression. That was our key point to put on the Alliance agenda. Whatever suggestions you made in the Alliance were backed up by others. It was a good process. There weren't tensions on race grounds in the Alliance. We were all in the same boat, and it was clear that we were after legislation and government response to address systemic barriers. On the pay equity issue, women of colour and immigrant women were totally left behind; we weren't included in the process, and our issues weren't raised. But on employment equity we were very involved.

Amy Go

I was involved in employment equity on behalf of the women's committee of the Chinese Canadian National Council. One of the key issues was how big a workplace needed to be, to be covered under the employment equity legislation in Ontario. We thought it should be fifty people. For fifty people, you would have full coverage; fewer than fifty, there should be a more simplified process. But in the end, the ministry made it a hundred, which left out the majority of small businesses in the province. The day the minister announced that, we were really upset. We called a press conference, and then the community groups all met and came out to say this was not what we wanted. We held rallies and we did a lot of lobbying. We met with sympathetic people inside government. Our strategy was multi-layered.

There was a piece of legislation, so that was success to a degree. Various groups had been talking about employment equity for years and years and years, and I think it happened because the NDP government came in. But to tell the truth, they brought the legislation in too late. They took too long trying to find compromises with the business community.

PAY EQUITY

Mary Cornish

I was a labour lawyer, and I started working on the question of pay equity in the early 1970s. Laurell Ritchie and I met in the sauna of my apartment building, and we decided that we should form a group in Ontario, which subsequently became the Equal Pay Coalition.

The Conservatives were in power in Ontario at the time, and we lobbied them and the two opposition parties. The coalition had connections with both the Liberals and the NDP, which was unusual. The union movement liaised only with the NDP, but we had business and professional women's organizations within the group too, along with the YWCA and other community agencies. Partly why we had these groups was because we didn't want anybody saying, "Oh, but you know what would be okay? If we just had some education, then employers would learn how to pay women better." Our common message, and keeping people together, was the key. When the Tories were defeated in 1985, the Liberals formed an accord with the NDP to rule. Because of our lobbying, equal pay for work of equal value was on the platforms of both parties. We then went into intensive lobbying of the government around what the content of the law should be. Because people had different interests, this kind of lobbying was a fairly tricky thing, but we managed to keep it together.

The law was passed in July 1987 and came into effect on January 1, 1988. Manitoba had a law that covered only the public sector, but one of the key things in Ontario was that we had a law covering both the public and the private sectors. Once the business community sorted this out, it was appalled. There was fierce opposition, and we ended up having consultations around the province.

It was a stunning victory when we actually got the law. The fact that it applied to the private sector was extremely important, as was the fact that employers had a proactive obligation to go out, make plans and address the adjustment. In other words, they were not allowed to sit around and wait for somebody to complain against them. They had to review their own classifications. The federal system is still complaint based. People have been lobbying ever since it came into effect to make the federal law proactive.[4]

---

4. Since 1977, section 11 of the Canadian Human Rights Act has specified that it is discriminatory to establish or maintain different wages for men and women doing work of equal value in the same establishment.

If you look at the implementation of the legislation in Ontario, all kinds of women didn't get enough. The people who got money were essentially unionized workers. Non-unionized workers had much more difficulty accessing the act. The private sector, with its small workplaces, was very, very difficult. So the law wasn't a panacea for achieving immediate income equality, but it went far beyond what anybody else had ever gotten. After we had finished lobbying for the bill, I started litigating a whole number of the original early cases.

From the point of view of a strategy for the women's movement, the Ontario law provided significant sums of money to women who had never had it before. Pay equity also required people to rethink the value of women's work. That had a significant effect in the workplace.

SEVENTEEN

AIN'T I A WOMAN?
DAWN Canada

Sojourner Truth told you already, "Ain't I a woman?" She asked the white feminist movement on our behalf, a hundred years ago, and the white women of North America have yet to face the answer. She served up the question; we need do no more.

—LEE MARACLE, *I AM WOMAN*

THE DISABLED WOMEN'S NETWORK Canada (DAWN) was established in June 1985 when a group of feminists with disabilities met in Ottawa to discuss women's issues. As the organization took shape, DAWN identified six key areas of concern to women with disabilities: mothering, self-image, empowerment, health, sexuality and violence. DAWN's mission since the beginning has been to end the poverty, isolation and discrimination experienced by women with disabilities. In addition to the discrimination against them as women, which they share with their able-bodied sisters, women with disabilities face massive barriers to their full participation in society. DAWN became a lifeline for women all across the country.

Many of DAWN's founding members were activists frustrated with the sexism of the disability rights movement. But DAWN's goal of creating a bridge between women with disabilities and the women's movement was not easily met. By demanding both physical access to women's services and events and the right to be heard, women with disabilities forced the women's movement to look at a whole new set of issues. For example, DAWN's exposure of the widespread violence against women with disabilities added tremendous depth to the feminist analysis of sexual abuse and violence as an issue of power. But despite tremendous progress, the battle for access is ongoing. The women's movement was less open to women with disabilities than to many other groups. The battle for access has not yet been won.

Pat Israel

All the years I was in the disability movement I was fighting the disability movement, because it was extremely sexist back then, extremely. For example, you couldn't get disabled people to use the word chair, or chairperson; it was like, "Pat, the term is chairman; that always includes women." I'd be having this struggle over one little word, but to me words are what change the world.

Back when women's shelters were developing and on a roll across Canada, we weren't there. We weren't there in the groups meeting about them, we weren't there pressuring them to be accessible, so most women's shelters across Canada were inaccessible to us. We had big issues. We didn't even have ramped curbs back then. We were facing curbs this high in any city in Canada, in any town. There was no transportation for persons with disabilities. There was no housing. So we were working on really basic issues.

I was in this major disability group, COPOH, the Coalition of Provincial Organizations of the Handicapped, but I didn't know another disabled feminist. Then all of a sudden people started saying, you need to talk to Pat Danforth. She is just like you. And I went, okay, I'll keep that name in the back of my head. And then I heard, you need to talk to Yvonne Peters. Finally I met Yvonne at a meeting. I was like, thank god there is someone else, because it was really lonely. It was really lonely being disabled, feminist, and literally the only one in Canada. Yvonne was a blind woman with a guide dog. She is a lawyer now, a smart, articulate disabled woman and a total feminist. So there it was. Finally we had two. And when we reeled in Pat Danforth, there were three. Pat was from the West, and so was Yvonne. I still didn't know anyone from out East. We were meeting at COPOH meetings, and then running off and talking. That was the beginning.

It was at least another year before the official DAWN Canada would have had its founding meeting. First we decided we needed to have a women's section within COPOH. That's what women always think—we can do it within the main group. You can't. You can't do it. COPOH were trying to be nice and trying to be open, but they were like, you can't put radical feminists in a mixed disability group. What they really meant was that women's issues were not their issues. They didn't want to hear about the abuse and rape of disabled women—that stuff is pretty darned scary. Not that they didn't deal with sexuality—they did. But the abuse stuff, which surfaced really fast within DAWN, shocked a lot of people, scared a lot of people. It didn't scare us. It did not surprise disabled women that there was abuse of disabled women. But the system that was supposed to help women was totally blown away by it.

Our first real meeting of disabled women was funded by the Secretary of State. Sec State funded both women's groups and disabled groups. We had a hard time getting funding, because we claimed the right to get funding from both sectors. We said, we are women with disabilities and we are women. We want money from the disability program and we want it from the women's program. People kept trying to pigeonhole us by saying, you are disabled people. We would say, no, we are not. We are women first and we are disabled women, and that is different from being disabled men. We have children, we are abused, etcetera. We were going into people's brains in a way they had never seen.

So it came to the first meeting, in 1985. It was supposed to be national, and it was going to be in Ottawa. The Secretary of State was trying to pick who came to this meeting. And we said, how do you know who the disabled feminists are, 'cause we don't even know them. They'd say, there is a woman in a wheelchair in Halifax, and we think she should come. And I'd say, why should she come? Well, she is in a wheelchair. Yeah, so? What has she done in the women's movement? How is she connected with feminists? Is she connected with feminists? No. They were designing it so it would fail. You can't bring a non-feminist into a meeting with feminists and expect her to fit. And I was adamant that we have disabled lesbians at that first meeting. We had Joanne Doucette, and she was very forthright, very open about being a lesbian. We didn't have any identifiable disabled bisexual women then. I identify as bisexual now, but I didn't back then. But at least we had Joanne. Some of the other women turned out to be lesbians as well. That was really important. I didn't want us to have to fight that battle later on within DAWN. I wanted lesbians front and centre at the first meeting.

At that first meeting, we had fifteen or twenty women. The odd woman brought her husband. These guys were attending caregivers who sat in at the evening reception, but we told women, no, they are not sitting in on the meeting. We were very forceful on that. The first night one woman started screaming, "You hate men," la dah dah, which we knew would happen. But the meeting was amazing, and it was facilitated by a really neat facilitator who helped the group gel over the weekend, as a good facilitator does.

That was the beginning. That meeting was to bring disabled women together to help set up DAWN. We figured out the name there—DisAbled Women's Network Canada. We agreed to go out and form groups in our provinces. A good core was there: Joan Meister and Shirley Masuda from out West, Joanne Doucette and me from Toronto. Pat Danforth. Yvonne Peters. Gwyneth Matthews, who didn't end up doing a lot of work on disabled women's issues, had written that book which was interesting, stories from women with disabilities.[1] So DAWN Toronto, DAWN Ontario, DAWN BC, DAWN Saskatchewan formed, and a number of groups started having meetings. Each one had its own distinct flavour.

DAWN Canada was the national group. We identified abuse as the top issue, right there at our very first meeting. Women sat there and said, yeah, I was abused. Almost every woman said something, so we knew that was the biggest issue surfacing right then. DAWN Canada got funding to write position papers, make contact with women's groups, that sort of thing.

I had gone to a NAC meeting a couple of years before DAWN started. I checked with them first. I said, I'm in a wheelchair. Will I have to use any back doors? Will I have to travel in a freight elevator to get to the room? No, no problem. I checked several times. Then I get there. The first night the meeting is at the Château Laurier hotel, in a huge room. There are hundreds of feminists in this room. I can't even get in. There is a little wee balcony with stairs on each side to go down. So I am sitting there saying wow, isn't this an interesting picture.

Women of colour fought for the right to be included in the women's movement. If there had been a sign that said "Women of colour must sit behind this barrier at the NAC meeting, and they are not to go any further," do you know how many women would have stood up and walked out of that meeting, saying, "This is wrong," "This is racist," "This is unjust"? My barrier was the stairs. If you turned and looked and wondered why there weren't disabled women on the floor, you would see me up there behind my barrier. No one came up and asked, are you okay? No one came up and said, this is really bad, how can we help you? Nothing. I just sat there and thought, wow, this is a lot of work. It is a real, clear indication of how

---

1. *Voices from the Shadows: Women with Disabilities Speak Out* by Gwyneth Matthews (Women's Press, 1983).

unwelcoming the women's movement is to us. I had to use the freight elevator to get to some meeting rooms. When I say freight elevator, I'm talking, you go through the kitchen, you get into a stinking freight elevator in which they move garbage, where there is food on the walls and there might be broken glass on the floor. That is how I got to many of the meetings with this women's group.

A couple of years later, Yvonne and I went to another NAC AGM. Of course, Yvonne had no Braille offered to her. They knew she was coming, but there was no Braille offered to her. I again had the freight elevator bullshit routine, and I was really angry. We asked the head of NAC, why did you pick this hotel? She said, well, we got a really good deal. And I said, well, you got a really good deal on the backs of disabled women, because they couldn't come to this. That was a top leader in the women's movement. Not all top women were like that. You would always find women who were ready to say, I understand your issues, and how can we make them better? But we had to raise our issues ourselves. I did sit on the board of NAC for a couple of years. I thought it was important to get in, right in a women's structure, in a women's group, be there at the meetings. I had no trouble getting elected and no trouble serving. I think when women heard me give my talk about wanting to be on the NAC executive, they understood. That was after a couple of years of DAWN being highly visible, highly there.

Sec State started saying to women's groups, you must make sure DAWN is invited to your meetings. So you'd get a call from a women's group and they'd go, "Um, we're having a meeting and we've been told to call you. Can you send a blind woman, because we have a lot of stairs where we are meeting." And I'd say, "So you are having an inaccessible meeting and you are asking me to send a blind woman, so that she can walk up the stairs. I, as the rep who lives in Toronto, cannot come to this meeting." After a while, big meetings did get better, they did become more accessible.

We did start to see agendas for conferences that would say "women with disabilities," blah blah blah. After a number of years I stopped presenting workshops at NAC conferences, because I got fed up with non-disabled women not showing up. I would go off to do a workshop on, say, how you can incorporate disabled women into your organization. Two women out of eight hundred would come to my workshop, and one of them would be disabled. That showed me that women didn't want to learn. They were willing to let us come or to organize all the access, that was okay, but for them to learn for themselves and start doing it right, they were not willing to give up an hour or two at a NAC meeting. We used to get calls all the time: How do you plan this? How do you do that? We put together a brochure, "How to Plan a Meeting to Include Women with Disabilities," because we got so many requests. But when you would actually have the workshop, you'd get a complete lack of interest. Finally I just started saying, don't ask me to do a workshop at your conference; you do the investigation, and you do the workshop. It was kind of like women of colour would say, white women need to educate themselves about racism; they need to learn; they don't need to have us come in every time to educate them. I started to feel that way about non-disabled women.

As DAWN developed and grew strong, the disability groups were growing a little worried about us, a little worried that we were taking money that they should have gotten. So we were fighting that on the other hand. Disability groups would say, you should not have your own group, you don't need it. So I'd go to a meeting and ask, have you tackled the rape of disabled women? How come all of the women's shelters are not accessible? DAWN had to struggle with every women's shelter across Canada, almost individually, to try to get them accessible. The disability movement never did a thing, and yet here they were trying to make sure that we didn't develop.

The strength of the disabled women who formed DAWN Canada was formidable. We also presented an amazing example to the world, because I think we were the first disabled women's group to develop. Eventually, there was a DAWN Jamaica, and you did get disabled women's groups in Europe developing, but DAWN was one of the first—if not the first—to be a recognized, disabled women's feminist group. If there was one thing that would break my heart, it was hearing that a disabled woman could not get into a shelter and had to go back into an environment where a man could hurt her even more or possibly kill her, or that a deaf woman couldn't get access to a sign language interpreter at a rape crisis centre and was turned away. We worked to get a real understanding of the abuse issue and a true acceptance that we must do something about it. We started to see the shelter movement say, the new shelter must be accessible; we must be able to make sure that disabled women can get in here. And the police started calling us and saying, "We want you to come down and teach a course about women and disabilities." We were totally shocked by that. I had one police officer who was almost crying, saying, "You can't be telling me that a guy would rape a woman with a disability." And I said, "Men have raped women with severe cerebral palsy, and these women are in diapers, cannot speak, cannot move. They are raped several times by the same man, because he knows no one is going to do a thing."

So police really started to understand, and so did the whole abuse movement. That was a direct result of DAWN. We got really well known, and the issues of disabled women finally came to the forefront. We had a disabled moms' conference, because I thought some of the most isolated women would be disabled women who got pregnant. Now there are starting to be disabled parents' groups and independent living centres in Canada that have caught the issue, so that is good. But we were the first to say, there are disabled moms out there who are getting no information about disability and pregnancy.

The women in DAWN totally enjoyed each other. They clicked as friends. It probably changed those women's lives forever. And it encouraged us to keep up the work. Another thing we wanted was to be role models for disabled girls. The role models for disabled girls in Canada were not disabled women. They were disabled men. We wanted girls to be able to look at a disabled adult woman, and go, wow. How do you handle your life? But I don't think we've been able to make the huge impact we wanted to on girls.

The lesbian issue was a contentious issue within DAWN, because you had straight women who were not accepting. I had people call up and say, "I have heard DAWN is a lesbian group, and if it is a lesbian group I don't want to come." I would say to them, "Well, lesbians and bisexual women with disabilities are always welcome within DAWN. If you are uncomfortable with that, you don't need to come to the group." If you are racist or homophobic we don't want you as part of DAWN, either, because DAWN doesn't need women like that. Disabled women are no different from any other group. People are funny; they think people with disabilities will be more understanding of other minority groups. But people of colour groups are no more understanding of disabilities. Feminists are no more understanding of disabled feminists. That's human nature, so you will always get the struggle.

A couple of years ago, I started to get tired of fighting. At that point, I shouldn't have had to be fighting anymore. I should have been able to call up any women's meeting and say, I want to come down, and it would be automatically accessible. But it never got that way. I always thought that was tragic. It was still fight after fight after fight at the local level. We would try to stop the International Women's Day organizers from booking an inaccessible facility. We'd say, book it at the Y; the Y is fine. They'd say, "We don't like the atmosphere at the Y." So you would have "we don't like the atmosphere" winning over disabled women being able to go, which really drove me crazy. A number of years ago, I heard that the International Women's Day party was going to be held at an inaccessible bar. I called the bar and I said, "I want to talk to you about wheelchair access." The woman said, "Well, we are laying plywood on top of the stairs." I said, "You are laying plywood on the top of six stairs going straight up? Does your bar have good insurance for the falls that are going to happen? Even non-disabled women are going to fall on that. What about the washroom— can we get in?" Finally she said, "You people are making my life hell." I've heard that a number of times to my face, "you people," meaning women with disabilities are the biggest pain in the butt. I knew this woman was stressed out, had gotten a couple of calls. But I said, that's it. I hung up and that ended my activities in the women's movement for a long, long time. I was fed up. This woman threw it in my face that I was not welcome, that I was a pain for even calling, that as a group we were never satisfied. It broke my heart.

When you're a disability rights activist and a feminist, you have two cores. The disabled women's one is the mesh of the two. I've never lost my will to help women, and I never will, no matter how angry I get. I've always meant to write an article saying goodbye to the women's movement and saying, hey, do you miss me? 'Cause nobody's ever called. Nobody has ever said, Pat, why did you back out of all this stuff? We want you here. No. I don't know why. But then maybe lots of other women find that they back out slowly and leave.

I've always thought disabled women are a plus to the women's movement, because we add so much. With our lives, with what we go through, with what we learn, many of us come with expertise that you can't get anywhere else. The women's movement protects women. It empowers them. It supports them. It gives women role models they can't get anywhere else. So when disabled women hear that we are a bother, we are a pain, we are the disease of the week, probably nothing hits us so much. Every movement has its struggles. Every movement has its ups and downs. But if you are callous, it will drive women away. I should never have to call a women's group and ask, are you accessible? They just should be by now. Any group should be.

Joan Meister

That first meeting of women with disabilities in 1985 in Ottawa was very exciting. The time had come for us to become more vocal and to articulate our needs. I had spent much of my life in Vancouver being a feminist and an activist, and the women's movement didn't care that I couldn't get to meetings. The disability community wasn't interested in women's issues. One wasn't interested and the other was inaccessible, so we formed our own group. We had a great meeting with a good facilitator, and we got a lot done.

We had several priorities for the meeting. We wanted to talk about health, sexuality, self-image, employment and violence. We wanted to talk about the violence in our lives, because we knew it was different. I hadn't felt that much solidarity with a group of women since my early union days. The feeling in the room was intoxicating. We were exhausted, but we got the work done well.

We went back to our various regions of the country to found provincial groups. What we didn't get after that initial meeting was any funding to sustain us. The government didn't give us any support. We could get project money, but none for board development. We formed a steering committee for DAWN Canada by using an arcane email system. Our mandate was to represent all women with disabilities.

We had a conference in '87 and adopted some bylaws. At our first AGM, we discussed the fact that to survive as a group we had to have a structure and principles. We had to do research so that people could find out about us. We decided to produce four position papers, which may have been the first such papers on women's disabilities anywhere. We did papers on employment, violence, parenting and self-image. Everything hinged on the issue of self-image. Out of these papers, we developed policy. We knew what we were doing, and we did it, but we got zero support from anybody. Not the feds, not the women's movement, not the labour movement. No one stepped up to the plate. That was profoundly disappointing. We didn't formally ask for support; I just thought people would do the right thing. But I realized they needed to read our position papers and get the information. We weren't sophisticated enough to have a campaign. We had these positions on these four areas, and that stood us in good stead for a long time. DAWN formed an alliance with a lot of other organizations that were equality seeking. We didn't have a national office or a phone number. We didn't have a staff and couldn't keep adequate records. That continues, which is a shame, because we have so much to contribute.

We had conference calls among DAWN members. We decided on our first board of directors, and I became national chair. We started having meetings with women with all kinds of disabilities, including mental health and hearing disabilities. With no money, we had meetings with all these incredibly diverse women and tried to do something on a national level, including having members from Quebec. We flew by the seat of our pants and had fun meetings and learned a lot, but it would have been easier if people were more helpful. I saw us as an educational group. We did networking, too. I wasn't a good speaker, and I felt that was a weakness of mine. We didn't have big debates, because we were often in agreement. We wanted to address a kind of discrimination that exists in our lives. There were no women on the left to talk to about being disabled, and within DAWN a lot of women didn't know what I was talking about when I raised the issue of strategy. I had a great woman I was working with, our senior researcher, and I could bounce anything off her. Otherwise it would have been isolating to be the national chair.

You could almost say that DAWN was the first virtual organization. Now the electronic aspect of our lives is pervasive, but then it was groundbreaking. Occasionally we had AGMs, but they weren't always paid for. We did make demands of the women's movement for access and accommodation. We were invited to meetings and events but wouldn't go unless they were accessible. We didn't make demands for our positions, just for accessibility.

I remember being warned about NAC by Pat Israel, who said they reduced her to tears at all the meetings. She said they were really mean. They weren't mean to me, though. I had been an activist for thirty years, and then I became a disabled activist, which in a way was a privileged position. I had to get DAWN on NAC's agenda so we could be allies; otherwise, they wouldn't know anything about us. I served as secretary on the NAC executive, and it was a wonderful experience. I was responsible for internal relations.

Things are changing slowly. The women's movement is coming around now on disability issues, as is labour. The women in Quebec don't seem to get it around this issue; year after year, I hear the same complaints. In B.C. there are some well-placed women who do seem to get it. DAWN has been terribly difficult on all levels, and we've survived because we were an idea whose time had come. Money would help a lot and might overcome some of our health concerns. We work way too hard.

PART IV
The 1990s and Beyond

14 women died
in Montreal
December 6, 1989.

119 women died
in domestic violence
In 1989 in Canada.

First mourn.
Then work for change.

But we've come so far; *that's the thinking.*
So far compared with fifty or a hundred years ago.
Well, no, we've arrived at the new millennium
and we haven't "arrived" at all.
We've been sent over to the side pocket
of the snooker table and made to disappear.

—CAROL SHIELDS, *UNLESS*

THE 1990S WAS THE DECADE of corporate globalization. With the fall of the Berlin Wall, capitalism embraced the globe with triumphalist right-wing intellectuals declaring the "end of history," by which they meant the end of any struggle for an alternative economic, political or social system. Communism had failed to create a viable alternative and social democracy was everywhere beginning to embrace the neo-liberal reality. The 1991 Gulf War, led by U.S. President George Bush Sr., prefigured the military enforcement of globalization that was to come. At the beginning of the decade, it really did look like the left was dead. With the singular exception of the end of apartheid in South Africa, there wasn't much hope for those struggling for a better, more equitable world.

Among activists, the emergence in 1994 of the Zapatistas, a Mexican Aboriginal movement savvy in the ways of global media and reaching out to the still-underground anti-corporate youth of the North, signalled the beginning of a mass worldwide movement against corporate globalization. The movement would emerge into the media spotlight at the end of the decade, in a colourful and militant march against the World Trade Organization meetings in Seattle. The internet permitted grassroots groups around the world to communicate with each other and their supporters in a way they never dreamed would be possible and to create a growing number of alternative sources for media.

Canada's constitutional wrangles continued in the early 1990s. In 1992 Brian Mulroney's Charlottetown Accord, supported by the premiers and all the major political parties, failed to win a majority in a national referendum.

Negotiations on the accord had included Aboriginal leaders because of the national spotlight that had been shone on their issues by the armed standoff between Mohawk warriors from Kahnasatake and the Canadian army at Oka, Quebec, two years before. The failure of Charlottetown, which included an amendment permitting Aboriginal self-government, led to a Royal Commission on Aboriginal Peoples.

In June 1993, with Mulroney's resignation, Kim Campbell became leader of the Progressive Conservatives and the first female prime minister of Canada. That summer she basked in popularity, speaking publicly about being a role model for girls, although feminists were less than enthusiastic about Campbell's leadership, since the Tory record on women's equality was poor. Once a federal election was called, Campbell paid the price for the by-now-widespread hatred of her predecessor. The Bloc Québécois and the Reform Party gained the most seats in the election, transforming Parliament in the process. Canada now had five major political parties, two with regional bases. Quebec's election of a Parti Québécois government in 1994 led to another referendum on sovereignty association the following year. That referendum also failed, but only by a hair's breadth this time, with 50.56 percent of those voting saying no.

Despite the crushing defeat of the Tories in the 1993 federal election, the 1990s was a decade of triumph for neo-liberal economics, with the election of Mike Harris's Conservatives in Ontario and the engineering of a national deficit hysteria that permitted the destruction of Canada's social safety net. Even though they ran on a platform of protecting social programs, the Liberals, under Prime Minister Jean Chrétien's leadership, cut even more deeply than the Tories had. According to the National Council on Welfare, welfare rates for a single parent with one child were reduced by between 30 and 40 percent in most provinces between 1989 and 2003; in Newfoundland and Quebec, reductions were in the 10 percent range. Everywhere, the poor were getting poorer. By the time Finance Minister Paul Martin released his 1997 budget, the deficit dragon, never as frightening as the propaganda made out, had been slain, and the tax cuts had begun. The already rich were to get richer still.

After two decades of steady and sometimes dramatic progress in women's rights across North America, a vicious backlash began to take hold. American writer Susan Faludi's book on the subject describes how the U.S. media spun sensational tales to undermine feminism, such as the notion that a single woman of forty had a better chance of getting hit by lightning than of getting married. In Canada, the backlash emerged first on campuses. Employment equity practices in the universities were threatening male dominance, and reports on the "chilly climate" for women and minorities in academia were met with ferocious opposition from male professors, creating a moral panic about "political correctness." The epithet was taken up in the mainstream and applied to almost every attempt to establish measures for gender or race equality. But the most devastating blow came when a man who was angry at feminists shot and killed fourteen young women in Montreal.

Yet, despite the backlash, and perhaps because of the shock of the Montreal Massacre, the women's movement in Canada continued to make gains during the early 1990s. The government of Brian Mulroney brought in gun control and appointed what it called with unintentional irony a "blue ribbon" panel on violence against women. An all-female parliamentary committee called for an end to the War on Women. When the Supreme Court struck down the rape shield law in 1991, then Justice Minister Kim Campbell met with women's groups to develop new legislation. The resulting "No Means No" law defined consent as feminists had requested, and Campbell then instituted a yearly consultation with feminist groups on violence against women. These changes constituted one of the most successful lobbying efforts in the history of the women's movement. Another success was the campaign to get the Immigration and Refugee Board to include gender persecution as grounds for refugee status.

The abortion struggle took on a new challenge at the end of 1989, when two men, one in Ontario and one in Quebec, took their girlfriends to court to try to stop them from terminating their pregnancies. The Ontario court threw out the case, but the Quebec court allowed an injunction against the abortion of Chantal Daigle. Pro-choice activists organized right across the country. By the time the Supreme Court of Canada overturned the injunction, Daigle had gone to the United States to get her abortion. The Tory government used these two cases to introduce a bill recriminalizing abortion in 1990, but women crossed party lines to work together to defeat it. After passing in the House of Commons, the bill was defeated in the Senate by a single vote.

New technologies began to expand the contested ground for women's reproductive rights. Feminists organized against sex selection clinics in Vancouver and Toronto, and a network of feminist scientists and women's health activists lobbied for a royal commission. It was the hearings held by that body, the Royal Commission on New Reproductive Technologies, that brought the issue to the attention of the general public. NAC's report to the Royal Commission hearings, entitled "A Technological Handmaid's Tale," warned that these new technologies could result in a "breeder class" of women and posed an even greater threat of "designer babies." The organization's provocative approach, including calling commercial surrogacy "reproductive prostitution," pushed the issue onto the front pages, but it alienated infertile women who were looking to the commission for support. In the end, the commission recommended banning some of the worst practices, but it would be another decade before legislation was in place.

Severe cuts to the Secretary of State women's program, which had funded most feminist advocacy groups since the days of Trudeau, had been instituted in the late 1980s. The initial cut to women's centres was turned back by a magnificent struggle that started in St. John's, Newfoundland, and spread across the country. But the deficit hysteria of the 1990s deepened the cuts, and most women's advocacy groups had either disappeared or were seriously diminished by the end of the decade. Both the cuts and the anti-feminist backlash coincided with the increasing participation and leadership of women of colour in the women's movement at the national level.

Many activist young women were turning away from the women's movement and toward the anti-globalization movement for their inspiration. But they took a feminist politics and sensibility with them. In the 2001 protest in Quebec City against the Free Trade Area of the Americas meeting, a collective of women organizing an event called Weaving a Web of Solidarity stated in their call:

> We will, as women, weave together our hopes and dreams, our aspirations, our indictments, our testimony, our witnessing, our demands, our visions. We will write on ribbons, on strips of cloth, on rags. We will draw, paint, knot cords, braid yarn, whisper into pieces of string. And from these materials we will weave our web. If they ignore our voices and continue their deliberations, the cries of women will haunt them and undo all their plans.

EIGHTEEN

REACTION AND RESISTANCE
The Backlash

*The American woman is trapped on this asymptotic spiral, turning
endlessly through the generations, drawing ever nearer to her destination
without ever arriving. Each revolution promises to be "the revolution" ...
but each time, the spiral turns her back just short of the finish line.*

—SUSAN FALUDI, *BACKLASH*

THE BACKLASH AGAINST FEMINISM emerged everywhere: in the
media, where anti-feminist male columnists appeared even in mainstream papers such as *The Globe and Mail;* in the courts, where men argued
that custody laws were biased against fathers; and in accusations that reports
by women of childhood sexual abuse and violence were false or grossly exag-
gerated. Feminist groups were portrayed as "special interest groups," supposedly representing only a narrow range of women pushing for measures that
would discriminate against men.

One of the major demands of the New Right, which emerged in Alberta
through the Reform Party and federally in the backbench of the Progressive
Conservative Party, was to cut funding to these "special interest groups."
Newfoundland women led a brilliant resistance to the Mulroney govern-
ment's announced cuts that saved funding to women's centres for a time. But
public funding of women's advocacy would end within a few years. And in
Edmonton and Calgary, the staff at the Alberta Status of Women Action
Committee were charged with fraud for periodically going on unemployment

insurance, a strategy feminist and other community groups had long practised to supplement the underfunding of their organizations.

The most violent expression of the backlash to women's equality was the
Montreal Massacre. On December 6, 1989, a lone gunman who blamed
feminists for his problems walked into École polytechnique at the University
of Montreal and systematically slaughtered fourteen young women. These
women died because they were engineering students wanting to take on what
once was considered a man's job. The gunman, Marc Lépine, finally turned
his weapon on himself, leaving behind a hit list of prominent Quebec feminists he had wanted to kill. Responding to a two-year lobbying campaign,
Parliament finally declared December 6 a national day of commemoration
and action against violence against women.

In the days following the Montreal Massacre, a poster appeared with red
roses and the slogan "First mourn, then work for change."

THE MONTREAL MASSACRE

Monique Simard

I remember the events at École polytechnique precisely. I was in Quebec
City when it came on the news and I thought it was a mistake, what I heard
on the radio. It was something that was not believable. It is so extraordinary
that you cannot imagine something like that happening. Then, after that,
it was very personal, because I was on the list of women that the gunman
wanted to kill. There were twelve, I think. My name was there, and Diane
Lavallée, and Lorraine Pagé, Francine Pelletier—these were the most
well-known public figures, and then there were names of policewomen
who we did not know. So there were two levels.

There was the tragedy that was happening, and it was awful to feel that
someone wanted to kill you. My husband and children reacted very, very
badly to that, especially my husband. He was scared, so traumatized by this.
We were at that time preparing the celebration of the fifty-year anniversary
of women's right to vote in Quebec, and many of us were honoured as
godmothers of the event. There was a meeting scheduled for two or three
days after. I've never been to such a sad meeting in my life, profound
sadness. In a way, these young girls were killed because he could not have
access to us. We were the symbols. Quebec is a small place, and we also
knew Thérèse Daviau, the mother of one of the girls who was killed. She
was a city councillor.

There were so many levels of sadness and outrage. And, of course, what made us mad as feminists was that, publicly, nobody wanted to interpret it as an attack against women, feminism, the progress of women. They reduced it always to the act of a madman. Of course he was a madman, but in his madness he was representing the resentment of society and of men toward the progress women had accomplished. That made us very mad, how they wanted to downplay that in public discourse in newspapers and editorials.

Also scheduled during December 1989 was a big meeting for the right to abortion, in support of Chantal Daigle. We held it. It was at the Métropolis de Montréal. It was very difficult, and all these young women at Polytechnique stood up to say, "We are not feminists, we are not feminists." So I would say that le 6 décembre had many, many consequences.

I would say that December 6 was the event that most marked the generational difference in terms of feminism in Quebec. For a lot of us, it was a traumatizing experience. It was the message that was sent, you know, that these old bitches are really the ones responsible for what is happening in society, but I am going to kill you instead. It was to try, in a way, to reverse the progress of feminism in society. To push us back into our "place." Also it was a moment where we realized, for our daughters, that they took for granted what they had. They took for granted access to education. They took for granted maternity leave. They took for granted everything like that. And they did not associate with the struggles of feminists. That was hard to swallow. I think this was the first time that we started giving thought to the heritage of feminism, how our actions had influenced, or penetrated, because now we were old enough to have daughters who were starting into adult life and were expressing their thoughts and analysis. On a personal level, I had to have a bodyguard for many months, because there was a copycat after the massacre who threatened me. That was not made public.

The shootings did not affect at all my positions on feminism—on the contrary. But you tend to measure the consequence of your actions in a pragmatic way. We had always evaluated our influence in a much more positive way. You don't think about the perverse effects of your actions. That is not something that you want to analyze, that you want to look at. So this was something that just blew up in our faces, the extreme, perverse effects of everything that we've achieved.

For example, in Quebec, we always talk about the Quiet Revolution. It was quiet politically, economically, but there was a revolution, and it was done quite smoothly. On the other hand, personal relationships, the structure of family, religion—nothing was quiet there. We went in a single generation from the highest birth rate, the highest rate of weddings, one of the highest rates of religious practice in North America to the lowest. This leaves huge marks on individuals, because their traditional guidelines disappear. Not all individuals are equipped to deal with that in a responsible way. A lot of people were damaged, not knowing exactly where to go.

And the feminist movement also had perverse effects. A lot of women are alone. A lot of women have suffered as a result of that, of not having children, of realizing at one point that they have missed out on something important in life. I was very fortunate, since I have always put a lot of importance in family. I don't know how, but I did.

Francine Pelletier

I think I will never really get over the Montreal Massacre. I didn't know this at first, because I'm a stiff-upper-lip kid. I'm tough. I'm a tough broad. I didn't know this until I worked on a documentary on the tenth anniversary, for CBC's *The Fifth Estate*. I remember trying to do the opening for the piece, and I was shaking like a leaf. It did me in somehow.

My world came crumbling down. I had sailed into this lovely ocean called feminism, sisterhood. I had discovered who I was, I had discovered women, I had built a magazine. It was a success. I was a success. I had great friends. We were all sinking into the sunset. I was convinced that despite a few irate male chauvinists, society was generally accepting of this great revolution called feminism. I never thought there would be such a price to pay. That's what the killings said: It was a crime against women. It had never happened before anywhere in the world. And to make it worse, my name was on the list, so in a way, I was sort of responsible. Not really responsible, but he had killed other women thinking he would prefer to kill me and Monique Simard and the others on the list. So what do you do with that? There is nowhere to put in this society that someone wants to kill you. To be singled out was … It didn't scare me. It was just that all of a sudden everything was crumbling. My reaction was to fight back. But I will never, ever forget that day. And I will never, ever forget everything that happened around it.

The worst for me was the aftermath. Suddenly the war of the sexes made sense. I had never seen it before. There was a huge chasm between men and women. For example, it was the first time that my editors wouldn't publish my column in *La Presse*. They said it was anti-male. On the day of the funeral, I had received a phone call at home and a guy said, "If you want to interview Marc Lépine after his death, interview me." So I said all right. We met in a coffee shop, and the guy said how he was angry at feminists and how his partner, who is a feminist, had ruined his life. I wrote everything he said. But they wouldn't publish it. They didn't want to know that this was to do with men and women and feminism. It was crazy. It was like the tower of Babel. It was mind-fucking. There were excesses on both sides. But the fact that we could not communicate because there was suspicion on either side was terrible. It was like being in a war.

It was acute for at least a few months afterward. A year later, once I realized there was a suicide note, I tried to get it. I said I thought it was important to know what was going through this man's head before killing fourteen women. Plus I was on the list, so I had a right to see the note. I got nowhere with the police. I went to access to information, and they took the police line that it would dangerous to publicize what this "crazy" man had in his mind. I was not going to get the note. Then someone mailed it to me anonymously. Someone in the police was on my side. There was never any question of not publishing it. It was front page. It was a scoop. But I think there is still a huge taboo around the event, a huge taboo. It's worse here in Quebec. I noticed it immediately. Just the editorials the day after it happened. I remember *The Globe and Mail* asked, "Why were women in the gun's sights? Well, women are still targets in the society." Whereas *Le Soleil* and *La Presse* said it had nothing to do with women. It was denial with a capital D.

The best story I heard was from friends who had been together for a long time. They're in bed together, and she is on the phone talking to her girlfriend. He is this very sensitive male and doesn't understand at all. I had a boyfriend at the time. It wasn't a serious relationship, but I remember the need of having a man to take me into his arms, and I ran to his apartment and he said, "Get over it. What's wrong with you?" I don't think a lot of men understood the vulnerability that welled up collectively in women. Don Macpherson of *The Gazette* wrote a wonderful column about walking behind a woman in the dark and realizing that she was afraid and making a parallel with the Montreal Massacre and saying, "I suddenly understand." But a lot of them didn't. The next day I went to Radio Canada to be on

Peter Gzowski's show. Gzowski did a great job on this, but I passed two technicians who were saying, "Ah, they should have killed them all, ha ha." Polytechnique was the trigger for making it okay to be anti-feminist. It was suddenly all over the talk shows.

Of course, we were naïve. You don't make a revolution and there's no price to pay. Men were threatened, and why didn't we think they would be? I think it puts a finger on why I was such a late bloomer in the feminist world. Men and women are supposed to love each other, and feminism in the minds of many people puts a wrench into that. We are supposed to be partners. Even if there's domestic violence, people can say they love each other somehow. But if on a public scale men are attacking women just because they are women, it says terrible things about your prospects for love. It puts a terrible damper on our deepest wish to be loved, and for most of us, it's by the opposite sex. That's another part of the thing that happened. Plus there was the factor of these young women who said they didn't want to be seen as feminist. Publicizing the suicide note a year later didn't do what I had hoped and make everyone realize that yes, Lépine was an anti-feminist. But ten years later, yeah. Everyone sees it now.

Kam Rao

For me, December 6 was radically contextualized by what had happened earlier on our campus at Queen's University in Kingston, with the backlash against the No Means No campaign. The student government had run an anti–date rape campaign, fairly simple and straightforward. But men in an all-male residence put up signs that mocked the campaign and threatened women, like, "No means kick her in the teeth," "No means on your knees, bitch." Complaints were laid with authorities to deal with these guys, but nothing happened, so young women took it upon themselves to protest, and it culminated in a sit-in at the president's office. That sit-in was seen as radical at the time, and it was.

A group of us felt under siege. We felt like feminists were being blamed for things. When the Montreal Massacre happened, we were at a party, and someone burst through the door and told us. Of course there was disbelief and a kind of shattering. I felt sick to the pit of my stomach. As much as we'd imagined terrible scenarios, this was beyond our comprehension. We strongly identified with the women in Montreal. These were young women who were a little older than us. These were engineering women who were not deeply politicized or trying to attract attention to themselves. Lépine identified feminists as the reason he was doing this. Some of us were distraught that anything we had done might have brought out this response. For other women, it was a sense of fear, feeling quite vulnerable. There was no consensus on the meaning of it.

Here we are a decade later talking about this and knowing there is now a national day of remembrance. Maybe the massacre was the act of a madman, but he was a madman who was politically lucid. It is really peculiar to be fighting for the meaning of those events even as you recognize them as a deep personal tragedy. For some reason, we live in a time and a place and a particular cultural context that wants to believe tragedies are not political things. So it's hard to avoid the feeling that you are cheapening or devaluing an experience when you ascribe a political analysis.

At the time, when I spoke publicly about the massacre, I was quite sure-footed, quite confident in my rhetoric. People would have said I was strong, and I was. But so much of what you're drawing on is this sense of doing the right thing, being righteous, being noble after a fashion. What was going on was a war against women, an attempt to roll back so many things that women older than us had worked on. Things like the No Means No campaign and the December 6 massacre were the crest of a wave. If we didn't resist it, we would be overtaken. It really felt like that.

The meaning of the massacre was contested on campus. It was deeply shocking to people. The fact that this had happened to engineering women meant that all of a sudden the universe at Queen's shrunk to be only the engineering school there and the feminists, who had been polarized before. People had difficulty seeing this as an act of misogyny without saying that it was about all men. We don't have highly developed language about this kind of stuff. It was desperately, desperately sad, and at the same time it was the worst kind of vindication that such a thing could occur. It was an instance of the kind of mad misogyny that is quite routine but is not usually so spectacularly demonstrated. Here it was. It's almost irrefutable.

The St. John's Secretary of State Occupation

Dorothy Inglis

In the early spring of 1990, the word went out that there were going to be enormous cuts by the federal government to women's centres. All the activists in town heard that we needed help—our centre was going to be closed if we didn't do something about it. There was meeting after meeting after meeting about what we were going to do. About thirty to forty women met almost daily. Once we had decided to occupy the local Secretary of State office, our meetings were on a daily basis. We planned it carefully, and then we just went in and did it. At the beginning there were forty-five women and twelve children. We said to the staff that they might want to go home, because we were taking over the office. Some of the staff were our friends, and we said we were terribly sorry, but we were taking over. They got up and left. The fire department came in after we were there for a few hours and showed us where the exits were and where we could smoke, and they brought booklets for the children to colour in.

This is the Newfoundland solution to things. There's nowhere else in the world where the fire department and police would be so helpful. We wanted this to be a non-partisan issue, and women from all political groups were united to do it. It got out on the floor of the House of Commons that we had taken over the Secretary of State office. We got tremendous support. The provincial minister on the status of women came down to the centre and took out a notebook and said, "Tell us what we should do." We had total support in the Newfoundland legislature, too. People understood the reason for women's centres. The transition houses were recognized for how much they did. The support came from everywhere. The Atlantic premiers met in Corner Brook and they gave us total support. It was a high point.

What was it about the women's movement in Newfoundland? Word travels faster here. Because our communities are smaller, we have a kinship thing. There were a number of women's centres elsewhere in the province. People heard and understood what this was all about. If you have the networks in place, then you can get to each other. We had shifts during the occupation, and hundreds of women were involved. Then women across the country started to occupy their own centres. It took off like wildfire. We had no leaders. There were many spokespeople, and many voices were heard.

The occupation lasted six days and five nights, until the police and the courts finally said we had to get out or serious charges would be laid. There was going to be an injunction. So we got out, but we won. We won for centres across the country, although the government went on later to do its chopping. Things like that are once in a lifetime.

Joyce Hancock

By the time the cuts came to the women's centres, we knew what we did was saving the government money. We were delivering services and doing advocacy. We knew what a woman needed if she came with a black eye. So when the cuts were announced, women said, no way; we need these services.

All the women's centres in Newfoundland were involved. I remember the president of our women's centre in Stephenville went to St. John's to sit in for a few days. I was the regional representative for NAC, and I had also been appointed to the Canadian Advisory Council on the Status of Women. The first board meeting of the advisory council was in Corner Brook, at the same time as the Atlantic premiers were meeting, so we staged a protest. When the premiers drove up to the hotel, we were standing in the hotel parking lot. The council members each went to our own premiers. I went to Frank McKenna. By the end of the day, we had a letter from the premiers condemning what the feds had done and demanding that it be reversed.

I remember that on International Women's Day that year we had a beans and rice dinner to which we invited the mayor and wore black arm bands. We won lots of local support. Everyone may not have agreed with us on abortion, but they knew the women's centres supported poor women. There were mini protests all over. If someone knew an MP was going to their area, they would organize a protest. It was such a small amount of money, and women and children were losing all these services.

NAC was way too slow to respond. I was almost embarrassed to be the NAC rep. Women from St. John's were calling me and asking what was going on. Weeks were passing, and I remember feeling very torn, because I agreed with the women in St. John's who really felt that NAC had let them down. We had about twenty-four member groups in our province at that time. This was one of the biggest fight backs that we'd ever had, and where was NAC when we needed them? There was real angst at the AGM later that year about NAC claiming any piece of our victory. It was Newfoundland women who put all the energy into that fight back. It was great leadership on behalf of the women's centre in St. John's.

Alberta Status of Women Action Committee

Nancy Miller

I was on staff at the Alberta Status of Women Action Committee for seven years. I think the most important contribution ASWAC made was that we forced the media to take note of issues that had been ignored. We created a diverse network, and our work around poverty was important and innovative. Through coalition-building and making connections, we were a lifeline for women in rural communities. It wasn't easy to find like-minded women out in the rural areas. We started by building personal relationships. We would sign women up for our newsletter and then they would sign up other women. It was interesting that even the most isolated woman always found another woman, even if she was fifty miles away. We would go to a farmhouse and have a weekend-long meeting. Women would bring friends to join us for the potluck in the evening. The women had so many issues in common, like child care and reproductive health care, and those issues mattered whether a woman was a feminist or not. Lots of women started to think they were feminists after those meetings. It was difficult for us to do our work that way, though, because of the expense of travel.

ASWAC was a provincial organization with offices in Lethbridge, Calgary and Edmonton. Our newsletter reached about a thousand women. We knew how to use the media to create interest. I remember doing a radio show with Ralph Klein. That wouldn't happen now, but there was a place for feminism on the media's agenda then.

We held hearings about poverty in Calgary, Lethbridge and smaller locations in 1987 and '88. We called them "pover-teas." Poor women came and made presentations. There were Aboriginal women, women on welfare, single mothers. We prepared booklets about the issues that simplified the information so that all women could access it. Eventually, a book was published with individual women's stories and stats.

Money was the most difficult thing for us. The federal government made a point of providing just enough money to keep organizations destabilized. They never gave us money to operate year-round or for travel. We had to do fundraising, and our constituents were poor women. We spent all our time raising money, so how could we lobby? We promoted women taking individual action and meeting with their MLAs. We felt if we helped women understand the issues, then encouraged them to lobby, it would have a bigger impact. But women leaving abusive relationships needed more. We'd get loaded down because there were no services for women with personal needs. There was no infrastructure around, and we had no one to refer them to.

It became harder and harder for ASWAC to function financially. Eventually, three staff members—two in Edmonton and me in Calgary— were laid off on a regular basis, and we would collect UI. We'd try to rotate the layoffs so we weren't all off at the same time. We didn't stop doing political work or community work when we were collecting; we were volunteers before we were employees. But in the end, a board member reported to the UI office that we were working while collecting unemployment insurance, and my two co-workers and I were charged with fraud. Our bookkeeper was charged as well. The case dragged on for years and destabilized the entire organization. Board members were afraid they'd lose their houses. Those of us who were charged spent a lot of money on legal fees. The investigator from UI went after us with relish. He made comments to individual women about "getting the lesbians." It became a political hot potato. The government spent an enormous amount of money investigating this thing, and I think if we hadn't been a feminist organization, it would have dealt with us differently.

The feminist community abandoned us. Everyone stepped back and treated us like we were guilty or something. I wonder whether it wasn't fear that they would be dragged in and punished, too. So many women had done the same thing in their organizations. We never had one penny donated to help us with legal fees. The women we knew who were privileged left the ship the fastest, because they had the most to lose. I hoped someone would organize a fundraiser, but no one did. It took a real toll on our lives. I was angry and terribly sad, but I comforted myself with the fact that you have to pay a price for doing good work. In some countries, women get killed for the work we did. We bore the brunt of the feminist backlash in Alberta. When we weren't convicted, there was no mention of it in the media. It was a relief to get off, but frustrating not to have our names cleared.

It is really right wing in Alberta, and the moment Big Brother slammed his fist on the table, everyone backed off. ASWAC was so spread out. Decentralization was our strength when we were dealing with individual women, but it hurt us during this crisis. The crime we were accused of was keeping something running for women at our own expense. I felt that the people who had gained from ASWAC let it go so easily.

NINETEEN

SHARING POWER
Women of Colour Take the Lead

If you are going to hold someone down, you're going to have to hold on
by the other end of the chain. You are confined by your own repression.

—TONI MORRISON

I SERVED AS PRESIDENT of NAC from 1990 to 1993. One of the reforms in NAC during that time was the decision to pay the president a salary. Up until then, the presidency had been a full-time voluntary position, ensuring that only women of considerable privilege could even consider the post. Deciding to make it a paid position opened the road for marginalized and working-class women to run for election.

In 1991 NAC adopted affirmative action measures by designating places on the executive for underrepresented groups, including women of colour, immigrant women, women with disabilities and Aboriginal women. If no one from a designated group filled the spot, it would remain empty. With more women of colour and Aboriginal women on the executive, NAC's priorities started to change. The strong leadership of Aboriginal women allowed the organization to take the position it did on the Charlottetown Accord. When Brian Mulroney appointed the "blue ribbon" panel on violence against women in 1991, it was women of colour who argued that NAC should not participate on the panel's advisory committee because women of colour were underrepresented. What the media called NAC's boycott of the panel hurt the organization's credibility with the media and government, but it showed women of colour that NAC was ready to stand with them in fighting racism and demanding more representation. The next obvious step within the organization was to elect a woman of colour as president. In NAC's twenty-year history, all its presidents had been white women from either Toronto or Montreal.

After considerable discussion among women of colour on the executive, Sunera Thobani, a feminist who had been very active in the Vancouver women's movement, agreed to run. Many white women on the executive saw Shelagh Day, NAC's vice-president, as the obvious candidate for next president. The executive was divided, and after a major discussion, it was recommended that both women run for the job. When Shelagh Day decided to withdraw, Sunera Thobani was acclaimed as president for the 1993–95 term.

Sunera Thobani

I came to Canada from England in 1989. By that time I had worked in many women's organizations, and when I came to Vancouver I tried to join as many women's groups as I could, to find out what was happening politically. I recognized and still value having South Asian women's groups, but I wanted to get involved and active in mixed organizations as well. So many times I was the only South Asian woman at a mixed event. That was my experience in Vancouver around reproductive technology and abortion rights.

Running for the NAC executive in 1991 came from the work I had done on sex selection. A doctor trying to open a sex selection clinic in Vancouver was targeting the South Asian and Chinese communities. I got involved with other South Asian women to try to stop the opening of his clinic. It became a huge media event, and there was a very racist framing of it: that these two communities had brought their backward values to Canada and have a preference for males. Also, the Royal Commission on New Reproductive Technologies was starting to travel across the country, so the whole issue was getting a lot of attention. I realized that I wanted to be active against it at the national level. So that was my major reason for wanting to get involved in NAC: to work at the national level and hook up with other women doing work on the issue.

I was very intimidated by my first NAC meeting. There were all these feminists around, some of them very high-powered. There were very few women of colour there, but it was really exciting to connect with them. The presence of women of colour from Ontario and other parts of the country was small, but still enough for me to get excited. I met a lot of women I wanted to work with, and it seemed politically urgent, very important to be doing this kind of work.

The women of colour meetings at NAC were important to me. It was meeting women like Winnie Ng that really left a mark on me—here were these women who had done this for a long time. Also, learning how important immigration issues were to women of colour in this country. Personally I understood it, because I had immigrated, but now also politically. My first NAC AGM was about Aboriginal women and NAC's position on the three nations, and that debate also had a big impact on me, seeing Reanna Erasmus and other powerful Aboriginal women. And I was blown away by the NAC lobby. I couldn't believe that NAC had that kind of presence in the country.

I think we first talked about having a woman of colour run for NAC president at the CRIAW conference on racism in 1992.[1] There were enough women of colour on the NAC executive by that time. Fely Villasin had been elected, Winnie was around, and Carolann Wright was there. I can't remember who the suggestion first came from. But I do remember everybody thinking that it was really important. And I remember discussions about whether Fely should be the one to do it or Carolann. I'd done enough work in B.C. and was known well enough in Ontario that I would be able to get support from white women, so we all came to the conclusion that I should be the one to run. We thought there would be an election for the position, so we had to put up someone who could face a serious challenge.

When I look back, I can't believe how naïve I was. I don't think I ever thought about what it would be like if I got elected. I'd been in the country for a short time, although I had a lot of understanding of some of the key issues. Another concern for me was my family. I was doing a Ph.D. at that time, and so interrupting my studies was a personal consideration. But I thought it was an important enough political project for women of colour that other things could be put on hold. It meant moving, but I was prepared to do that. I knew I could get connected with other feminists in a way that wouldn't happen in B.C.

---

1. The Canadian Research Institute for the Advancement of Women was established in 1976. In 1992 they held a conference in Toronto called "Making the Links: Anti-Racism and Feminism."

One of the turning points in my deciding to run was being with my mother when some boys were throwing snowballs at her. I was so furious at how women of colour who work here, who work in other people's houses and care for "Canadians," get treated in the streets. Experiencing that kind of racism was an important thing for me at that time.

Shelagh Day decided before the nominations closed in April 1993 that she wasn't going to run. I heard about it from a reporter who phoned me and said, "Well, you are going to be president of NAC, what's your platform?" I didn't know what to say. Then, of course, everything went crazy with that illegal immigrant charge. As soon as it became public that I was going to be acclaimed as president, John MacDougall, an MP, stood up in Parliament and claimed that I was an illegal immigrant and said that NAC's funding should be withdrawn. That started this huge public attack on NAC and on me. I was defending myself against the charge of being an illegal immigrant and at the same time against my presidency being a "politically correct" decision on NAC's part. It was implied that no woman of colour would ever be in that position otherwise. I had to confront that without being able to speak openly about some of the intense fights that had gone on in NAC. And I was shocked at the level of racism that had been unleashed. I remember getting a petition from a group of women who didn't want me to wear a sari in public. I was so taken aback by things like that.

I felt really isolated. It's every immigrant's worst nightmare that you are going to be accused of being illegal, and that the charge will stick. There is all this insecurity around migration. You are never secure in the place where you arrive. It can all be wiped away in an instant. That fear is central to immigrants' lives. I think I went into a state of shock, but thank god my immigration papers were in order.

That level of public attention and that level of racism really prepared me for the whole September 11 thing eight years later.[2] I had my experience to fall back on, and the first time it happened, I had a whole organization to support me.

I still get complaints that I sold out to white women by becoming president of NAC. Some women of colour thought that now that I was in this position, I was only going to care about the issues that white women

---

2. Thobani, speaking at a women's conference a week after the World Trade towers were hit on September 11, 2001, was critical of American foreign policy and got widely attacked in the media.

care about, that I was some kind of token figure and had done a terrible
disservice to the anti-racist movement in this country. A lot of women of
colour did rally around me at that time. I remember when I moved to
Toronto, Winnie Ng organized this wonderful evening and a lot of women
of colour came and were supportive and recognized that this was an
important moment for us. But I also met women of colour who had been
in struggle with white women and had walked away from it, so there was a
certain anger around. There was also some feeling of anger that, here is
someone who does not have the history of battling over the years.

The biggest internal conflict, which was very intense throughout the first
year, was about whether I was legitimately president of NAC. That was the
most difficult thing to deal with, to try to hold the executive together with
people who thought that Shelagh Day should have been president and were
treating her like she was. Some of it was to do with race and some of it was
not. People having concern about my lack of experience at the national
level, I think those were legitimate concerns. But those concerns could have
been dealt with by providing support and expertise. So I did see it as a
question of racism, really. And I mean racism in a really profound way that
I continue to experience. I don't want to generalize, but many white women
are just not convinced that women of colour are capable, despite their best
intentions. They don't want to have prejudice, they want to support women
of colour, but at heart there is this discomfort and this sort of wondering,
"Are women of colour really capable or not?" That comes from a long
history—I mean, how many women of colour do you actually see in these
positions? How many women of colour do you see as leaders? There is just
not much experience for white women to look at and learn from. There
isn't the experience of having worked with women of colour on the job and
seeing that not only can they do the job, but their politics will be there.
There is always this fear: "Will their politics only be about race?" It's such a
profound, deep thing, it's beyond a conscious form of racism. As long as
the women's movement is not able to change that, we will continue to fight
and have these battles.

When I decided to leave after one term, I felt that I had done everything
I could do for NAC and as NAC president. There were a lot of women of
colour on the executive. We had built a good relationship with the labour
movement and with other organizations. Financially, NAC was stable.
We had seen it through a certain crisis. And I felt what I had to do politically
I had done. There were also very serious issues that NAC was not prepared

to deal with and that I was no longer prepared to live with. As long as I was NAC president, it was my job to work with the positions adopted by the AGM, and I knew that the organization was not ready to reopen those positions.

We were trying to do something in the women's movement that nobody else was trying to do in the whole of Canadian society. We were grappling with issues of power, representation, who gets to speak for whom. We were dealing with issues of "diversity" in a profound way, and I haven't seen that kind of struggle in any other sector of Canadian society. It was an incredibly important issue to struggle over. We're going through a setback now, but we're going to have to deal with these issues. They haven't been resolved in society, and they haven't been resolved in the women's movement.

I think when I look back that women of colour were not strong enough to carry it. There were enough differences of politics among us that it undermined the potential of what we might have been able to do. Plus, the general attack on the women's movement in terms of funding cutbacks made it impossible. We did elect another woman of colour as president, Joan Grant Cummings, but the politics of NAC changed, and in my view they were not very radical. If the politics had stayed radical, I think my presidency would have made much more of an impact.

I think the future of all of us depends on our dealing with racism. So it's a bit like being an ostrich to say no, I'm not going to deal with racism, especially now with the whole war on terrorism and the incredible racism attached to that. It's imperialism on the rampage again. If at this moment we say we can't deal with racism, then we're finished. I think you have to deal with it. NAC really tried to do that. NAC didn't die as an organization because of women of colour; NAC went into decline because of the politics. And it wasn't just NAC, it was the whole left that went into decline, not only in Canada but internationally. The left internationally is almost dead. It was a much larger attack on social movements and progressive politics, and NAC got hit with that, too. If anything, to have kept the radical politics of the radical women of colour going is what would have saved the women's movement at that moment.

Winnie Ng

I joined the NAC executive the year before Sunera became president. I was a regional rep, and that was the first time I had worked in a mainstream women's group. I had always worked in the area of anti-racist human rights before that.

I put my heart and soul into making support on the ground for there to be a woman of colour as president at NAC. The anti-racist work NAC was doing had led to a woman of colour as head. This was huge for me, significant and substantive. In a way, it spoke to the maturity of an organization that was willing to take that risk. It spoke to the courage of both the outgoing and incoming presidents. It spoke to the courage to recognize and fully embrace our issues as immigrant women and women of colour. It gave us a voice. For the first time, it wouldn't be someone speaking on our behalf but someone speaking in our own voice.

I remember the strategy sessions where we worked to minimize the resistance. Where were the white women activists at? How could we make sure they stayed involved? There was the fear that it would be seen as the women of colour taking over and the white women backing off. That's what happened, to the detriment of the organization, but we were trying to minimize that. If I reflect back, maybe we shouldn't have done so much talking among ourselves, at the women of colour caucus. It was quite sectoral and a bit holier-than-thou. It could have been a more healthy and open process if we'd had the dialogue with all the women and had the discussion as a group. It would have been painful and challenging, but it should have taken place.

It was a bit of a set-up, too, by some of the women of colour who wanted to divide the organization to increase their own influence. Not consciously. It was more the reality that this was the first time we were taking the power, and we wanted to protect it. Now it seems a bit paranoid. Using power and then dividing "us" from "them"—we could have expanded the "us" more. It happened because we were all new in this. We missed some good opportunities and could have confronted some of the white women and asked them why they didn't come back.

Sunera was a brilliant communicator, but there was no one for her to fall back on. The leader became isolated even among her supporters. I backed away in '95 because of further divisions and fragmentations. There was a problem among the white women, but the women of colour were so busy treasuring the moment that we forgot to challenge each other. We took on some of the nonsense. The whole "hierarchy of oppression" became another point dividing the group. First we had the withdrawal of experienced white women, and then the removal of our funding. There wasn't a base constructed to deal with these new challenges.

Jackie Larkin

It was not an easy discussion in NAC leading up to choosing Sunera—trying to weigh the different factors and qualities needed to lead an organization and determining who had those qualities, how important those qualities were weighed against the importance of having a woman of colour lead the organization. As a member of the executive, I thought that Shelagh Day had better organizing capacity and more experience with the media, but in the end I thought it was more important to give Sunera the support. It was time for a woman of colour to lead NAC. Looking back, I may have underestimated Sunera and her capacity to deal with the media—she was a good communicator.

I had an idea it would be difficult for Sunera to be president, but I don't think I realized it would be so difficult in relation to the dynamics that played out between the women of colour and the white women. My sense was that it would be hard to lead NAC because of its inherent weaknesses as an organization. I was concerned about Sunera's organizing skills, but organizations aren't built by one person. The polarization started to happen as I was leaving the executive. There was support needed, and it wasn't there.

I remember a meeting where the tensions were so great that women could hardly talk. When transition is happening, women of colour are taking positions of leadership and other people have trouble giving up power and resolving differences, then people stop talking. Sunera also didn't feel she was getting support from the staff. I think it did great damage to NAC when Sunera's leadership wasn't met with an integrated team to help make it happen. If there's a big shift from white women to people of colour, and then the white women drop out because of the challenge of making it work, because they don't have the wisdom, it is very hard. I supported Sunera running for president, but I didn't choose to stay on the executive when it would have been important to do that, so I contributed, too. It weakened NAC—the executive was divided in half on who should run. If I could go back, I would be much more willing to take responsibility for making it work. It's a huge regret to have to say that we supported Sunera but then many of us didn't follow through—

that's my regret, not having her as president. Sunera was the right woman to reflect the aspiration of including women of colour. She was courageous. But no one is perfect, and it's the teams we build that take us through the difficult times.

If there had been a couple of white women committed to making Sunera's presidency work, that might have made a huge difference. That was a turning point in NAC. It coincided with the downturn, although we would have faced the downturn anyway. It was a combination of the victory of conservative governments, the fact that the abortion fight had been won, the aging of the NAC leadership and the gap between us and the next generation. Sunera's leadership should be addressed in that context.

TWENTY

WOMEN ON THE MARCH
Fighting Poverty and Violence

Du pain et des roses, pour changer des choses.
Bread and roses, to change things.

—MARIE-CLAIRE SÉGUIN AND HÉLÈNE PEDNEAULT[1]

I N 1995 IN BEIJING the United Nations held a world conference on women. A conference for non-governmental organizations (NGOs) preceded the main conference in a nearby town. For a few days, it was a multicultural village of women, almost all of them feminists. Thousands of women from almost every country on earth met in workshops and plenaries. They discovered that wherever they came from, their issues were similar—even more similar than they had been at the U.N. women's conference in Nairobi, ten years earlier, because of corporate globalization. Women from the Fédération des femmes du Québec arrived in Beijing with a provocative proposal for a World March of Women. The FFQ had organized an enormously successful march of women in Quebec in 1995, and their proposal for a world march spread like wildfire around the globe. It was an idea whose time had come.

---

1. From the song "Du pain et des roses," written by Marie-Claire Séguin and Hélène Pednault for the march against poverty in Canada.

In October 2000 a World March of Women took place in more than 150 countries around the world. Two thousand women marched in Winnipeg, and events took place in almost every Canadian city. More than thirty-five thousand women marched in Ottawa, in the largest feminist demonstration in Canadian history. In many countries, the World March of Women was the first-ever visible feminist protest. Yet, despite that it was led by Quebec feminists, the march received almost no media coverage in English Canada. At a time when the women's movement in Quebec was at a high point of influence, the women's movement in English Canada had become increasingly marginalized. Nonetheless, thanks to the leadership of the FFQ, there is now a visible global women's movement in the streets.

DU PAIN ET DES ROSES

Françoise David

I was vice-president of the Fédération des femmes du Québec in the early 1990s when we began to revitalize the FFQ. The Secretary of State was threatening to stop our funding, and our membership had shrunk enormously. There was a lot of work to do. We had an orientation conference in '93 where we developed a new politic to support poor women, give advantage to women in the regions, etcetera. At our annual conference in 1994, we changed the statutes and opened two positions for women facing double discrimination. We abolished all standing committees, because the same women were always on these committees—usually intellectuals. Not that I have anything against intellectuals, but we wanted all women to participate. So we switched to temporary committees for the different issues we had to focus on at different times. Hundreds of women might be involved on a particular issue.

The FFQ always had both group and individual members, but up until '92, it was always individual members who were on the executive, on the board and, above all, on staff. In 1980 the FFQ had 120 member groups, but by 1992, they had only 60. It was as if they couldn't really deal with the group members. Sometimes the FFQ didn't consult their member groups on an issue. A number of times, this posed a problem, because the FFQ said one thing and the member group, often experts on the topic, said something else.

The FFQ was excellent at lobbying. They knew how to find the right connections, but lobbying is not enough. You need a balance of forces. You

have to mobilize the membership. The government has to have the sense
that if your organization says something, there are a lot of women saying the
same thing. And the government has to feel that if it doesn't do something,
it might not be the government next time. For me, that's a good lobby,
supported by the strength of the membership. The FFQ was not that good
on mobilization, and that's what we wanted to change, three or four of us
who came at the same time in '92. We were from the large women's groups,
and we told them, "If you don't want the FFQ to die, we have to work with
the groups. Maybe you think the FFQ is open, but poor women don't
think so." So poverty became a central theme. The rate of unemployment
in Quebec at that time was 14 percent. There was enormous poverty, so
when you talked about poverty it mobilized a lot of women.

The executive was astonished when, in 1994, I suggested a women's
march. I was looking for a way to unite the women's movement. One night
I saw a report on TV on Martin Luther King, and I realized that's what we
needed, a big march. And we needed a theme and winnable demands so
we wouldn't be discouraged.

Everyone found the idea very exciting, but they wondered, how could
we do it without money? I had been in the women's movement for about
seven years at that time, and I knew the women of Quebec well. It was my
feeling that people were ready for this. The Liberals had been in power in
Quebec for seven years. There was a recession. Life was really flat and grey.
It seemed to me that people were ready to mobilize. So we pulled together
a meeting and invited about twenty women's groups. I told them the
proposal: a march against poverty, from Montreal to Quebec, in about a
year's time and with winnable demands. At the end of the meeting we
formed logistics, content and finance committees. Six months later we
launched the call for the march. We had our demands, and we had
financing from a fundraising campaign.

The march of 1995 really captured the imagination of Quebec. It was
a leap of faith. I didn't doubt for a second that we would win. I had the
naïveté of a person who does something for the first time. By then there
was a new PQ government, which had promised pay equity laws and
other things. In addition, I had another intuition. The march took place
six months before the referendum, and M. Parizeau needed the support of
women.

An *acte de foie:* yes. Eight hundred women registered to march. And it
wasn't just marching; they had to be fed, they had to be housed. In the

regions they looked for money, and we looked for money. One funny thing was that after the march was over and the bills were paid, we still had $5000. We put it in a special fund for the whole women's movement and used it to fund other actions.

The Bread and Roses March lasted ten days. We marched through sixty cities and villages in Quebec. We were on *Téléjournal* every night. It was like ordinary people had discovered feminists. They realized we were not all extremist, radical lesbians. It is certain these prejudices exist here like elsewhere. People found out that the women who were marching seemed like their wives, their mothers, their girlfriends. We are not anti-male; that's not our game. So they saw us as very sympathetic.

It was quite moving. We would arrive in a village, and the priest would sound the church bells. The Church is patriarchal, but it found us sympathetic, and I had nothing against that. Teachers brought children out of elementary school with flags and sang for us. The feeling was incredible. We expected ten thousand people to march on the Plains of Abraham in Quebec City at the end. We were going to rally in front of the National Assembly, where Jacques Parizeau had accepted to respond to the march outside in front of everyone. Instead of the ten thousand we expected, there were eighteen to twenty thousand. That support was built during the march.

There were gains from the march on several levels. We had nine demands. We didn't get everything we wanted, of course. We made a gain on the sponsorship of immigrant women. We had already won the reduction of time of sponsorship from ten years to three years, but it wasn't retroactive; a woman who had arrived in 1993 had to be sponsored for ten years, but a woman who arrived a year later only had to wait three years. So we won, through the march, our demand that it be made retroactive. For the population, it was hard to understand, but for the immigrant women, it was fantastic. We also won a forty-five-cent raise in the minimum wage. We were really angry about that, because we had demanded an eighty-cent increase. But it was the first increase in the minimum wage in twenty years, so I think now that it was an important win. We won $250 million for social economy projects such as co-ops and other non-profit provision of goods and services. We confirmed pay equity with a timetable. We got supported housing also.

The second level of gain was to unite the whole of the women's movement. I think, as a result, it is much more united today. The third gain, which was amazing, was the support of the population. It was Michèle Rouleau, former president of the Quebec Native Women's Association, who had an intuition about that. A lot of what we did was based more on intuition than analysis. She said to me, "Françoise, we should not call this the march against women's poverty. We should call this the women's march against poverty." Otherwise, we exclude poor men. And when we gain, for example, an increase in minimum wage, we gain for everyone. With the support of the population, the FFQ became an important actor politically. In all future consultations and social summits, the views of the organization were very important. We gained the respect of the population, of the media and of the political class, even if we didn't always agree. It was clear that the march was a turning point.

There is a particular dynamic in Quebec. We are a small people, seven million. Everyone listens to the same news, discusses the same things. It is so true that we are a distinct society. The advantage is that when a march lasts ten days and is on the news, 100 percent of the people know about it. Quebec is like a big village, so it's much simpler to mobilize there than in the other provinces. Even among Quebec federalists there is a national consciousness. In the rest of Canada it's Ottawa that's important, but here that is not true at all.

Why did the march strike the imagination of the population? First it was the issue. We were just out of a recession and people were happy that we raised the question of poverty so openly. It had been at least ten or fifteen years since we had talked about poverty. So lots of people were glad we put the issue on the table. The other thing that struck people was the women. These women, to talk about poverty, are prepared to march ten days, twenty kilometres a day. That impressed people, and the majority of these women were older than thirty-five. We had women of fifty or sixty years.

The other thing was that the march was beautiful. The theme was bread and roses, the famous theme song of Marie-Claire Séguin. We sang the song ten times a day. The march and the song were on television. A rose producer from Drummondville really liked us, and he delivered ten thousand roses free. So instead of placards, women held roses in their hands. We also had small sticks with purple ribbons, twenty thousand of them. We asked that no group have more than one banner. The unions found that hard, but it was fairer. So instead of placards we had roses and ribbons, and the sun was shining. It was fabulous.

Another thing was the artists. We had the support of women artists from the age of twenty to the age of eighty. Very well-known artists would talk about our demands. It was an affirmation of women in a serene and friendly way. We didn't attack anyone, but we said, look, there are things to do and we have to do them. A large part of the population, I believe, is more sympathetic to activists who propose something positive. Of course, I understand that we have to denounce things sometimes; we don't have a choice. But you win the support of ordinary people more when you say yes to peace rather than no to war. Ordinary people saw our human side on this march.

WORLD MARCH OF WOMEN

Diane Matte

The idea for a World March of Women first came up during the organization of the Du pain et des roses march in 1995. I was the coordinator of Du pain et des roses. We saw how successful that march was at organizing women, and given globalization and the U.N. World Conference on Women coming up in Beijing, it seemed to us that a global march made sense. Du pain et des roses was a new kind of engagement for the women's movement in Quebec. Through this kind of big public event, we got women involved who were not in the groups. So we thought that, at an international level, it would be useful to have this kind of activity.

When we first started talking about a world march, there were eighteen women visiting here from around the world who had been invited by international development groups. We tested the idea with them, and they found it very interesting. They were surprised by our march against poverty in Quebec because for them, being from the global South, the idea of there being poverty here was a bit strange. I think for a few of them it was the first time they realized there was a similarity between what women experienced in the North and in the South. After that, Michèle Asselin, who was the FFQ president, and Françoise David, accepted to present the idea at Beijing at the parallel NGO forum before the official U.N. conference. In fall of 1995, at the AGM of the FFQ, Michèle proposed the idea of a world march, but Françoise thought it was not realistic. So we decided to set up a committee to test the feasibility of the idea.

I started to work on this committee with a group of seven or eight women, and at the AGM in 1996 we came back with a fully developed position on the World March. We wrote a letter that was sent to all kinds of networks to launch the idea. What came back was that we needed a march against both poverty and violence against women. These are the two issues that affect women most in their daily lives. So we proposed an action for 2000 on these themes. By June 1998 we had women in sixty countries in five regions of the world committed to it. The date was set for the autumn of 2000. The FFQ had not done international work up to that point, but a lot of our member groups had international contacts, and we also worked with international cooperation groups. We used progressive women in the churches, too. We functioned by email and regular mail, since some groups didn't have electronic access.

We held the first international meeting of the World March of Women in Montreal in October 1998. It was a fascinating experience. For example, the Japanese women were talking about democratization in the family, but the women in Quebec were not aware of this terminology. Our preoccupations are the struggle for rights and equality. There were other issues that we had been dealing with in Quebec for a long time or hadn't thought about at all.

In the end, 161 countries and territories were involved in the march, and 5300 groups participated. About a hundred countries had national coordination. The effect of the march was very important. Tens of thousands of women marched on October 17. We collected five million signatures protesting violence and poverty. Women met with top officials of the World Bank, the International Monetary Fund and the United Nations. In Quebec, as in many countries around the world, the impact was to strengthen the women's movement in relation to the state, in relation to other social groups and, of course, in relation to globalization. Many women profited by working in coalition. In certain countries it helped to consolidate a more pluralistic women's movement. In Brazil, for example, where there had been mainly an elite women's movement made up of thinkers, the march stimulated a more popular kind of feminism. There was some hostility over that from the more traditional feminists, as they call them. In other countries, women used the march as a way to advance demands they already had. In three Asian countries, women were able to develop the first bill on conjugal violence. In India, they were able to put such a bill to a first reading. In Burkina Faso, women established a committee with the government to which they can bring their demands.

At the end of the World March, it was pretty obvious that we couldn't stop there. We are now working outside the FFQ to plan another world action.

EPILOGUE

We have chosen each other
and the edge of each other's battles
the war is the same
if we lose
someday women's blood will congeal
upon a dead planet
if we win
there is no telling
we seek beyond history
for a new and more possible meeting

—AUDRE LORDE, "OUTLINES"

ONE OF THE LINES in the feminist anthem "Bread and Roses" is "Hearts starve as well as bodies, give us bread but give us roses." Feeding our hearts as well as our bodies is the promise of feminism, a lofty goal in this world obsessed with greed and power. Poetry is one way to feed our hearts; solidarity is another. The women's movement gave us a place to connect with other women and feel what we could give each other and the world. It also helped us to think about the world in a way different from that of powerful men. It is only in the rising of social movements that we get this different perspective. When workers rose up at the beginning of the twentieth century, we had a glimpse of a world in which everyone would receive according to their need and give according to their ability. The many rebellions of people in colonies and underdeveloped countries have opened our eyes to the massive inequalities in the world and showed us how the poorest and most oppressed can find new ways of organizing and inspiring depths of humanity in struggling for their rights. The battles of Aboriginal peoples around the world reveal a radically different way of seeing the relationship between humans, animals and the environment. The rising of women in the latter part of the twentieth century showed us for a moment a world where, whatever your gender, race, disability or sexual orientation, you could do anything, be anyone, and where relationships would be based on caring and co-operation, not competition and domination. But capitalism, colonialism and patriarchy have proven much more enduring than any of these movements expected.

Change is like the tide: Every once in a while, a huge wave washes over everything, but mostly it is a slow and steady wearing away. The second wave of feminism in Canada was an enormous wave of change. The power of the women's movement has faded now, but the changes described in these pages affect the life of every woman and man in the country—in our work, our schools, our families, our friendships and our love relationships. Almost nothing is the same as when I was a girl. And these changes were brought about by thousands of women joining together to push down barriers and create new ways of being. Yet so much remains to be done to achieve the vision we had for an egalitarian world.

There is much conventional wisdom about the decline of the women's movement in Canada. Many blame it on identity politics. If feminists had only focused on what united women, they say, instead of what divided them, the women's movement would have remained strong. It is true that the cross-class alliance of the women's movement was an important part of its power. That there were a handful of women in positions of power to promote the feminist agenda was critical to our success. But feminism would have betrayed its vision, and therefore lost its purpose, if it had continued to marginalize the poorest and most oppressed women to favour those more privileged. The battle against racism pioneered in Canada by the women's movement is one of the most important battles of our time. There were excesses, as there always are in the struggle for something new. Women have never been united in their views; it was our ability to unite across differences of class, age or politics while maintaining the debate that was our strength. If uniting across race proved more difficult, the fault lies not with those demanding that their voices be heard but with those who walked away. As neo-liberal globalization increased the gap between rich and poor, the challenge of maintaining a common vision among women became much greater. The backlash against feminism and the funding cuts to women's groups made dealing with these difficulties even harder. The women's movement in Canada worked hard to find new ways to unite across differences. Today, the "war on terror" and the security state are further isolating already marginalized communities of colour. In a globalized world, dealing creatively with difference and learning to share power and resources are essential to our survival. As long as the George Bushes of the world believe they know what's best for everyone, we will continue down a path of human and environmental destruction. Feminism can lead the way to finding alternatives.

Women today continue to face common problems. Feminists fought for universal child care and for men to assume their full share of child rearing, but neither battle has yet been won. The reality today is that most women are working longer hours outside the home and still taking primary responsibility within it. Women's equality will be possible only in a world that accepts nurturing and caring as important roles for both men and women. Gloria Steinem has said that her generation of feminists made it possible for women to do what men did traditionally, and now it is time for the opposite to occur. Men who want more time to be with their children and to enjoy their lives will be our allies in the challenge to this society where only career and money are truly valued. We need a strategy that includes child care, a shorter work week and improved parental leave for both men and women. Most of all, women must decide to stop carrying such an unfair share of the work of society.

Another continuing, and related, problem is the intractable hold of men on power. Second-wave feminists put on armour to enter the battlefields created by patriarchy. Some of us tried to act like men; others facilitated the leadership of patriarchal men by cleaning up their messes. It is no accident that the only senior management field in which women are in the majority today is human resources. To challenge the way power is practised, we need to challenge the men who hold it. Resistance is the first act of rebellion. But we also need to explore new ways of decision making that involve cooperation rather than domination, inclusion rather than elitism, and new kinds of leadership that involve empowering others rather than aggrandizing ourselves. Speaking truth to power, it turns out, is not enough. We have to change the very nature of power.

How do we play the game but change the rules? As the poet Audre Lorde so famously said, "The master's tools will never dismantle the master's house." But neither can we make change exclusively from the outside. The success of the women's movement was in its ability to work both inside and outside the system: as some writers have put it, in and against the state. Once you are inside a system, however, the pressure to conform is tremendous. My generation started as kick-ass radicals but were slowly co-opted. Italian philosopher Antonio Gramsci called it hegemony, the way that capitalism maintains its ideological hold. Seeing social movements and progressive political parties as two equally important vehicles for change, and structuring an ongoing relationship between them, may be one way to proceed. More important is developing participatory democratic processes both inside our movements and within the political system. The principle must be the participation in decisions of those whom the decisions affect. Elite control makes co-option that much easier.

The World March of Women defined the priority of today's women's movement as fighting poverty and violence. Feminist strategies for protecting and empowering women have saved thousands of lives, and attitudes that blamed women for the violence against them have changed radically. Yet male violence continues almost unabated, in Canada as elsewhere. The horror of the hundreds of Aboriginal women who have disappeared not only from Vancouver's Downtown Eastside but across the country illustrates that some women's lives are still considered dispensable by authorities. And poverty among women is increasing and becoming more racialized, along with the gap between rich and poor.

At the beginning of the twenty-first century, a global movement for social justice united the youth of the North with those fighting for change in the South. From Seattle to Chiapas, from Quebec City to Mumbai, so many millions of people hit the streets to protest corporate globalization and war that even *The New York Times* was forced to recognize a new superpower. The *Times* called it global public opinion; I prefer referring to it as the global movement of movements. It's hard to know yet what this movement will achieve, but it has already pulled the veil away from savage capitalism and American imperialism, leaving naked the cruel exercise of corporate power.

The uppity women of this new generation are mostly active in the anti-globalization movement. Those active as feminists valiantly maintain anti-violence services and local women's groups and publish magazines such as *Bitch*—"It's a noun, it's a verb, it's a magazine," says the publication's website. Third-wave feminists in Canada have produced books such as *Turbo Chicks* and *Girls Who Bite Back*. Never again can anyone say that feminists don't have a sense of humour. In addition, third-wave feminists are dealing with issues of sexuality and body image. The oppression of what American author

Naomi Wolf calls the beauty myth is probably more severe today than thirty years ago, with girls as young as ten dieting and models of beauty becoming thinner and thinner.

The new feminism will find many male allies. I believe there is a critical mass of mostly younger men who want to reject their privilege and join with women in combatting patriarchy. Whether we still need a woman-only movement or whether a new feminist movement will include men is something a new generation will have to figure out. Even feminist notions of gender are being challenged today, by transgendered male to females. New forms of coalition like the World Social Forum, in which groups unite on certain values and respect diversity of opinion and practice, might provide a model for a new feminist movement.

It was at the World Social Forum in Pôrto Alegre, Brazil, in 2001, that I heard Indian writer Arundhati Roy talk about confronting empire. When you read the excerpt from her speech that follows, please add the word "patriarchy" to her word "empire." I feel sure she wouldn't mind.

Our strategy should be not only to confront empire but to lay siege to it. To deprive it of oxygen. To shame it. To mock it. With our art, our music, our literature, our stubbornness, our joy, our brilliance, our sheer relentlessness—and our ability to tell our own stories. Stories that are different from the ones we're being brainwashed to believe.

The corporate revolution will collapse if we refuse to buy what they are selling—their ideas, their version of history, their wars, their weapons, their notion of inevitability.

Remember this: We be many and they be few. They need us more than we need them.

Another world is not only possible, she is on her way. On a quiet day, I can hear her breathing.

BIOGRAPHIES

Doris Anderson is a journalist and activist. She was editor of *Chatelaine* from 1957 to 1977 and is a past president of NAC. She is the author of *The Unfinished Revolution*, an account of the women's movement in twelve Western democracies, and of *Rebel Daughter*, an autobiography. Doris is president of Fair Vote Canada.

Bonnie Beckman is a feminist, artist and entrepreneur. Having worked as an artist-for-hire into the 1980s, she now owns and operates Beckwoman's, a one-of-a-kind store with a political edge, and a landmark on Vancouver's Commercial Drive.

Akua Benjamin is an educator and activist working on issues that impact on women of diverse backgrounds. She was a founding member of the Coalition of Visible Minority Women, past president of the Toronto chapter of the Congress of Black Women, and a member of NAC's equity committee. Akua is currently director of the Social Work Program at Ryerson University.

Lillian Bouzane is an award-winning writer and a founding member of the women's movement in Newfoundland and Labrador. She has received two international awards for her poetry, and her first novel, *In the Hands of the Living God*, was nominated in 2002 for the Man Booker Prize. Lillian is working on her second novel about the life of fifteenth-century visionary Girolamo Savonarola.

Dionne Brand is a poet, novelist and essayist. She won the Governor General's Award for Poetry and the Trillium Award for Literature in 1997, and the Pat Lowther Award for Poetry in 2003. Dionne lives in Toronto.

Varda Burstyn is an award-winning writer known for her critical and prescient work. She has written about the politics of science, the environment, genetic engineering and reproductive technologies; government, public administration and freedom of expression; and the politics of film, fine art and sport culture. Her first work of fiction, *Water Incorporated*, an environmental thriller, will be published in February 2005.

Barb Byers is a progressive and dynamic leader in the Canadian labour movement. She began her career as a social worker and went on to become president of the Saskatchewan Government and General Employees' Union and of the Saskatchewan Federation of Labour. Barb is currently executive vice-president of the Canadian Labour Congress.

Barbara Cameron is an academic, educator, and advocate for child care and women's economic equality. A founding member of Organized Working Women, she served on the executive of NAC and currently sits on the Women's Committee of the Canadian Association of University Teachers. Barbara teaches in the political science and women's studies programs at York University.

Marcy Cohen has worked as a front-line employment counsellor, college teacher, community-based researcher and educator. She currently works as the research and policy coordinator for a large health care union in British Columbia. Marcy lives in East Vancouver.

Marjorie Griffin Cohen is an economist, educator and author. She has published extensively in the areas of public policy and economics, and served on the executive boards of NAC, the Coalition against Free Trade, and the Canadian Centre for Policy Alternatives. Marjorie is a professor of political science and chair of women's studies at Simon Fraser University.

Susan G. Cole is a writer, editor and activist. She authored *Pornography and the Sex Crisis* and *Power Surge: Sex, Violence and Pornography,* as well as the hit comedic play *A Fertile Imagination.* She also founded one of Canada's first all-women bands, Mama Quilla II. Susan is a columnist for *Herizons* and senior entertainment editor of Toronto's *NOW* magazine.

Sue Colley is a social policy consultant, community organizer and dedicated women's equality and children's rights advocate. She was the executive director of the Ontario Coalition for Better Child Care for eight years and has been a consultant on many early childhood education–related projects. Sue is currently project director of the Integration Network Project at the Institute of Child Study, OISE/University of Toronto.

Mary Cornish is a feminist lawyer and senior partner with Cavalluzzo Hayes Shilton McIntyre & Cornish, a leading public interest law firm. An international expert in the fields of justice reform, human rights, pay, employment equity and labour, gender and social protection issues, she has provided legal advice to international organizations and governments. Mary is chair of the Ontario Equal Pay Coalition.

Judy Darcy is a passionate advocate for peace, social justice, and women's and labour rights. She stepped down as national president of CUPE in 2003 after twelve years of representing over half a million working men and women. Judy lives in Vancouver, where she has immersed herself in community activism and the local political landscape.

Françoise David is a community organizer and feminist activist. She was the coordinator of the Regroupement des centres des femmes du Québec and president of the Fédération des femmes du Québec. She now works as a speaker and consultant and is the spokesperson for Option citoyenne, a political movement seeking to unite the left in Quebec.

Sandra DeLaronde has advocated for Aboriginal women's issues with NAC and with Aboriginal organizations. She is director of the Aboriginal Courtwork Program at Manitoba Justice, and a full-time mother, coach and cheerleader to her daughter, Sarah. She credits her mother, Kathleen, and grandmother Mary for her strength and clarity of vision to participate fully in this world.

Barbara Doran has produced and/or directed twenty-four films since 1981. Founder of Morag Productions and Passage Films, her work has been broadcast nationally and internationally and featured at film festivals around the world. She currently sits on the boards of the Academy of Canadian Cinema and Television and The Documentary Organization of Canada. Barbara lives in St. John's.

Ginette Drouin Busque has long been a women's rights advocate. She has been president of the Fédération des femmes du Québec and vice-president of the Canadian Advisory Council on the Status of Women. She currently works as a researcher in the Quebec government's Secrétariat à l'action communautaire autonome, in the Ministry of Employment, Social Solidarity and the Family.

Muriel Duckworth has advocated for peace and social justice for more than sixty years. She remains active in Voice of Women, the Quakers, the Canadian Research Institute for the Advancement of Women, Oxfam and in the Raging Grannies. She is also part of a campaign raising money for the Johanna Oosterfelt memorial fund. Muriel lives in Halifax.

Margo Dunn is a feminist, writer and bibliophile. She taught women's studies at Langara College and owned the Vancouver-based feminist bookstore Ariel Books. She is largely responsible for the preservation of the papers of the early Vancouver women's movement at SFU Archives. Margo frequently contributes opinion pieces to local newspapers, TV and radio; performs her creative work; and updates www.margodunn.ca.

Mary Eberts is a scholar, litigator and activist in the fields of human rights and equality law. Among her many accomplishments in the women's movement, she was a founder of LEAF. Mary practises law at Eberts, Symes, Street, Pinto & Jull and is the Gordon F. Henderson chair in human rights at the University of Ottawa.

Carolyn Egan remains active in the Ontario Coalition for Abortion Clinics. She works at a sexual health clinic and is president of the board of the Immigrant Women's Health Centre. She is also the president of Local 8300 of the United Steelworkers and is on the executive of Women Working with Immigrant Women, which organizes International Women's Day in Toronto.

Caroline Ennis has reached an age where she can now do the projects she prefers to do. Some include talking circles with her husband and those connected with landscaping and gardening. Caroline lives in Tobique, New Brunswick.

Frances Ennis is a feminist and social activist with a background in community development, participatory research, women's health and adult literacy. She is a program consultant with Health Canada. She recently learned the art of rug hooking, which will become her next career. Frances lives in St. John's with her husband.

Debbie Field is an activist in a variety of social movements, including labour, feminism, environment and international solidarity. She was Canada's first equal opportunities coordinator, working for the Ontario Public Service Employees Union, and was the first woman to work in Stelco's coke ovens since World War II. Currently, she is executive director of FoodShare Toronto.

Ursula Franklin is a distinguished researcher and professor, and a devoted activist for women's rights, peace and social justice. She is a Companion of the Order of Canada and has received countless other recognitions and awards for her advocacy work. Ursula is an active public speaker and the author of *The Real World of Technology.*

Martha Friendly is actively involved in advocating for universal child care and other progressive social policy. She has written many popular and scholarly publications on child care and is currently coordinator of the Childcare Resource and Research Unit at the University of Toronto. Martha immigrated to Canada in 1971 and lives in Toronto.

Deirdre Gallagher is a feminist and a labour activist. She currently works for the Public Service Alliance of Canada as a political assistant. Deirdre was born in Dartford, Kent, England, and lives in Ottawa.

Pat Gallagher worked in the trade union movement for twenty-six years. She recently retired as executive director of operations for the Saskatchewan Government and General Employees Union. She is on the Saskatchewan Labour Relations Board, co-chair of the Saskatchewan Health Coalition and the first vice-president of the Saskatchewan Federation of Union Retirees. Pat lives in Regina.

Amy Go is a social worker by training and is active in the women's and anti-racism movements. She was national president of the Chinese Canadian National Council and secretary of NAC. Currently, she is the executive director of a long-term care facility. Amy lives in Toronto.

Gwen Gray is a feminist activist and lawyer. She was the chairperson of the Saskatchewan Labour Relations Board from 1997 to 2003, and is a founding member of Herstory. As a labour lawyer in Saskatchewan, Gwen earned a reputation as a fair, intelligent advocate of working people, a reputation she continues in her private practice with Chivers Carpenters, in Edmonton.

Pat Hacker, forever a feminist, is currently living in Prince Edward County making and marketing Slickers homemade ice cream. Retired from the marketing department of the National Film Board, she has continued to work for women's rights globally, for peace and for the environment. Pat is also a practising certified hypnotherapist and therapeutic touch practitioner.

Audrey Hall has worked in nursing and in post-secondary education. A feminist since the 1970s, she was active in Saskatchewan Working Women and represented women's organizations on the Saskatchewan Labour Force Development Board. Over the next few years, she hopes to spend more time enjoying the roses. Audrey lives in Saskatoon with her partner, Ed, and their son, John.

Joyce Hancock has worked in the feminist movement for more than three decades on issues of social justice and gender equality. She is a founding mother of the Bay St. George Women's Council and the Women in Resource Development Committee. Joyce is serving her third term as the president of the Newfoundland and Labrador Advisory Council on the Status of Women.

Chaviva Hošek is a former professor of English literature and a past president of NAC. She was Ontario's minister of housing and director of policy and research in the Prime Minister's Office from 1993 to 2000. She is currently president and chief executive officer of the Canadian Institute for Advanced Research. Chaviva lives in Toronto.

Dorothy Inglis is active in feminist and peace organizations. She is a member of Voice of Women and served on the executive of NAC and the board of the Council of Canadians. She holds an honorary LLD from Memorial University and the Governor General's Persons Medal. Dorothy published a compilation of her articles, *Bread and Roses,* in 1996.

Fran Innes has worked as a teacher, journalist, writer-broadcaster and city councillor. A foremother of the Newfoundland Status of Women, she was a founder and first president of the Newfoundland Family Planning Association (now Planned Parenthood). She has authored many articles, book reviews and a children's book. Born in Grand Falls, Newfoundland, Fran has a son, daughter and granddaughter.

Pat Israel has been active in the disability rights and women's movements for the past thirty years. A founding member of the DisAbled Women's Network, she has worked to make the women's movement more inclusive to women with disabilities. She currently works for a non-profit organization promoting active living for older adults. Pat lives in Toronto.

Bonnie James is an advocate for women's rights and social equality. She has worked to establish women's shelters, has been active with NAC and with provincial and national NDP governing councils and women's committees. Bonnie currently works as a health care data analyst with the Workplace Health, Safety and Compensation Commission of Newfoundland and Labrador.

Bonnie Sherr Klein is a feminist documentary filmmaker and was part of the National Film Board's Studio D. In 1987 she survived a catastrophic brainstem stroke, which she later described in her book *Slow Dance: A Story of Stroke, Love and Disability.* She is currently making a film about disability representation. Bonnie lives in British Columbia with her husband, Michael. They have two children, Seth and Naomi.

Denise Kouri is a policy analyst and adult educator. She directs a health policy research unit and also manages a health promotion program in Mozambique. Involved in various civil society organizations, she was president of Saskatchewan Working Women in 1980–81. Denise lives in Saskatoon with her partner. They have two adult children and one grandchild.

Ellen Kruger has worked as a teacher, consultant, community clinic administrator and mental health client advocate. She has been active in the women's movement since 1971, was a founding matron of Women's Health Clinic, and was chair and spokesperson for the Manitoba Coalition for Reproductive Choice. Ellen lives in Winnipeg and is currently enjoying retirement, her family, yoga and Argentine tango.

Lee Lakeman has organized with women resisting abuse since 1973. A founder of the Woodstock Women's Emergency Centre and Ontario Association of Interval and Transition Houses (OAITH), she has worked for twenty-seven years within the collective at Vancouver Rape Relief and Women's Shelter. Lee recently authored a report, excerpted in *Not for Sale: Feminists Resisting Prostitution and Pornography,* analyzing women's attempts to use the Canadian government to protect themselves.

Frances Lankin has advocated for social equality and women's rights both as a politician and as a community activist. She was an NDP member of the Ontario Provincial Parliament (1990–2001) and served as a senior cabinet member. Currently, she is the president and chief executive officer of United Way of Greater Toronto.

Jackie Larkin is a popular educator and active in the labour and women's movements. She facilitates a wide range of workshops for a variety of social justice organizations, works at the British Columbia Nurses' Union as the education coordinator and also plays an education coordination role for the Canadian Federation of Nurses Unions. Jackie lives in Vancouver.

Salome Lukas is a political activist dedicated to the anti-racist struggle and the plight of immigrants and refugees. Of Greek-Cypriot origins, she was active on the board of NAC and, as an artist, designed political posters and postcards, including the poster for the Women's March—For Bread and Roses, for Jobs and Justice. Salome lives in Toronto.

Flora MacDonald is a pioneer feminist, activist and politician. She served as Member of Parliament for Kingston and the Islands (1972–88). A Companion of the Order of Canada, she is the recipient of numerous awards for her contributions to public service. Among her many current commitments, she is chairperson of the Shastri Indo-Canada Advisory Council, Future Generations and Partnership Africa-Canada.

Julie Mathien has worked for more than thirty years in Canadian social policy at provincial, municipal and school board levels, and as a community volunteer. She is currently a policy development officer in the Social Development and Administration Division, Community and Neighbourhood Services Department, City of Toronto, working in the areas of children's policy and immigration and settlement.

Diane Matte is an energetic feminist and global justice activist. Trained as a teacher, she coordinated the Quebec women's anti-poverty march, Du pain et des roses, in 1995. An instigator of the World March of Women in 2000, she continues to coordinate this feminist global solidarity action network against poverty and violence against women. Diane lives in Montreal.

Marilou McPhedran is a lawyer, consultant and women's rights advocate. Member of the Order of Canada and recipient of the Governor General's Persons Case Commemorative Medal for her women's equality work, she founded and co-directs the International Women's Rights Project. Based in Toronto, Marilou recently co-authored the first Canadian legal guide for health professionals on preventing sexual abuse of patients.

Joan Meister was a fierce disability rights advocate, passionate feminist, union organizer and independent spirit. Joan was a founding member of AUCE, the Association of University and College Employees, and a union activist until she was forced onto long-term disability by multiple sclerosis. She continued her activism through DAWN Canada. On January 10, 2004, Joan passed away after a courageous battle with cancer.

Susanna June Menzies has been active in many provincial and national women's organizations. She is Member of the Order of Canada and recipient of the Governor General's Persons Case Commemorative Medal for her research and activism on women's equality rights. Now an "old crone in polyester," Susanna lives in Winnipeg and remains engaged in social justice issues.

Nancy Miller retired from "professional activism" and went back to school. She now works as a multimedia production coordinator for "really cool" online learning projects. Nancy remains deeply connected to issues around choice, sexuality and human rights through the Calgary Birth Control Association and Planned Parenthood Alberta. She continues to live happily with her partner, Pam Krause, in Calgary.

Greta Hofmann Nemiroff is a writer, educator and feminist activist. A founding member of the New School of Dawson College, she currently teaches women's studies, English and humanities. She is a member of many feminist groups in Canada, including Quebec, and the United States, and was president of the Sisterhood Is Global Institute (1999–2004). Greta lives in Montreal.

Winnie Ng is a community and political activist and a leading advocate on human rights and anti-racist change within Canada's labour movement. Winnie is currently the Ontario regional director for the Canadian Labour Congress. She lives in Toronto.

Myra Novogrodsky is an educator and advocate for progressive education. A founding teacher of City School, she has published widely and co-authored

Claiming an Education: Feminism and Canadian Schools. She has also worked extensively on Holocaust education with the non-profit organization Facing History and Ourselves. Myra is a course director at the Faculty of Education, York University.

Deb Parent is a community activist, educator and organizer. An ally in diverse communities, working with the Toronto Rape Crisis Centre/ Multicultural Women against Rape and teaching Wen-Do, a women's self-defence program, she is also a Gay Games gold medal athlete and part of a women's drumming group called WombBOOM! Deb joyfully continues to be a rebel without a pause.

Madeleine Parent is a legendary trade union activist and feminist in Quebec. An active organizer since 1942, she is widely recognized as one of the pioneers of union rights in Quebec. In addition, Madeleine served many years on the executive of NAC with a particular focus on Aboriginal women's rights.

Ghislaine Patry-Buisson is a feminist and union activist. She has been with the Quebec Human Rights and Youth Protection Commission since 1977, focusing on issues relating to women's rights. Still active within the women's movement, she is a founding member of the Thérèse F. Casgrain Foundation and is vice-president of the Léa-Roback Foundation. Ghislaine lives in Montreal.

Francine Pelletier is an independent documentary filmmaker and screen-writer. She is a co-founder of the feminist magazine *La Vie en rose* and spent five years as the co-host of CBC's *The Fifth Estate.* Pelletier's work has earned her many honours, including several Geminis, a Gabriel Award and the New York Documentary Festival's Best Human Relations Award. Francine is from Montreal.

Helen Fogwill Porter is an author, active feminist and long-time member of the NDP. Her book publications include *Below the Bridge, A Long and Lonely Ride* and *January, February, June or July.* Her stories, poetry and articles have been published both in Canada and internationally. Helen was born and still lives in St. John's.

Jean Rands is an active socialist and feminist and has been a clerical worker for over four decades. A founding member of Vancouver Women's Caucus and of the independent feminist unions AUCE (Association of University and College Employees) and SORWUC (Service, Office, and Retail Workers Union of Canada), she is currently involved in organizing another independent office workers' union. Jean has for forty-three years shared her life with Al Engler.

Kam Rao is a Toronto-based broadcast journalist and also a graduate student in political studies.

Laurell Ritchie is involved in the union, women's and social justice movements. She was a co-founder of the Equal Pay Coalition and the Coalition against Free Trade, and active in NAC. She has been a representative with the Canadian Auto Workers Union since 1994. Laurell lives in Toronto.

Sheila Roberts is an activist with peace, socialist and anti-imperialist efforts, the women's and labour movements, and the arts. As a researcher, educator and consultant for government, the film industry, and arts and cultural organizations, she has been responsible for the development of training initiatives and the founding of several key cultural organizations in Saskatchewan.

Laurel Rothman is an advocate for children's issues. She works at the Family Service Association of Toronto where she coordinates Campaign 2000, a cross-Canada coalition that holds governments accountable to their promise to end child poverty in Canada. Laurel lives in Toronto.

Nancy Ruth is a feminist and social activist and has run twice in Ontario elections for the Progressive Conservative Party. She was instrumental in the founding of several organizations working for women's rights, including the Ad Hoc Committee on the Constitution, LEAF and the Canadian Women's Foundation. She also "co-mothered" www.coolwomen.com.

Norma Scarborough is a retired school secretary, mother of five, and grandmother and great-grandmother of seventeen. She was one of the founding members of the Canadian Abortion Rights Action League (CARAL) and was its president through most of the clinic period and court battles in the 1980s. Norma lives in Toronto.

Priscilla Settee is an educator and advocate for feminist, environmental and Aboriginal rights. A former secretary of NAC and federal NDP candidate in the 2004 elections, she has more than thirty years experience in local and international community development. Priscilla, a Cree from Northern Saskatchewan, is currently completing a Ph.D. and is program director of the Indigenous Peoples Program, Extension Division, University of Saskatchewan.

Kay Sigurjonsson is a founder of NAC and of the Canadian Women's Foundation. She is retired from the senior staff of the Federation of Women Teachers of Ontario, which was a unique women's professional organization/union, as well as a powerful force in the women's movement. Kay lives in Toronto.

Monique Simard has produced over twenty-five documentaries. She was active in the labour movement for nearly twenty years, and has been an outspoken feminist for more than thirty years. She heads Productions virage, a leading documentary production company, and is president of the board of directors of Alternatives, an international action and solidarity organization based in Montreal.

Muriel Smith has advocated for women's rights from both inside and outside of government. As an NDP member and a minister in the Manitoba government (1981–88), she worked hard on all feminist agenda items. She remains involved in women's organizations such as the University Women's Club; UNIFEM, the United Nations' Development Fund for Women; and UNPAC, the UN Platform for Action Committee. Muriel lives in Winnipeg.

Sarah Spinks has been both a union and community organizer. She has been making documentaries for the last twenty years at the CBC, and with her own company, Spin Free Productions. She wrote a book, *Cardiac Arrest*, about the deaths of children on the cardiac wards of Toronto's Hospital for Sick Children. Sarah has three children and lives in Toronto.

Gail Stacey-Moore is still active in fighting for Aboriginal women's rights and human rights. She teaches social work at McGill University in the Aboriginal Certificate Program. She is also an intake worker, clinical coordinator and therapist at the Aboriginal Healing Clinic. Gail is from Kahnawake, Quebec.

Michèle Stanton-Jean has worked as a journalist, senior public servant (provincial and federal), educator and historian. She has published on ethics, women's history, health and adult education. She is currently adviser for programs development at the University of Montreal's Faculty of Graduate Studies, chair of the International Bioethics Committee and vice-chair of the Canadian Commission for UNESCO.

Sunera Thobani is an outspoken advocate for social justice and women's rights. She was the first woman of colour to serve as president of NAC. She is currently an assistant professor in women's studies and gender relations at the University of British Columbia. Sunera lives in Vancouver.

Martha Tracey is a feminist and activist in her community and union. She has facilitated courses at the Prairie School for Union Women at Fort San, Saskatchewan. Martha is a probation officer in Moose Jaw and a member of the Saskatchewan Government Employees Union.

June Veecock has been a labour and community activist both in Canada and in her native Guyana for over twenty years. She is currently director, human rights, for the Ontario Federation of Labour, with responsibility for anti-racism and equity programs. June is a member of several community organizations but is particularly committed to working with the Congress of Black Women.

Frances Wasserlein is a feminist, historian and social activist. Her research and social activism have focused on issues surrounding women's liberation. She has taught women's studies at Langara College and women's history and lesbian studies at Simon Fraser University. Frances is currently the executive producer of the Vancouver Folk Music Festival.

Betsy Meadley Wood has been active in women's and prisoners' rights, Canadian sovereignty and civil rights issues. A founding member of the Vancouver Status of Women, she fought for daycare and abortion rights. She more recently co-founded the Defense of Canadian Liberty Committee. Betsy lives in North Vancouver and has developed a keen interest in the relationships among brain chemistry, nutrition and behaviour.

Ellen Woodsworth has fought long and hard for the rights of women, for the gay and lesbian community and for seniors. Among her achievements is a successful campaign for the inclusion of questions about women's unpaid work in the 1996 census, making Canada the first country to do so. Ellen is a city councillor in Vancouver.

ACKNOWLEDGMENTS

THIS BOOK has been a collective project from the start.

My first thanks go to the women who so honestly and thoughtfully shared their stories, their analyses and their reflections. Sisters in struggle, opponents in various feminist battles and women I had never met before were all incredibly open, articulate and wise. I thank them for trusting me to present their stories. Not all of the 103 women interviewed appear in the book, because of space restrictions. Nevertheless, their wisdom helped to guide the book even if their names do not appear.

My old friend Sue Colley helped me to get a handle on an enormous project. My brother Alvin transcribed the interviews and gave me the first feedback on the treasures within them. My new friend Kim Elliott stepped in to help with the interviews when I got sick close to my first deadline and then continued to assist in myriad ways with skill and generosity. Andrea Nene, my research assistant at Ryerson University, helped with the fact checking and read the first draft of the manuscript with the eye of a young woman. Then Denise Campbell, Annahid Dashtgaard, Lisa Rundle and Audra Williams gave me critical feedback on an earlier draft from their experiences as young feminist activists.

The book was also a collaboration with my editors Andrea Crozier at Penguin Books and Barbara Pulling. Andrea insisted on more context so that the book would be accessible to readers who knew nothing of the women's movement. Barbara worked with me intensively in the best feminist fashion, challenging me to produce what I hope will be a book that speaks to the women who were part of the magnificent struggle for women's liberation as well as to the women and men who know only its legacy and mythology. Finally, a thank you to my agent, Linda McKnight, who has guided me for many years through the publishing world and, in the case of this book, through a couple of different publishers before finding a home at Penguin.

The women's movement saved my life, as it did for thousands of women of my generation. I hope that I have done it justice.

PHOTO CREDITS

INDEX